21.95

Gender-Responsible Leadership

I dedicate this book especially to the men
in my circle
of family, friends, and colleagues—and beyond—
who are often interested in gender equity,
usually sensitive to their own privilege,
and will sometimes initiate change.
It is my hope that
our journey through these pages
will generate, in both women and men, enough
. . . spark to raise awareness
. . . light to inform and educate
. . . warmth to affirm and support
. . . heat to challenge,
and
. . . flame to inspire action
toward a more gender-just society.

Gender-Responsible Leadership

DETECTING BIAS,
IMPLEMENTING
INTERVENTIONS

Catharine Herr Van Nostrand

SAGE Publications
International Educational and Professional Publisher
Newbury Park   London   New Delhi

For information address:

SAGE Publications, Inc.
2455 Teller Road
Newbury Park, California 91320

SAGE Publications Ltd.
6 Bonhill Street
London EC2A 4PU
United Kingdom

SAGE Publications India Pvt. Ltd.
M-32 Market
Greater Kailash I
New Delhi 110 048 India

Printed in the United States of America

Library of Congress Cataloging-in-Publication Data

Van Nostrand, Catharine Herr.
    Gender-responsible leadership : detecting bias, implementing
interventions / Catharine Herr Van Nostrand.
      p. cm.
  Includes bibliographical references and index.
  ISBN 0-8039-4049-1 (cl.).—ISBN 0-8039-4050-5 (pbk.)
  1. Sex discrimination against women—United States.
2. Leadership. 3. Sexism—United States. 4. Sex roles—United
States. 5. Group relations training. I. Title.
HQ1237.5.U6V36 1993
305.42'0973—dc20   92-33931

93 94 95 96 97 10 9 8 7 6 5 4 3 2 1

Sage Production Editor: Astrid Virding

CONTENTS

PREFACE AND SNEAK PREVIEW

The Problem

We are all supposedly "enlightened" human beings; we recognize that others depend on us for gender-fair leadership. We know we should treat girls and boys, women and men with equal respect, and that sexism is unethical. We are especially aware of impenetrable "glass ceilings" and other formidable roadblocks inhibiting the full advancement and empowerment of females. However, in spite of our sophistication about discrimination, we may not recognize how our own biases actually fortify some of these roadblocks and create very inhospitable environments for women, and sometimes even for men.

Why is it, as we chair a committee, teach a class, advise a client or customer, present a seminar, converse with colleagues, or supervise our work teams, that we sometimes laugh at misogynist remarks, suffer sexist comments without intervening, allow gender-driven power maneuvers to sway decision making, and even manage to ignore the "different voices" (Gilligan, 1982) in our midst? And why is it that those who usually bear the brunt of the jokes, and whose voices are often not heard, are female?

As leaders, we know that our resolve to remedy sexism occasionally fades into oblivion, and our noble intentions to promote equity fall precipitously by the wayside. What we fail to recognize, however, is how our methods may be contaminated by our own favoritism—how, by our subtle bias, we sometimes trivialize females, minimize their participation, and marginalize them to the fringes of the very groups that not only depend on our wise leadership, but hope to benefit from women's expertise.

In my 25 years of experience as educator, workshop facilitator, keynote speaker, and principal consultant of a human resource development firm, I have noticed how my own favoritism toward men aggravates women's disadvantage in mixed-sex groups, creating environments even more inhospitable for females. This problem is also recognized by other professionals.

Why, ask committee chairpersons, are our meetings so often dysfunctional? Why are women put down, patted on the head, or otherwise patronized, and how do we leaders contribute to this disparagement?

Why, question educators, do female students submit incisive, well-researched papers, yet often fear speaking up in class? Worse yet, what gives some male students the right to think they can sleep through our lectures? Do either of these phenomena have anything to do with our personal favoritism or biased pedagogical methods?

What varieties of harassment, worries parent after parent, are causing our discouraged daughters to leave law firms, professorships, upper management, and other promising positions and go into business for themselves? What male-centered policies prevail in these institutions, anyway? And, perish the thought, what male privilege did our daughters observe in their own families of origin that allowed them to tolerate mistreatment for as long as they did?

Why, ask seminar leaders and training specialists, did my recent workshop fall flat? Was it because females and males were segregated by gender? Because discussion groups chose only males as leaders? Because I allowed certain women to get away with making derogatory cracks about men? As a "professionally trained" facilitator, where was I supposed to have learned skills to deal with these gender issues?

As this book shows leaders coping with sexism—in U.S. Senate hearings, conference breakout sessions, sales meetings, support groups, and other environments—it is my hope that we will develop more awareness of our own biases. We will then be ready personally to face some tough issues:

- covert ways in which we show favoritism toward, and collude with, one gender
- how, with subtle glances and gestures, we persistently acknowledge, and give credence to, one gender more than the other

- which persons we most often laugh at, argue with, try to discredit, show approval of, or ignore, and how our behavior is inexorably intertwined with our own prejudices
- how we fail to intervene when group members make comments that degrade others on the basis of sex, race, age, religion, creed, physical ability, affectional preference, or other immutable factors
- whether we take proactive steps to create environments that promote the strengths and encourage the involvement of all persons

This volume is aimed toward refining our understanding of the confusing interplay among rigid sex roles, power differentials in mixed groups, our collusion in these power maneuvers, and how all of this mirrors a culture that, in general, condones male entitlement, privilege, and violence—especially violence against women. It presents a review of our knowledge about how stereotyped behaviors skew group process, how we play into these imbalances, and how our biased assumptions perpetuate the trivializing and depersonalizing of women.

The primary goal is to develop appropriate, well-timed intervention strategies for remedying our own sexism and confronting it in those we lead. These techniques will help create learning and working environments in which females have the same advantages as males, and in which the ideas and talents of women are valued, respected, and actively sought out. Watching us implement these gender-responsible methods, other leaders—also alarmed about the drain of valuable female talent from their organizations—will be motivated to begin critiquing their own attitudes, behaviors, and policies.

Personal experience, dialogue with and observation of other professionals, and formal research in areas as diverse as education, sociolinguistics, organizational development, law, radical feminist therapy, and speech communication provide the basis for this sourcebook. I have maintained an ongoing study of, and involvement with, women's issues. But perhaps the most eye-opening experiences in my field research have involved visits to men's centers, interviews with male activists, presentations at conferences on gender scholarship, and an extensive investigation into the current "men's movement." This background has helped me develop a deeper understanding of the issues with which both women and men are struggling as we approach the twenty-first century.

Although interdisciplinary research, personal observation, and case studies from professional colleagues shape the core of this text, some of the most provocative testimony has come from casual acquaintances or perfect strangers. In informal conversation I had merely to mention that I was writing a book about gender bias in leaders, and all sorts of people simply "came out of the woodwork" with their tales about discrimination. These accounts were spontaneous, unsolicited, and unrehearsed. Given a sympathetic environment, people (most often women) want and need to spill their experiences as victims of sexism.

Personal testimonials take on a special urgency when we realize that victims or their loved ones have been betrayed by supposedly "responsible" leaders in whom they had placed implicit trust. Indeed, the sensitive nature of these incidents cannot be overestimated. As a matter of fact, even though I had quoted one woman anonymously, I was asked to suspend her particular case study from the manuscript temporarily because the case might be going into litigation.

It is evident that the crucial juxtaposition of gender, power, collusion, and leadership is not only a contemporary issue, but has essential and poignant significance for many people. Although most of my sources choose to remain anonymous, I am deeply grateful for their openness and trust.

ACKNOWLEDGMENTS

I wish I could release the names of all the colleagues, friends, and acquaintances who shared with me their experiences of gender bias; however, for reasons of politics, propriety, delicacy, or fear of reprisal, many of them prefer to remain anonymous. Their candor, which gives certain case studies in this book even more authenticity and intensity, is greatly appreciated.

In addition to these unnamed individuals, I am deeply grateful to the following colleagues whose creative suggestions and thoughtful criticism helped shape this volume. (Since many of them are affiliated with St. Cloud State University [SCSU] in St. Cloud, Minnesota, or with the University of Minnesota [U of M] in Minneapolis/St. Paul, I will list those institutions' full names only in the initial citation, using acronyms in subsequent citations.)

First of all, special recognition is due Rita J. Johnson, whose enlightened editorial expertise honed the final manuscript. An independent consultant, writer, and community activist, Rita possesses incisive judgment and a thorough grasp of the subject matter that are evident throughout the book.

Heartfelt thanks are also extended to the following colleagues who read a preliminary draft, submitted in partial fulfillment of a master's degree in human development: Patricia Samuel, J.D., feminist activist and women's studies director, St. Cloud State University, served as primary adviser on this project, provided incisive criticism, numerous resources, and suggested the manuscript be submitted to Sage Publications. Roberta Hall, higher education consultant, Minneapolis; former associate director for programs at the Project on the Status and Education of Women of the Association of American Colleges, Washington, D.C.; and coauthor of *The Campus Climate: A Chilly One for Women* (and its sequels), provided helpful suggestions and careful editing. Anne Truax, then director of the Minnesota Women's Center and currently assistant to the director, Office of Equal Opportunity and Affirmative Action, University of Minnesota, Minneapolis, provided valuable feedback. Charles Niessen-Derry, director of the St. Cloud Intervention Project and facilitator of groups for male batterers, radicalized my thinking about the connections between male privilege and the oppression of, and violence toward, women. Karen Schmid, instructor, Department of Interdisciplinary Studies, and interim assistant dean, College of Social Sciences, SCSU, suggested numerous resources.

These two good friends and colleagues critiqued a later, more extensive draft of the book: Helen Gilbert, Ph.D., therapist in private practice, St. Paul, Minnesota; and Gail Hanson, Ph.D., lecturer, Department of Speech Communication, U of M. Helen and Gail asked stimulating questions, provided experienced editing, and lent consistent support and encouragement.

The following colleagues critiqued one or more chapters, provided a case study, suggested additional resources, brainstormed with me, or allowed me to quote from their presentations and/or our conversations: Nancy Rule Goldberger, Ph.D., coauthor of *Women's Ways of Knowing,* member of psychology faculty of the Fielding Institute, and consultant, Housatonic, Massachusetts; Jean Houston, Ph.D., psychologist, scientist, philosopher, teacher, seminar facilitator, Pomona, New York; Sally Gregory Kohlstedt, Ph.D., professor and associate dean, Institute of Technology, U of M; Mary A. Dwyer, Ed.D., professor of psychology, SCSU; the Honorable Elizabeth A. Hayden, district court judge of the Seventh Judicial District, Minnesota; Bill Vossler, free-lance writer, St. Cloud, and member of the North Dakota Writer-in-Residence Program; the Reverend Jean Boese Dickson, director of Alternatives to Domestic Violence Program, YWCA, Janesville, Wisconsin; Jane Downey, M.S., associate professor, Department of Technology, SCSU; Mary Martin, Ph.D., professor of mathematics, Winthrop College, Rock Hill, South Carolina; Steve Penrod, professor of law, U of M; Jesseli Moen, Journey Home program coordinator of Recovery Plus, a program for chemically dependent women, St. Cloud Hospital, St. Cloud; Glen Palm, Ph.D., associate professor, Child and Family Studies, SCSU; Toni A. H. McNaron, professor of English and women's studies, U of M;

Sudie Hofmann, Ph.D., associate professor, Center for Human Relations and Multi-Cultural Education, SCSU; Shirley Johnston, D.V.M., Ph.D., associate dean, College of Veterinary Medicine, U of M; John Mason, Ph.D., Department of Applied Psychology, SCSU; Rich Chandler, author risk management consultant and workshop facilitator, St. Cloud; Peter Schwenger, Ph.D., professor, Department of English, Mount Saint Vincent University, Halifax, Nova Scotia; Linda Scott, Ph.D., assistant professor, teacher development, College of Education, SCSU; Carolyn Desjardins, Ph.D., director, National Institute for Leadership Development, Phoenix, Arizona; Deborah Tannen, Ph.D., professor of linguistics, Georgetown University, and author of *You Just Don't Understand: Women and Men in Conversation*; Sandra Z. Keith, Ph.D., associate professor, Department of Mathematics and Statistics, SCSU; Annabel Nickles, graduate student in materials science and engineering; Jim Lovestar, former chairman of the Twin Cities Men's Center, Minneapolis, and Karen Jurgens, therapist, St. Cloud.

I also wish to recognize these colleagues who provided special expertise: Jeanie Wilkens, Professional Development Associates, St. Joseph, Minnesota; Patricia Jensen, Lake Country Consulting, St. Cloud; Roseanna Ross, Ph.D., associate professor of speech communication, SCSU; Jan Stanley, M.A., then coordinator of the Multicultural Gender-Fair Curriculum Project, SCSU; and Jane M. Olsen, director of the Women's Center, SCSU.

Special thanks are due the authors who allowed portions of their copyrighted work to be reprinted here. Carol Pierce and Bill Page, coauthors of *The Male/Female Continuum: Paths to Colleagueship* (1990), permitted me to use an abbreviated version of the Continuum in Chapter 2; concepts from their book, plus my conversations with Pierce, are referred to throughout this volume. Cooper Thompson granted permission for me to quote an excerpt from his book, *As Boys Become Men: Learning New Male Roles* (1985), reprinted as Table 2.1.

The following authors granted me permission to quote from their unpublished papers (which were subsequently published): Dr. Michael Obsatz, associate professor of sociology, Macalester College, St. Paul, and therapist in private practice, allowed me to quote liberally from his paper "Boy Talk: How Men Avoid Sharing Themselves" (1975), which was subsequently published in a "men's survival resource book." Virginia Goldner, Ph.D., senior faculty,

Ackerman Institute for Family Therapy, New York, permitted me to quote from her paper "Feminism and Family Therapy," subsequently published in *Family Process* (1985, vol. 24, pp. 31-47). Amy Sheldon, Ph.D., associate professor of linguistics, U of M (and also affiliate, Center for Advanced Feminist Studies, and affiliate, Center for Research on Learning, Perception and Cognition), provided me with a copy of her article "Pickle Fights: Gendered Talk in Preschool Disputes," later published in *Discourse Processes* (1990, vol. 13, pp. 5-31).

I especially appreciate the efforts of the specialists who helped determine the book's form and style. William Kemp, Kemp Laser Graphics, St. Cloud, executed the 10 computer-drawn figures based on my designs. Ann West, acquisitions editor at Sage, was a genius at consistently nurturing, gently prodding, and highly motivating an author. Also at Sage, I thank Christine Smedley, Aquisitions Editor; Judy Selhorst, Copy Editor; Megan McCue, Editorial Assistant; Astrid Virding, Production Editor; and Laury Greening, Promotion Manager. Charles Garvin, Ph.D., School of Social Work, University of Michigan, and series editor for Sage Sourcebooks for the Human Services, provided incisive criticism and much-needed advice about what "tone" an author can set while writing on the sometimes controversial issues raised here.

To my sister, Susan (Herr) Engberg, herself an accomplished writer of fiction, I extend special appreciaton for her helpful suggestions and loving motivation. And finally, I express deep gratitude to my family: Our three daughters furnished frequent "You can do it, Mom" cheers; Laura Van Nostrand Caviani provided a careful critique of several chapters; Catharine Louise Van Nostrand helped to tape-record my presentation at a National Women's Studies Conference; Maren Thyra Van Nostrand not only critiqued several chapters, but patiently rendered preliminary sketches of the illustrations. My husband, David Van Nostrand, with good humor, tolerated manuscript excerpts on every horizontal surface (including the dining-room table), and willingly and frequently served in the role of chief cook and bottle washer.

To all those I have forgotten, who cultivated the book's growth along the way, thank you for your questions, challenges, stimulation, support, and empathy.

—Catharine Herr Van Nostrand

INTRODUCTION

Male Privilege, Power,
and Process in Mixed Groups

Inequality between the sexes [is] "the severest illness of our social organism."
(Alfred Adler, 1914/1980; quoted in Rigby-Weinberg, 1986, p. 199)

As professionals who lead mixed groups, we may find ourselves unwittingly colluding with one gender at the expense of the other. By *collusion*, I mean we condone behaviors of (or show favoritism toward) a certain person or faction. This favoritism, whether conscious or unconscious, is driven by our own biases, our need for approval, our desire to avoid confrontation, and multiple other factors.

We reveal our collusive sexism through myriad behaviors: We address members of one gender by their first names and allow others to remain anonymous. Sometimes we dialogue extensively, using intense eye contact, with one gender while virtually ignoring the other. We have excessively high standards for some persons, allowing sloppy or inappropriate behavior from others. We permit some persons to dominate a discussion, not knowing how to involve the rest of the group. Or we realize that a room setup and chair arrangement seem to favor one gender while isolating the other, but we do nothing to change them. Maybe we laugh at a sexist joke while neglecting to confront the inappropriate humor. Worse yet, we crack such jokes ourselves.

The group to whom we pay the most attention—the gender with whom we are most preoccupied (and for whom we reserve privileged status)—is very often men. It does not seem to matter whether a leader is female or male; both tend to favor men. The problem with this "attention discrepancy" is that it perpetuates male privilege; it treats women as if they are inadequate or invisible. In other words, we leaders are not being as responsive toward—and responsible for—women as we are toward men; we are not demonstrating gender-responsible leadership. By our bias, we treat women as second-class citizens.

As noted in the Preface, my goals in this volume are as follows:

(1) to help us all to become more aware of sexism, in ourselves and others, that denigrates primarily women, but also men

(2) to promote the design and implementation of gender-fair intervention strategies for confronting this bias

(3) to encourage the creation of workplace and learning environments in which the voices and opinions of females carry as much weight as those of males

My purposes are to make possible less "chilly [group] climates" (Hall & Sandler, 1982, 1984; Sandler, 1986), to discourage the "continuum of dominance and subordinance" (Pierce & Page, 1990), and to encourage mutually respectful female-male interactions that promote "linking," not "ranking" (Eisler, 1987).

The focus is the juncture of gender, power, collusion, and leadership—that is, how gender affects group process, how we leaders "buy into" these power dynamics, and what we can do about it. Special emphasis is placed on actions that *men* can take to support and promote gender equity. This volume is intended as a sourcebook or manual; the leader self-audit checklists, discussion questions, tables and boxes, appendices, illustrations, and case studies presented here are all practical tools for identifying with and absorbing concepts.

Although most of the group examples that I cite in this volume take place within the four walls of classrooms, therapy sessions, committee meetings, workplaces, and private homes, the sexism in these settings is but a symptom of our overall patriarchal, misogynist, and sometimes violent culture. Therefore, I will occasionally step outside of the confining microcosm of these small groups and focus on events in our society at large, because women's powerlessness in the microcosm is but a reflection of extensive male entitlement and privilege in the macrocosm.

How do we define this entitlement? What is this privilege? It is a privilege, explains therapist John Driggs (1990), that men obtain "simply by virtue of their being born male":

> Male privilege is the social system . . . that encourages men and women to believe that men are entitled to special treatment simply because they are men. . . .
> When male privilege is pointed out to men, they act confused, deny that it exists, or claim that they are being misunderstood. Women thoroughly understand male privilege, often defend it, and silently feel devalued by it.

Knowing that society in general winks at and condones male privilege, it may seem an overwhelming assignment to ask leaders to remediate permanently the gender-driven power imbalances in their private professional spheres of influence. However, this is precisely what I propose: I suggest that our everyday brief but significant contacts with clients, students, employees, and even our own children are the very places to start challenging bias. The *personal* thus becomes the *political*; we think globally, act locally.

Resistance to Gender Equity

While some men are showing heightened awareness of women's second-class status and are working to overcome discriminatory attitudes and behaviors, it has been my experience that, for the most part, many men *do* expect "special treatment," and prevailing male attitudes are discouragingly sexist and patriarchal. I repeatedly observe disparaging treatment of females, with a concomitant tendency by males to excuse themselves from responsibility for this very sexism. For example, I encountered this blatant bias as I facilitated a training seminar on "time and stress management" for company officers:

> **Van Nostrand** [leading discussion about how company priorities can affect worker productivity]: Women are *tired* from balancing

home, career, and child care. The futuristic CEO of the twenty-first century will provide employees with *paternity leave.*

Chief executive officer [seated prominently in the front row]: Why would he [*sic*] want to do that? Then the men would be just as *tired* as the women!

Upon hearing this remark, I was dumbfounded as to how to respond appropriately. His comment was a prime example of what University of Minnesota linguistics professor Amy Sheldon (1990a) calls "male-centered attitudes that perpetuate the trivialization, marginalization and invisibility of female experience" (p. 4). As workshop leader in this situation, what does one do? Does one ignore the chief executive officer? Gloss over his remark with humor or sarcasm? Stop the seminar process and ask other participants if *they* want to comment? (Do you think they would, given their boss's authority over them?)

My sense of outrage at the CEO's sexism was matched only by my own sinking sense of inadequacy: My repertoire of leadership skills simply did not equip me to respond appropriately in this situation. And by my silence, I was condoning and perpetuating his discriminatory attitudes. I began to ponder: If seasoned facilitators like me have trouble dealing with such *blatant* sexism, is it any wonder we are often confused about how to respond to the more *subtle* innuendoes of group dynamics, such as eye contact, gestures, levels of responsiveness, and which gender sits where and what language they use? Neither my research nor my experience had provided me with concrete tools to deal effectively with the misguided misogyny of people like that CEO.

Professional Applications of Gender-Responsible Leadership

A variety of organizations and institutions continue to request training in techniques of gender-responsible leadership. Attorneys have sought proposals on "gender diversity training." [1] Industrial arts teachers want to design their subject matter to be more accessible (and encouraging) to prospective female teachers and students. Chambers of commerce and community colleges are scheduling seminars about female-male "gender politics" in the workplace. Health and human services professionals see applications in their work, whether with battered women, veterans, disturbed youth, or in a host of other service areas. Some organizations sponsor roundtables on educational equity, while others request speakers on the connections among leadership, sexism, and violence (Van Nostrand, 1992a). University faculty recognize the need for teaching methods that will empower women, especially in such traditionally male subjects as law, forestry, and mathematics, as well as in veterinary medicine and other health sciences, among many other disciplines.

That my thesis is contemporary and necessary has also been confirmed by other professionals:

> I know some [biased] teachers who need more information on gender-fair leadership. I just saw a training film depicting a classroom teacher saying to her students: "When you get home, ask your *mothers* to help you with this homework. . . . " Her remarks make it sound like women are the only ones who *parent*; she excludes men. . . . Educators need this stuff. But do you know who needs it more? It's the clergy— they're the worst of all! (teacher)

> Gender sensitivity is a very prevalent topic at all our conferences right now. Social workers are very alert to gender issues, and many would agree that men are insensitive and women are oppressed (Charles Garvin, professor of social work, personal communication, August 14, 1989)

> I'm becoming more aware of my own bias. For instance, the other day I was leading a training seminar and a male participant cracked a very offensive joke about gay people. I said nothing at the time. But during the break, another participant approached me and said she was deeply offended by this man's remark, and wanted to know why I hadn't confronted him about it.
> What should I have said? What's a good way to let participants know before the seminar starts that you won't tolerate such bias? How do you set guidelines for fair behavior? (training and development specialist)

Overview

The leadership qualities of *awareness* and *action* provide this book's framework. In Part I, Chapters 1 through 5 address learning to detect bias—how leaders can become more aware of and sensitive to the connections among patriarchy, power, leadership methods, and group process. The focus is on how both blatant and subtle discrimination marginalizes women in mixed groups, and how leaders perpetuate this by playing favorites, usually colluding with males (and—rarely—females) in a variety of professional settings. Responsible leaders are shown attempting to create group environments that empower women as well as men. (All names used in the leader profiles, case studies, and vignettes presented are fictitious, unless otherwise indicated. Some geographic locations have also been changed to further ensure anonymity.)

In Part II, Chapters 6 and 7 are about action: How we can develop proactive intervention strategies that will create more gender-fair climates for learning, working, and doing business.

Key to Figures

Many of the case studies presented in this volume are accompanied by illustrations that diagram the interaction between leader or observer and group, and among group members. As shown in Figure I.a, female and male *participants* are depicted by the familiar biological symbols, and the female or male *leader* by the same symbols, but with two concentric circles. If a woman or man is an *observer* of the session, this symbol is in boldface type. The dominating or *controlling energy* in the group is indicated by heavy curved arrows; the direction of the *leader's preoccupation* (the gender with whom the leader is colluding), by a jagged arrow.

How to Use This Sourcebook

The case studies, figures, tables, and checklists in this book may be used as instructional tools in classrooms, workshops, and leadership training sessions. For example, the instructor could implement a case study in this manner:

(1) Have participants read a case study in groups, using it as a springboard for discussion: If you had been the leader in this particular setting, how would you have challenged the sexism and bias? What

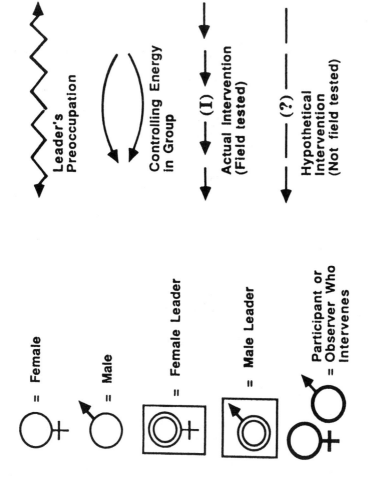

Figure I.a Legend for the Figures in This Volume

○+ = Female

○↗ = Male

▣+ = Female Leader

▣↗ = Male Leader

○+↗ = Participant or Observer Who Intervenes

⟿ Leader's Preoccupation

⫘ Controlling Energy in Group

↓ ↓ (I) ↓ ↓ Actual Intervention (Field tested)

↓ – – (?) – – ↓ Hypothetical Intervention (Not field tested) intervention would you have implemented? (See also Box 7.2, in Chapter 7.)

(2) Ask participants to role-play the "characters" in a case study. (Several scenarios include extensive dialogue that is suitable for dramatization; see especially Leader Profile 4.1 in Chapter 4 and Case 7.3 in Chapter 7.)

(3) Use the book's illustrations to trigger images of *other* gender-driven group imbalances experienced by participants. Then have participants draw similar diagrams on blackboards or flip charts, analyzing these images to stimulate discussion on group dynamics.

Tables and checklists may be implemented as personal self-audit tools, to sensitize prospective teachers or trainers; these instruments may also be used to evaluate other leaders (see, for example, Table 3.1 in Chapter 3, and Table 4.1 in Chapter 4).

Wording Choices

Inclusive Language

Inclusive, nonsexist, gender-fair language is used throughout this volume. Although it may seem cumbersome occasionally to encounter such phrases as "the leader should be aware of her or his favoritism," such gender-neutral usage is essential, especially in a book about bias!

Female Appellations in Ordinal Position

In most cases, I have consciously positioned words denoting females ahead of words designating males: for example, "she or he" is used, rather than "he or she." In choosing this device, I concur with Gary Powell, author of *Women and Men in Management* (1988), who employs the female, male sequence in his title to "call attention to the typical and unconscious order usually used" (p. 16). We are so accustomed to hearing *Mr.* and Mrs., *his* and hers, *men* and women; perhaps reversing the customary order in print can help to raise our awareness.

Focus on Mixed-Sex Groups

With rare exceptions, all the examples presented depict women and men interacting in mixed-gender groups. I realize that the power dynamics of *dominance* and *deference* that I will describe (see Box 1.1 in Chapter 1) may also play themselves out in gay and lesbian relationships and in same-sex groups. These dynamics will appear in any situation with a diverse population—diverse by level of education, socioeconomic status, or profession, much less by givens such as age, ethnic background, geography, sexual preference, and disability. It is this wonderful diversity that enriches any group, and it is the full empowerment of such disparate elements that is of concern on a macro level. However, the primary emphasis here is at the micro level of relatively small groups, such as the company training seminar mentioned above. The focus is precisely on the issue of whether women and their contributions are acknowledged and respected when they are in these groups with men.

Depiction of Extreme Stereotypes

I have deliberately drawn sex role behaviors in bold strokes, depicting behavioral extremes to make a point. Certainly none of the characteristics described is true of *all* women or *all* men in *all* situations, and when we add the many variables mentioned above, plus a host of other variables, such as personality type, we have a most interesting mix. "Gender and situation are confounded," observes linguist Sheldon (1990b). "Gendered behavior is situationally dependent" (p. 19).

Thus I want to make it perfectly clear that when I portray an extreme gender role classification, I do it to provide a medium for analysis, as a tool to shock us into realizing just how dysfunctional a certain extreme can be, not as a recommended or approved mode of behavior. I do not intend to use certain examples as a way to blame or scapegoat one person or gender. When I depict males throwing pencils, ignoring women's competencies, insulting women in front of their peers, or refusing to participate in group process, I realize that all men do not act this way. In a similar vein, when I portray women appearing unwilling or unable to protect their own interests, playing "nice girls" instead of expressing their needs, overprotecting males in groups, fuming silently and blowing up later, I acknowledge that all women do not fit these extreme stereotypes. Specific examples are chosen to raise awareness, stimulate discussion, and motivate us to design interventions that could lead to remediation—to better working and living relationships between women and men.

Men's Commitment to Women's Empowerment

It is my strong personal opinion that, in general, men would benefit by a more profeminist stance; that is, I believe many men need to develop more sensitivity about, acknowledge their part in, and take action to prevent the oppression of women. A professor who helped develop a college gender studies curriculum provides a rationale:

> It's really self-defeating for men *not* to be interested [in gender studies]. Women are already the majority in numbers, and men will be forced to deal with gender issues more than in the past. Beyond that, it's *right* that we should recognize the way our society works and how the most fundamental distinctions affect our behavior and our relations with each other. (Saunders; quoted in Moczygemba, 1990; see also Warch, 1990).

As we enter the twenty-first century, it is imperative that women become more visible, acknowledged, and enfranchised. Keeping our awareness at a level to detect bias is not women's task alone; the responsibility for awareness and action must also be shared by men. Detecting discrimination, developing sensitivity to name it, and implementing skills to assure fair treatment are everybody's jobs. We are all leaders; we can all spot injustice, and we can all mentor each other. This takes awareness, authenticity, commitment, and action. Gender-responsible leaders, like feminist men, are made, not born (Ognibene, 1987).

Note

1. "Gender diversity training" is becoming a priority in the legal profession, as in many other disciplines. For more information on the need for greater sensitivity to gender issues among attorneys and judges, see Minnesota Supreme Court Task Force for Gender Fairness (1989), Minnesota State Bar Association (1990; this document includes conclusions relating to perceptions of stereotypes of women as well as on parenting and family obligations and recommendations for action), Mattessich et al. (1989), Olson and Heilman (1989), and Halvorsen (1990).

Part I

AWARENESS

Detecting Bias

◀ 1 ▶

LEADERS IN COLLUSION

How Leaders Perpetuate Male Privilege

We are irresponsible [leaders] if we assume males won't assert their status in groups. . . . We are irresponsible if we put [participants] in any sort of mixed group—whether they be mixed by ethnicity, learning styles, gender, or any other reason—and we don't monitor the group's interaction. We need to watch for status control, dominance by the majority over a minority, dominance by verbal members over silent members.

(Linda E. U. Scott, Ph.D., assistant professor, College of Education, St. Cloud State University; remarks made during a 1989 workshop; see Scott, 1990)

You are leading a workshop when you realize that a male participant has consistently been calling attention to himself at the expense of the rest of the group. What do you do?

You are facilitating a support group, trying to involve reticent females in discussion; mostly, however, you find yourself preoccupied with a huddle of silently hostile males clustered in a corner. Do you modify your leadership methods?

You are a judge presiding during a trial when a male attorney makes a condescending remark about a colleague—"Ladies and gentlemen, can you believe this pretty little thing is an assistant attorney general?" (Schafran, 1989a, p. 12).[1] What do you do?

As leaders, do we condone, and thus perpetuate, these manipulative, demeaning, attention-seeking behaviors? Do we give

3

recognition to group members whose behaviors foster disrespect, division, mistrust, and competition? Or do we instead focus on those behaviors that promote mutual respect, cohesion, supportiveness, and connection? In setting an example for others, we may be so preoccupied with fulfilling our own stereotyped gender roles, or expecting others to fulfill theirs, that we fail to see what detrimental effects these rigid roles have on both our leadership and group process. We may enter into collusion with manipulators and controllers, or those who seem the most needy or popular at the time, while ignoring members who are attending, deferring, or clarifying. By protecting—or projecting—our prejudices, we encourage both subtle and blatant bias, some of it unrecognized by us, some of it within our control. Our collusion compromises the integrity of our leadership position and the group process goes awry. To become authentic gender-responsible leaders, we must first understand how we collude on a personal level.

What Is Collusion?

When we collude with someone, we are in covert agreement; we are secretly cooperating, conniving. We are indulgent of certain behaviors; we fail to take action against certain events. As individuals, women and men learn to collude on a very personal level. This collusion comes in two guises: We covertly agree with what others expect of us, and/or we also agree with what we expect of ourselves. A person "acts in order to fulfill others' [external] expectations rather than from his or her own needs" (Bunker & Seashore, 1977, p. 361). However, collusion can also mean that we act in accordance with our own internalized expectations (p. 364).

When we buy into certain assumptions, we discourage honest intergender communication. Often we collude unconsciously, especially when we play along with the expectations of others. In addition to behaving in accordance with external pressures from others, we may simultaneously collude with the sex role stereotypes we have internalized. At an informal business gathering, for example, a female executive, noticing a group of businessmen, might be inhibited by deeply embedded, largely unexamined role restrictions: I can't introduce myself and shake hands with those men—they might think I'm flirting [colluding with external expectations], and anyway, a real lady wouldn't do that [colluding with self-expectations]. At this same gathering a male executive might be operating on similarly unexplored restrictions: I can't introduce that woman over there to my friends—the guys might think I have something going with her [expectations of others]; besides, I was raised to wait until women speak first [expectations of self]. It is clear that these habitual and often unexamined responses will inhibit collegial networking that could benefit both genders.

Collusion is not always unrecognized, however. Sometimes we know exactly how and why we collude. The following account by a female executive director exemplifies self-collusion defined by a consciously, almost deliberately, internalized stereotype of the female role:

> I am standing in line for refreshments at a business reception. There are two men ahead of me whom I don't know. A bank executive whom I *do* know comes to stand behind me in line. My organization does business with him; he is my banker, and we are one of his larger accounts—we're talking about a lot of money here!
>
> This banker speaks to me and shakes my hand; then he leans right past me and talks to the two guys ahead of me. He carries on with them and ignores me—treats me as if I'm invisible—even though he knows me well, knows I'm an executive, does business with me regularly. He doesn't even introduce me, just talks right past me. I feel so insulted; he just ignores me!
>
> The whole situation is so difficult. Here you have men in front of and behind you, and one of these men is someone you do a lot of business with. He knows the other men, but you don't. Common courtesy says if you know others, you introduce the new person in the group. I could have taken the initiative to introduce myself, but it's uncomfortable for me to do that when I've already been overlooked and not included. That takes a lot of courage. *Besides, as a woman, I'm not socialized to do that.*

Sandwiched in the refreshment line, this executive colludes with what men expect of her while colluding with herself at the same time. She is shut out of a network established by the opposite sex—here an old boy network established as men talk among themselves. In spite of feeling ignored, invisible, insulted, and overlooked, this professional is still aware of how she is playing her part in an unequal system. Whether she does not introduce herself because she fears being perceived as overly familiar or aggressive or because she does not want to insult the banker by calling attention to his thoughtlessness, by failing to take action, she has colluded with being excluded.

This episode eloquently illustrates differences in male-female communication styles defined by linguist Deborah Tannen (1990) as *report talk* and *rapport talk*. Males frequently use language in a public way to report, reinforce their autonomy, and maintain status; women most often use language in a private way, to establish rapport and to develop intimacy. In an interview broadcast on National Public Radio, Tannen (June 6, 1990) described a husband who makes plans without consulting his wife: He invites a high school chum to be a houseguest for the weekend. The wife complains, "Why don't you tell him you have to check with me first?" The husband replies, "I can't tell my friend I have to ask my wife for permission!" The wife is hurt and insulted by her husband's *detachment*; she interprets his behavior as indifference, because to her communication means intimacy: We're married, we make decisions jointly, you should have asked me. The husband, on the other hand, interprets his wife's message as a parent-child interaction that puts him in a "one-down" position. Although many might regard the husband's behavior as thoughtless and inconsiderate, Tannen suggests that we try to understand that his primary concern is maintaining status—"He has his antennae out regarding status issues."

At the business reception, the banker and his friends may desire to connect respectfully with the female executive, but their male conditioning overrides the expression of mutual respect and collegiality; instead, they focus attention on themselves to reinforce status and *dominate*. The female executive may desire to introduce herself and be recognized as an equal colleague, but her female conditioning precludes self-assertion; instead, she colludes with the males' oversight and *defers*. The cycle of collusion is complete, as the males collude with her deference because it reinforces their need for dominance. Both female and males play rigidly stereotyped roles, colluding with each other to fulfill unexamined needs. While deference and dominance do have their place, these behaviors—when carried to the extreme—can damage group process.

To maintain status, privilege, and entitlement, males may try to control others through *dominance* or *detachment*. Like the businessmen in the above situation, males may dominate by calling attention to themselves and establishing a position of prominence. Or, like the husband who neglected to inform his wife about the houseguest, males may detach and not communicate their plans or feelings. Females, meanwhile, attempting to cope within this system of male privilege, may accommodate through *deference*: Maybe if I smile expectantly the banker will introduce me. Females may also, like the uninformed wife, seek some measure of control by *diagnosing*, questioning, and protesting the process: Why don't you tell him you have to check with me first? These behavior patterns are designated the "Four D's" of gender role extremes (see Box 1.1.)

Mixed-group process is complicated enough, given these gender role extremes (the Four D's), widely divergent communication styles (report/rapport talk), and a tendency of each gender to form old boy or old girl networks. Asymmetrical dynamics are thrown even more off balance when leaders collude.

Leaders in Collusion

As we lead groups, we may collude by condoning the behavior of, or showing favoritism toward, a certain person or faction. This favoritism is a problem in itself, but the collusion is even more dangerous when there is a power differential in the relationship. It is one thing for a leader to collude with a colleague of supposedly equal standing—business executive with banker, committee member with another member, spouse with spouse—but the situation becomes much more complicated and more damaging when the person with whom the leader is colluding is someone who trusts the leader implicitly, or over whom the leader has authority and power, such as teacher with student, boss with subordinate, therapist with client. Those in our care may unquestioningly buy into our words and actions because they believe in us—we have more expertise and are expected to know what we are doing. They assume that we have gotten a grip on our own hangups and are ready to provide them with uncontaminated guidance. However, when our self-awareness is lacking, or even when we detect personal bias but neglect to stop it, the results of our collusion can be far-reaching.

This collusion—this willingness to indulge some people and not others—may be with the opposite sex, our own gender, or both.

BOX 1.1

The Four D's of Gender Role Extremes in Mixed Groups

Males may try to maintain privilege and entitlement.
Males may
    dominate discussions or
    detach and distance themselves from group.

Females tend to accommodate.
Females may
    defer to others or
    diagnose dysfunctional process (playing "diagnosing
    detective").

In the extreme, each of these behaviors—dominance, detachment, deference, diagnosis—could be used in an attempt to control group process.

Of course, persons with whom we are conniving may go along with us for many reasons, among which are the following:

- They deny or refuse to recognize the collusion, or are even totally unconscious of it.
- They benefit from the arrangement and thus hope we never cease providing our special kid-glove treatment.
- They trust our expertise implicitly and would never challenge our bias.
- They sense some discrimination, but fear confronting us because we have so much more power/authority than they.

Some of these considerations may apply in the following account of a hypothetical therapy session, which is a composite based on themes from therapists Virginia Goldner (1985) and Michael Obsatz (1975, 1989) and others. We observe the session through the eyes of the fictitious male therapist, who simultaneously colludes with both male and female client, each of whom is playing an exaggeratedly stereotyped role.

CASE 1.1

You're the female—you translate!

I was counseling a married couple—I'll call them Barbara and Norman. Barbara had requested the series of sessions; she seemed very angry because, in her opinion, her husband was ignoring and trying to downplay or deny some of the issues she considered crucial in their relationship.

This particular session was at a real stalemate because Norman seemed irretrievably detached, defensive, and hostile to the whole therapeutic process. Slouched in his chair, his facial expression and general bodily demeanor seemed to suggest, What a waste of time—who needs this!

Although I felt fearful of Barbara's overt anger, I was even more apprehensive about Norman's covert hostility. I didn't know how to approach the couple. Because she seemed more receptive and even pliable, I tried to get on her good side. I found myself praising her for her insight, hoping to use her as a key to unlock what was going on. As we talked, I began to think she was right on; she seemed quite astute in her diagnosis of possible origins of conflict in their relationship. As a matter of fact, I even mentioned that during the session—I said, "Gee, Barbara, it feels like you're really *on* to something." Meanwhile I tried to ignore Norman; he just sat there with his arms folded across his chest, refusing to participate. But actually, even though I may have appeared to ignore Norman, I was very much bothered by his detachment—it felt like he was controlling the session with his silence.

I realized that Barbara and I were into some subtle level of communication that I didn't exactly feel comfortable with. It's as if we were both saying about Norman: I don't know what to do with him either! Barbara was easier to talk to—she seemed to have access into what was happening in the marriage. I felt like I was asking her to translate. In spite of the fact that she seemed bewildered by and even somewhat impatient with my questions, I kept asking and she kept answering. The way I was relating to Barbara certainly wasn't "hanky-panky," but it didn't feel entirely professional either.

Meanwhile, as I encouraged Barbara and urged her for more information, Norman sat in silence. I was getting more and more uncomfortable with the session—and I think both of them were, too. I didn't know what technique to use to motivate Norman to cooperate, or how to back off from my interrogation of Barbara.

It is to the therapist's credit that he recognizes how he aggravates some of the power imbalances in this dynamic. He suspects that by his overattention to Barbara he is using her to gain entrée into the family system (Goldner, 1985), and is thus colluding with her. The therapist also seems to recognize Norman's dominance through detachment ("It felt like he was controlling the session with his silence"), yet he colludes by not taking action to get Norman involved. Of course, Norman and Barbara are both colluding too: Norman believes it's his "manly" task to remain "independent and invincible" (Obsatz, 1975, p. 2), while Barbara thinks it's her "womanly" task to "help" the therapist. By colluding with the therapist, Norman meets his need to maintain status and establish autonomy, while Barbara meets her need to maintain connection and establish some level of communication. We therefore have the balance of power: One client is very detached and the other is very busy diagnosing the relationship, describing it to the overwilling therapist. The behaviors exhibited by Norman (detachment) and Barbara (diagnosis) exemplify the gender role extremes discussed above.

In addition to dealing with the self-collusion and internalized role-expected behaviors of Barbara and Norman, the therapist contaminates his leadership through his own hidden assumptions about what roles this woman and man should play. His biases serve to entrench more firmly the very behaviors that are already rendering the session unworkable, creating an even greater power imbalance, which he then further exacerbates by his collusion.

In his leadership, this counselor reveals the bias that females are better at connecting, sharing information, knowing what's going on—they have their finger on the family pulse. The therapist may as well be saying to Barbara, You're the female—you translate! Similarly, he assumes that males have every right to detach and withhold information—besides, they probably don't know what's going on in the family anyway: You're the male—you hibernate! These assumptions fit the unbalanced configuration of "maternal centrality, paternal marginality" described by Goldner (1985, p. 35).

While this therapist projects these outmoded expectations onto Barbara and Norman, he is also worried about what they expect of him. Obviously, Barbara has information she needs to share, he says to himself; besides, it's usually the woman who makes the diagnosis. She probably expects me to concentrate on her—if I turn to Norman, she may think I'm insensitive to her needs. Anyway, it's safer to keep talking to a pliable female than to try to get through a male's defenses (Goldner, 1985).

Meanwhile, as the therapist overchallenges Barbara's tendency to defer to his expertise (all the while worrying about her expectations), he overprotects Norman with another set of assumptions. Obviously, Norman has information he needs to hide, he says to himself; besides, it's a man's right to cover his vulnerabilities and remain silent (Obsatz, 1975). He probably expects me to concentrate on her—if I ask him to share himself I'll be breaking the rules of the old boy network. Anyway, he seems awfully hostile; it's better to "handle him with kid gloves" or he might "blow up" (Obsatz, 1989).

These attitudes contribute to the therapist's collusion with each client. He exploits one client's need to maintain rapport while protecting the other client's need to maintain status; he praises the woman for cooperating while protecting her partner from having to become involved. By his collusion, the therapist perpetuates Barbara and Norman's superstereotyped behaviors, which in turn impedes their personal development and causes the session to be counterproductive. Although this therapy session is a composite, it is not necessarily uncommon, and any professional who allows such extremes to persist promotes attitudes and behaviors in some people that may discredit, inhibit, disempower, or even exploit others. Gender-responsible leadership means empowering all persons in a group—both female and male.

The therapist here acknowledges his collusion, but is unable to deal with it appropriately; without full awareness of his own bias, he has become a colluding caretaker. As a human services professional, his responsibility requires responsiveness to both clients. Here, however, he is most concerned about protecting his own reputation, and thus permits each client to remain in a role-restricted mode.

This counselor personifies sexism: He expects a great deal of the woman while overprotecting and expecting less of the man. Such behavior—a form of *overchallenging* and *underchallenging*—can marginalize some individuals while it singles out others. Sandler (1986) calls this the "paradox of 'overattention' or 'underattention.'" When women receive such treatment, for example, it means "their comments may be ignored" or—conversely—"they may be continually called upon to present the . . . 'women's view'" (p. 13). The executive in the reception line received this paradoxical treatment: She was at first attended to with a word and a handshake, and then completely overlooked—sort of a now-you-see-her, now-you-don't phenomenon. In groups, when leaders are either unnecessarily effusive or noticeably negligent with their attention or expectations, it causes members to feel categorized and stigmatized; they feel they must perform at a certain level. Returning to our therapy scenario, Barbara was continuously engaged to provide information and diagnose the situation, while Norman was permitted to remain verbally uninvolved.

If, on the basis of gender, we expect either too much or not enough of an individual, we are not only colluding with but dishonoring that person. Excessively high or low expectations trivialize, discount, and disempower people without taking into account their unique capabilities. A teacher who performs a task for a female student—an experiment in a chemistry lab, for example—disempowers her. Similarly, a male student in a cooking class would be discounted if the instructor—assuming that his gender automatically rendered him inept—were to insist on preparing the recipe instead of letting him do it himself. We leaders can learn to recognize bias (both covert and overt) as well as the politics of group process (how men and women may go to extremes to dominate, detach from, defer during, or diagnose this process). Building on this awareness, we can then modify our leadership behaviors while continuously monitoring our own internalized assumptions; only then will we be ready to confront the sexism of others.

Socialized Sexism

The bias we encounter as leaders—on both sides of the podium—is the result of an ongoing process; society and our environment teach us how we are expected to behave. Linguist Amy Sheldon (1990b) videotaped preschool children settling disputes. She found that girls made more effort to maintain connection by "asking for or giving clarification about behavior, wishes, or intent" (p. 9), whereas boys argued longer, focused on self, insisted on getting their own way, and tried to assert their position of dominance through the use of language (p. 19).

One manifestation of this difference is report talk versus rapport talk, as mentioned earlier. When we understand that males frequently use language to maintain status while females often communicate to create connection, it is easy to see how women and men are sending and receiving confusing signals—and why leading a mixed group can be so difficult. According to Tannen, "Men and women grow up in different worlds. It's utterly essential that people accept and understand the differences, otherwise we end up blaming each other" (quoted in L. Witt, 1990).[2]

Carolyn Desjardins (1989a), building on concepts developed by Carol Gilligan (1982), uses a framework of analysis similar to that of Tannen and Sheldon. Although Desjardins warns that no behavior is gender specific, she suggests that females are more apt to operate in a "response mode" ("morality of response") that values connection rather than competition, caring rather than being objective. Males, on the other hand, tend to operate in a "justice/rights mode" ("morality of rights") that values autonomy rather than intimacy, analysis rather than synthesis (Desjardins, 1989b).

The Next Step

What are the implications of these theories for our leadership? If we want to create group environments in which connection is as valued as competition, building rapport is as valued as reporting, "linking" is as important as "ranking" (Eisler, 1987), what is the next step? Desjardins (1989a) believes *restructuring* is required to create climates that will encourage women's voices: "Equality requires changes in educational preparation, changes in the ways workplaces are structured" (p. 146).

Restructuring can be accomplished on a physical level: Maybe a certain committee is malfunctioning partly because the chairperson always sits at the head of the rectangular table. Maybe participation in a classroom is uneven because males and females are segregated. Once such tangible issues are addressed, restructuring must also occur at the more intangible level of values, beliefs, language, and behaviors. Leaders should ask themselves the following questions:

- Does our curriculum/agenda/policy reflect the diversity of our population, or does it primarily reflect the values of white males?
- How often do leaders overlook or condone degrading comments, harassing behaviors, and discriminatory practices?
- How many talented people have left this organization because of possible discrimination?
- Are decision makers willing to be critiqued for their possible gender bias—by peers or others?
- What instruments can be used to assess leader behaviors, institutional policies, and employee needs?
- Once a needs assessment is complete, are decision makers than committed to instituting training programs, hearing complaints, and resolving inequities?

Decision makers and leaders must be aware of their behaviors before they can change them. To create "diversity awareness" and institute such changes, those in positions of responsibility must consider which norms seem "normal" and decide if these are the standards with which they want their organizations to enter the twenty-first century.

Why should leaders consider restructuring? Does an organization benefit because of early detection and correction of inequity? "It's not only ethical, it's sound business practice," declares Rich Chandler, risk management consultant:

Gender-responsible leadership is the very essence of good risk management. Organizations carry unnecessary risk when they allow pay

. inequity, sexual harassment, or other discriminatory practices to
continue festering. These practices cloud the workplace atmosphere,
disrupt morale, and lower productivity. Therefore, organizations
that intend to control costs and retain valuable employees will head
off trouble by immediately identifying and correcting discriminatory management practices. (personal communication, fall 1991; see
also Chandler, 1992)

If we acknowledge that certain actions—by ourselves as well as
by others—will validate one individual while devaluing another,
why do these behaviors persist? In groups particularly, the interaction dynamic tends to favor males. Our culture rewards autonomy, objectivity, and competition (Belenky, Clinchy, Goldberger,
& Tarule, 1986; Borisoff & Merrill, 1985; Keith, 1987; Spender,
1980). As leaders, we usually reward report talk more than rapport talk; we pay more attention to status-seeking behaviors than
to synthesis-building behaviors. Myra Sadker points out that in
educational settings, "boys are eight times more likely than girls
to blurt out answers. Teachers are more likely to respond positively to boys calling out answers, but to tell girls doing the same
to wait their turns" (quoted in Griffin, 1990).

When educators employ such gender-biased methods, it reinforces society's message that the opinions of males are more
important than those of females. Sudie Hofmann, professor of
human relations, says that "classroom dynamics do nothing *but*
validate males" (personal communication, October 7, 1988). A
study that Catherine Krupnick conducted at an institution where
half the faculty members are women and females are a majority
in every class revealed that faculty members consistently take
male students and their contributions more seriously than females
and their ideas. In a class where they made up one-tenth of the
students, men did one-fourth of the speaking and were more impul-
sive. Women students, by contrast, wanted time to think about
questions before offering answers, and when they did respond,
women were more likely than men to "enlarge on the ideas of the
previous speaker rather than to challenge his or her initial assumption" (in Fiske, 1990).[3]

Krupnick's research also revealed that women tended to be
more uncomfortable using language in public, and were less proficient in holding an audience—skills that are essential for most
careers. Krupnick notes that "men need listening skills. They

must also be shown that when they give instant answers to complicated questions, mostly for the sake of social posturing, they are not getting a very good education" (cited in Fiske, 1990).

We leaders who give more credence to those who provide instant answers to complicated questions or who answer the questions most do not give the voices of those who want time to think before answering a chance to be heard. Because females tend to predominate in the latter group, their insights and experiences fail to become an integral part of a discussion. Females get the message that somehow they are not important to the group process: Developing rapport is not as valuable as being able to report; being responsive is not as valuable as being correct. As leaders, then, we must become aware of, and be willing to confront, behaviors in ourselves and others that place one gender at a disadvantage; we can find ways to substitute gender-fair methods for methods that devalue any individual.

When Leaders Do Not Act

While we may recognize our collusion, we may nevertheless fail to alter our—and participants'—behavior. Consider the following case study: Although the chairperson recognizes the inappropriate actions of one of his committee, he does not intervene to challenge that behavior.

CASE 1.2

"What's the big deal? It's easy to understand!"

The chair of a government commission, concerned with the confrontational tone of the group's recent public meetings, uncomfortably observes the interaction between one repeatedly obstreperous male and the only female on the commission. This woman, having earned her colleagues' respect as diligent and incisive, is asking for clarification on an issue. The male in question (who has established a reputation as one of the *least* productive members of the group) exasperatedly throws his pencil on the table with the remark, "What's the big deal? It's easy to understand!"

To the chairperson, the behavior is a lashing out; the man's attempt at dominance is childish—a tantrum. To the woman, her peer's blatant put-down makes her feel frozen and disempowered. Temporarily, at least, she defers. The chairperson says and does nothing.

The chairperson recognizes that this woman, whose insights he values and respects, is trying to synthesize meaning, to build rapport. She does not want quick reports or instant answers to complicated questions. Meanwhile, her male counterpart seems more interested in focusing on what he sees as her deficits, engaging in social posturing and trying to maintain status by putting her down. His behavior is similar to that of the male children in Sheldon's (1990a) study; as with the boys, this man is "asserting [his] position of dominance through the use of language." The pencil thrower uses aggressive language—both verbal and nonverbal—to trivialize and marginalize his colleague.

The chairperson, despite his discomfort at the man's rudeness and the woman's humiliation, does not intervene; he does not interrupt the inappropriate behavior, name the oppressive sexism inherent in it, or even state his disapproval. He may profess to support women's empowerment and equality; he may even categorize himself as a feminist. But when confronted with a situation where another male behaves "in ways based on hierarchy and control [and who] is exhibiting behavior which is oppressive to others and prohibits his own growth" (Moyer & Tuttle, 1983), this leader takes no action—except to collude with the offending individual.

When feminist theory is applied to linguistic research, explains Sheldon, we discover the following:

> In discussions involving males and females, male speakers with the same degree of expertise as women speakers tend to dominate and control the conversation by talking more, by controlling the topic of conversation, and by interrupting other speakers more. . . . Men tend to *disagree with or ignore* other speakers, while females tend to *acknowledge and develop* what other speakers have to say. In mixed groups of men and women, women ask more questions than men, which works to *distribute the chance to talk*. Men are more likely to try to monopolize the conversation. (paraphrased in Meier, 1989; emphasis added)[4]

We as leaders may perpetuate these extremes of dominance and deference. Because women tend to concentrate on acknowledging and developing what others say, using rapport talk rather than report talk, females may seem invisible to both the leader and other group members. With competition, aggression, and status-seeking behaviors being rewarded in our culture, such nurturing skills as attending to others and asking questions—distributing the chance to talk—may not be given credence. When leaders value easy answers and accept social posturing, the opportunity to cultivate listening, nurturing, and clarifying behaviors in *all* group members is lost.

How Leaders Collude With Males

Partly because of our socialization as females and males in our culture, we have all been trained to acknowledge and develop what men have to say. When we buy into male social posturing, we perpetuate the status that many men—and their leaders—believe entitles them to positions of privilege and dominance. Here *dominance* refers to how males attempt control, through either overinvolvement or underinvolvement in a group. They catch our attention by prevailing during a discussion or by remaining persistently detached from it. In these cases we, as leaders, usually become preoccupied with what the men are or are not doing, and this preoccupation is collusion. Through our collusion we exacerbate the exclusionary tactics used by males, and perpetuate the entitlement they derive from their privileged behavior—even when we know better.

Bernice Sandler describes her realization that she had been catering to males during presentations: "I examined my own habits as a lecturer and was shocked to realize that I looked at men and called on them more frequently than I did women in my audiences" (quoted in Schmidt, 1982, p. 102). Dale Spender (1980) reveals similar vulnerabilities:

> Blatantly I had declared that I preferred talking to women. Confidently I claimed "women made more sense." But in the presence of men I "unconsciously" reproduced the meanings I consciously deplored. . . . I was constantly discovering, to my own dismay, that while I *believed* that I did not give more attention to men than women in mixed-sex talk, that I did not turn to them for guidance, defer to their opinions, seek confirmation from them, or favour them at the

expense of women, the tapes which I studied told a different story. . . . [I and the other women] all *allowed males to be the center of attention and to determine the parameters of the talk.* (pp. 135-136; emphasis added)

Women perpetuate this kind of deference during everyday interactions, rehearsing these patterns of acquiescent behavior.

How Leaders Collude With Females

Because female participants may appear more docile, reticent, or nonassertive in mixed groups, leaders may try—misguidedly—to protect them, a phenomenon that Sadker calls "classroom chivalry" (in Griffin, 1990, p. 12). "A facilitator may be reluctant to call on women for fear of embarrassing them," asserts Roberta Hall (personal communication, June 1, 1988). On the other hand, a female leader, possibly because she feels more comfortable dialoguing with women, may find herself overattending to females, excluding males. This attention, however, is not always what it seems. Although a female leader may *appear* to favor women, it may be because underneath she is assuming men will not participate anyway, or she does not know how to involve men in the discussion. Her overchallenging of females, then, displays compensation for her discomfort in dealing with males; it also may be a way of setting men apart so she will not have to cope with their responses. In any event, she has become a colluding leader. The presenter in the following case study (a leader who had asked me to critique her presentation) reveals how even the most experienced and aware leaders can fall victim to such collusion.

CASE 1.3

"I gave away my power . . . "

A seasoned educator and consultant, Sharon, is guest lecturer for a university class on the subject of chemical dependency and intergenerational family communication. There are only three males in this class, one of whom is African American (see Figure 1.1). During

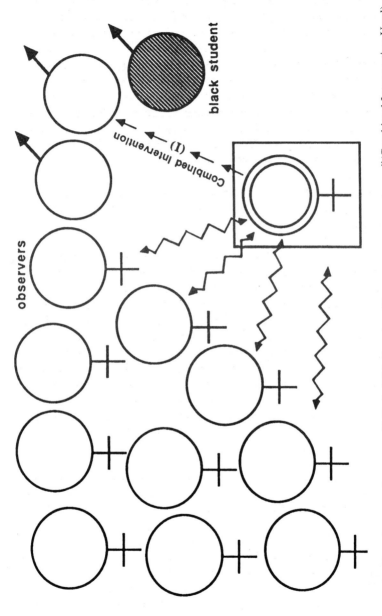

Figure 1.1. Guest Lecturer Appears to Collude With Females : "*I gave away my power . . .*"(Combined Intervention Used)

Sharon's one-hour presentation, she dialogues extensively with the female students—her gaze, gestures, and whole body are directed toward them. She has virtually no eye contact with the male students, who sit in the corner, acting disinterested, doodling in their notebooks, declining to participate. Only occasionally—with a slightly nervous, sidelong glance—does Sharon acknowledge the three men.

For nearly 40 minutes Sharon interacts exclusively with the women, who share personal family experiences. Suddenly the lone black student opens up. Taken aback, she responds with sarcasm, "We finally heard from a male!" Then, speaking to the black man, she continues, "Your nonverbals tell me you have something to say." Her next comment is directed to all the men in the group, "Up to now the men have not shared themselves, and I'm very aware of that." With this encouragement, the black student proceeds to reveal his own personal experiences.

Several issues evolved during this scenario. One primary concern is Sharon's preoccupation with the female students. In addition to her being a guest lecturer, the seating arrangement also affected participation: The women were grouped together, with the men off in the corner. This physical pattern, which Sharon could have restructured, contributed to her collusion. Another issue is the subject matter—a human services topic that the males may have felt uncomfortable discussing. Although Sharon later told me that racism should also have been considered a crucial concern, she felt the overriding issue was gender, because the males had chosen to sit together and as a group did not participate. Gloria Steinem (1983) writes:

> Males' silence (or silence from a member of any dominant group) is not necessarily the same as listening. It might mean a rejection of the speaker, *a refusal to become vulnerable through self-revelation,* or a decision that this conversation is not worthwhile. (p. 179; emphasis added)

Such controlling detachment creates a climate that discourages an equitable distribution of power, parity in participation, and a feeling of connectedness among group members.

Outwardly, Sharon appeared to focus solely on the women, while inwardly she was preoccupied with and protective of the men by allowing them to remain uninvolved. "I gave away my power to the . . . men," she confessed. This is *bias by default* and is sexism on a very subtle level, a level many leaders have only begun to appreciate. Such subtle favoritism can easily go unrecognized, especially when we often do not recognize our collusion with more blatant sexism. Only by becoming aware of such bias—both blatant and subtle—can we hope to avoid collusion.

These suggested gender-responsible methods sound all well and good, but leaders are often confronted with a multifaceted dilemma: It is difficult enough to teach a class, chair a meeting, or facilitate a workshop without having to worry every minute whether we are treating everybody fairly. For a leader to monitor both content and process, he or she must be both well prepared and sensitive. Becoming aware of gender-driven power imbalances, and our role in perpetuating them, calls for a whole new level of sensibility—and energy.

Content, Process, and Sexism

It is easy to see how any leader could be seduced by stereotypes. Male leaders may be so oblivious when other men control topics of conversation, detach themselves from group process, or put women down that they do not recognize these behaviors as power plays. Female leaders may be so afraid of criticism, or so exhausted by their own past efforts to protest mistreatment, that they become numb to the humiliation and exploitation of other women. Indeed, having been mistreated by a system that affords males first-class status, women may actually applaud, however wrongly, the humiliation of men. Despite pressures for women to conform to a male norm, "a woman's participation in behavior that contributes to a hostile environment doesn't mean it is any more acceptable or appropriate" (Martin, 1988).

Males and females learn differently. If we as leaders are to structure environments that are suitable to all participants, we must recognize that certain environments place women at a disadvantage, perpetuating their invisibility. Belenky et al. (1986) have determined that women do not learn well in a competitive/adversarial milieu. Keith (1987) agrees, adding that women do not benefit as much as men from the so-called advocacy mode, in which every point must be debated and defended. Rather, women benefit more from a "collaborative pedagogy" (Miller, 1980) or "connected knowing" (Goldberger, 1989; Noddings, 1984). Furthermore, such "cooperative learning" (Johnson & Johnson, 1988) can be advantageous to males as well as to females. To empower women, then, we must implement less adversarial, more collaborative methods. In this way we draw on women's natural predilections to see issues in context (Gilligan, 1982) and to use language for building rapport (Tannen, 1990).

Other studies show that when women are with men in class-rooms and similar mixed groups, men benefit more than women (Aries, 1976; Bernardez & Stein, 1979; Folkins et al., 1982; Latour, 1987; Megargee, 1969; Wright & Gould, 1977). Men interrupt more (Zimmerman & West, 1975) and control topics of conversation or, as Spender (1980) asserts, men "determine the parameters of the talk." Furthermore, if a woman *does* try to contribute to a discussion or state an opinion, she is frequently seen as aggressive and dominating (Geis, Carter, & Butler, 1982).

In the groups observed so far, males certainly *did* seem to control the process and determine the course of the discussion. Whether they were in the minority (college class) or the majority (business reception, therapy session, committee meeting), men's involve-ment—or lack thereof—distracted and preoccupied the leader's attention. Men's needs and actions took center stage, and male privilege was reinforced. Whether males controlled from the cen-ter or the periphery, leaders were drawn into these controlling maneuvers. Both dominance and distance were used as ways to rank and compete, to maintain status and entitlement. Partly because of our competitive culture and educational system, cou-pled with our own socialization as women and men, we allow ourselves to be controlled by dominators, attention seekers, and other manipulators.

When we leaders allow group process to validate only males, we undervalue not only *what* females have to say, but also *how* they say it. We ignore the insights girls and women bring to a discussion and the skills they use to deliver those insights. Syn-thesizing behavior, displayed by most of the women in the case studies here and commonly exhibited by females elsewhere, goes on all the time in groups. But do we as leaders reward it? Many observers suggest that these traditionally "womanly" modes of discourse are deprecated by our culture and need to be revalued (Borisoff & Merrill, 1985; Spender, 1980; J. L. Thompson, 1983). There is always the danger, however, that the pendulum will swing in the other direction, and women will be so depended upon for their connecting skills that others in the group feel shut out. Women could then be overchallenged and their skills exploited by the leader who, insecure about how to handle distant but dominant males, depends on females to do the interaction work, as we saw in Cases 1.1 and 1.3.

A leader who becomes preoccupied with one gender as a way to protect the other is not a gender-responsible leader. Women may be expected to remain silent, men may be allowed to report and control discussions; women may be expected to develop and maintain rapport, men may be excused from participating. Whichever the case, the power is out of balance, and males hold the advantage (see Table 1.1).

Interventions are necessary to prevent women from being disadvantaged in mixed groups, to keep stereotyped behaviors from distorting participation levels, and to discourage leaders from colluding with controlling males. If either gender is allowed to manipulate group process, the whole group suffers. Worse still, sex role stereotypes are permitted to continue, which impedes individuals' growth. The contributions of both women and men need to be sensitively recognized, actively solicited, and warmly supported. Gender-diverse viewpoints not only foster more richness of discussion, but permit all members to take interest in, and share ownership of, the group's process, to become "important 'shareholders' in the group's enterprise" (Quick, 1986, p. 57).

Unfortunately, however, we leaders lean one way or the other, colluding with, or appearing more sympathetic toward, one gender. Thus we find ourselves in a double bind: If we seem to favor either gender, participation levels become skewed, and both men and women are deprived of a satisfactory learning experience. When different voices are not heard, diversity is lost, and the group is less enriched. Collusion aggravates already tenuous dynamics in mixed-sex groups, and process becomes dysfunctional.

Implications for Leadership

What are the implications of these concepts for those who lead others? What behaviors do we reinforce? What do we value? If as management consultants and trainers we truly believe that women's time is as precious as men's (and that men can parent as well as women), then we will *not* tolerate CEOs—like the one mentioned in the introduction to this volume—who insist that males are too important to waste their energies on child care. As therapists and social workers who truly believe that every client should become fully actualized, we will *not* maintain environments in which silently controlling males remain at a detached distance while we overchallenge and even exploit their partners. If we espouse educational equity, we will *not* ignore girls who sit patiently with hands raised while we give absorbed attention to boys who blurt out answers. If we want to hold up the dignity of each human being, we will *not* tolerate committee proceedings in which some members are trivialized, degraded, or met with symbolic threats of violence. And if we treasure nurturing and connecting skills, we will encourage individuals who enlarge on the ideas of previous speakers, who acknowledge and develop what others have to say, and who demonstrate behavior that leads to linking and colleagueship.

Before we can convince others to be less sexist, we must ourselves be less sexist. Those of us responsible for detecting and correcting bias in others must demonstrate a standard of gender fairness first. It is to be hoped that we are approaching the time in our society when all persons in positions of power will exhibit the same sensitivity and no-nonsense leadership as Chief Justice Robert Wilentz of the New Jersey Supreme Court:

> There's no room for gender bias in our system. . . . There's no room for the funny joke and the not-so-funny joke; there's no room for conscious, inadvertent, sophisticated, clumsy or any other kind of gender bias. (quoted in Schafran, 1989a, p. 12)

Leaders need to go beyond merely making high-minded pronouncements about fairness. If they do not detect their own bias, group members will become so preoccupied with the leader's lack

Table 1.1   Rationale: How Leaders Condone, Collude With, and Perpetuate
                 Women's Second-Class Status

---

(1) *Patriarchal society:* We live in a patriarchal culture in which
    women and their achievements are frequently discounted or
    dismissed, and in which women hold less power. In government,
    business, and other institutions most decision-making positions
    are held by men. Society at large condones male power and
    privilege and cultivates an adversarial culture, one of "ranking"
    rather than "linking" (Eisler, 1987). Our institutions and
    leadership methods are often hierarchical and competitive,
    attributing more credibility to males than to females. Sexism,
    gender role stereotyping, and sexual harassment are rampant.

(2) *Sex role stereotyping:* Females and males, whether functioning as
    leader or follower, are socialized into predictable but limiting
    roles that often disrupt group process and cause unbalanced
    participation levels. In the extreme, these roles are played out by
    males who control by *dominance* or *detachment,* and by females
    who cope through *deference* or by trying to *diagnose* this
    imbalance (see Box 1.1).

(3) *Leadership methods:* Because leaders tend to lead in the ways they
    were led, or to teach in the ways they were taught, they may
    collude with controlling males, unwittingly condoning, and thus
    exacerbating, male entitlement. Females, meanwhile, are
    frequently treated by leaders and/or other group members as
    inadequate or invisible. This creates "chilly climates" (Hall &
    Sandler, 1982, 1984; Sandler, 1986) that further discourage and
    disempower women, placing them at even greater disadvantage.

(4) *Organizational systems/cultures:* Organizational cultures, systems,
    materials, and administrative policies are not always sensitive,
    gender fair, or even nonsexist. Leaders may not take time to
    critique their institutions' standards, much less their own
    methods. Furthermore, leaders may shun peer review and
    refuse critical feedback from colleagues who could help them
    develop more equitable methods. Many organizations thus
    remain chilly and even hostile to women.

The Process of Change

(1) *Gender-responsible leadership:* Change requires that leaders
    recognize bias and sexism in themselves and others and take
    steps toward remediation when favoritism overchallenges or
    underchallenges either females or males. Because of females'

second-class status, leaders need to place special emphasis on women's empowerment.

(2) *Women's ways of knowing:* Leaders can revalue women's ways of knowing (Belenky et al., 1986) and understand that women thrive on the use of "rapport talk" (Tannen, 1990), linking and connecting with others. Adversarial cultures, which emphasize ranking, may inhibit women because females learn and participate more readily in collaborative settings. If women's interaction styles are recognized, appreciated, and cultivated, then females can become more visible and instrumental in mixed groups.

(3) *Different voices:* It is essential to women's self-concepts and learning capacities that their voices be heard; it is crucial to the well-being of society that leaders develop sensitivity toward, and techniques to tap, the unique insights and talents of women. Leaders must devise and implement gender-fair strategies that will help create group climates in which women are as advantaged, and valued, as men.

SOURCE: Portions of this rationale were developed in dialogue with Jan Stanley, then coordinator of the Multicultural Gender-Fair Curriculum Project, St. Cloud State University, St. Cloud, Minnesota (1990).

of authenticity that the message becomes irrelevant. Leaders need to catch themselves in the very act of favoritism and collusion, to be aware of how they make assumptions, how group members attempt power plays. In order to reach this level of gender sensitivity, we all need to learn to *watch ourselves watching ourselves,* a process of meta-awareness known as "cultivating the observer":

> The ability to fully engage in our own [leadership] while maintaining a level of objectivity about it seems a challenging duality to hold. The knack of being able *to see* comes with practice. . . . Having established a platform from which to observe ourselves, we must then cultivate the one who observes. [This] means . . . seeing the truth about ourselves and how we interact . . . seeing the limitations, patterns, conditionings. (Findhorn Foundation, 1989)[5]

The focus in this chapter has been on leader behaviors. We have observed how leaders tend to be preoccupied with controlling males, whether these men are acting in a dominating, competitive manner or are controlling from a detached, apparently disinterested,

distance. We notice that dominance and detachment most often
garner more leader attention than the more connecting behaviors
that clarify or enlarge on what others have to say. It is understandable that our gender role socialization, our collusion, and our
busyness with content may cause us to be oblivious to biased
processes. Yet it is possible—indeed, it is utterly necessary—for
us to step aside and observe our leadership methods. We may
claim that we are gender sensitive, but prevailing research indicates that males continue to receive preferential treatment while
females become even more invisible and disempowered.

Being objective about ourselves, however, is not always simple.
As you prepare to analyze this volume's case studies and vignettes, ask yourself these questions:

(1) On the organizational level, what sort of climate exists in my insti-
     tution or workplace, and how does this environment contribute to
     the gender-driven imbalances that sometimes disrupt the groups I
     lead or to which I belong?

(2) On the personal level, what cultural and personal expectations,
     internal and external, occasionally blind me to my own collusion in
     these power plays?

(3) How can I cultivate the observer in myself and become more aware
     of how I may favor some persons to the exclusion of others?

(4) If I *do* recognize my favoritism and collusion, what prevents me
     from taking action when I see that one gender is disadvantaged?
     Why might I be afraid to intervene?

(5) What proactive steps can I take to improve my leadership skills so
     that I will be able to acknowledge and capitalize on the strengths of
     all group members, thus assuring that one gender does not become
     marginalized or invisible?

As leaders, how can we nourish gender fairness in ourselves and
model it for others? What does it mean to be a gender-responsible
facilitator? Do we practice what we preach, modeling nonsexist
language and behavior, interacting equally with both genders?
What leadership strategies can we cultivate that will optimize
learning benefits for both genders, with special sensitivity to
women's ways of knowing?

Notes

1. This example is from an article titled "How Stereotypes About Women Influence Judges," by attorney Lynn H. Schafran of the National Organization for Women's Legal Defense Fund. Such remarks—for example, a judge/attorney commenting on a female attorney's hairstyle—are dangerous because "comments about appearance made at particularly inappropriate moments can interfere with the effectiveness of an attorney's presentation," according to the Minnesota Supreme Court Task Force for Gender Fairness in the Courts (1989). (To receive a copy of this report, contact State Court Administration, Minnesota Supreme Court, 1745 University, Suite 302, St. Paul, MN 55104.)

2. Quotes from Witt in this chapter and Chapter 4 are from her article "Males Communicate in Authoritative Tone," which appeared in the *St. Cloud* (Minnesota) *Times* on August 16, 1990. Copyright © 1990, Gannett Co., Inc. Reprinted by permission.

3. Quotes from Fiske in this chapter and Chapters 2 and 5 are from his article "Survey Finds Pro-Male Bias at Colleges," which appeared in the Minneapolis *Star Tribune* on April 25, 1990. Copyright © 1990 by The New York Times Company. Reprinted by permission.

4. This quote is reprinted by permission of the Minneapolis *Star Tribune*.

5. This is taken from a description of a workshop titled "Cultivating the Observer," which was held at the Findhorn Foundation, Scotland. The actual quote is "fully engaging in our own *life*," but I have substituted the word *leadership*. Findhorn is a community that believes "the planet is involved in an evolutionary expansion of consciousness." The community offers educational programs that help people to "think globally, act locally."

◀ 2 ▶

WORDS, SPACE, AND SEXISM

How Males Enforce Entitlement
Through Language and Location

When I tried to communicate at a level that commanded respect, he was too threatened to hear me.

(the Reverend Jean Boese Dickson, director of a domestic violence program, describing earlier experience with a professor in divinity school, 1990)

A feminist assault on the politics of talking, and listening, is a radical act.

Gloria Steinem (1983)

In classrooms and workshops, committee meetings and social gatherings, boardrooms and dining rooms across the land, females and males are engaged in ever-so-subtle hierarchical positionings and denigrating verbal interchanges that might appear innocuous to the casual observer. However, these interchanges are not only distracting, they also create imbalance, disrupt process, and corrupt the possibility of egalitarian relationships. Process is disrupted because, instead of enjoying one another's presence, or focusing on the task at hand, people are preoccupied with why the interaction is so nonproductive. The following situations exemplify:

(1) "Have you ever noticed how the men do most of the talking in our evening discussion group?" declares a group member. She continues, "I'm thinking of leaving the group."

(2) "If you can't get that guy to shut up, I'm dropping the workshop," a disgruntled female participant warns the leader.

(3) A couple have weekend guests. The wife, in the midst of preparing an elaborate meal, has food and dishes spread all over the kitchen. Her husband, seated idly at the kitchen table and not lifting a finger, says, "Can't you cook without making such a mess? Look at this kitchen! There isn't one square inch of countertop space left."

(4) "Let's get this meeting wrapped up," demands a committee member. "I have to hurry home and beat my wife—otherwise she'll miss it." A female member retorts: "BITE YOUR TONGUE!" Another male member agrees, "Yes, that was a *very* sexist remark."

(5) A consultant meets with two male managers to plan training for supervisors, the majority of whom are female. The consultant asks, "Should the training be held in one session only, or should it extend to several sessions?" A manager answers, "One session is enough; we don't want those supervisors to have *too* much training—they might get smarter than we are!"

(6) A guest lecturer comments on the dynamics of the class discussion she is facilitating: "Up to now, the men have not shared themselves, and I'm very aware of that."

The Sabotage of Group Process
by Gender Role Extremes

What is going on? Are these just isolated cases, or part of a pattern? Do these scenarios have anything in common? For purposes of clarification and illustration, let us analyze the above examples of dysfunctional female-male interaction using the Four D's of gender role extremes introduced in Chapter 1: *dominate, detach, defer,* and *diagnose.* These categories are not always gender specific, and they are certainly not intended to limit us or lock us more rigidly into stereotypes. Rather, the Four D's can sensitize us about the self-defeating nature of extreme gender role behaviors, and how these behaviors create power imbalances in groups.

All of the interactions described above depict males in either a *dominating* mode (acting privileged, making condescending or

degrading remarks, controlling conversations) or a *detached* mode
(refusing to share themselves, lecturing rather than listening, remaining on the periphery of an activity). The males seem to be
trying to *control* a situation, either by overpowering it or by distancing themselves from it.

Females, meanwhile, seem to be in a *deference* mode that includes
playing *diagnostician*. Women defer by allowing males to take over
discussions, to manipulate from a distance, or to otherwise assert
privilege verbally and spatially. Females also play another very
significant role: They assume the role of a "diagnosing detective" by
sniffing out, identifying, naming, and describing what is happening
between the lines. They report on what they perceive—the subtleties
of interaction: "Men are doing all the talking"; "Up to now, the men
have not shared themselves." The one man who does diagnose an
interaction ("Yes, that was a *very* sexist remark") is prompted first by
the woman who had initially confronted the inequity.

This act of *naming*, commenting on, and diagnosing what one
perceives follows the guidelines suggested by Pierce and Page
(1990, pp. 36-38): The value of naming is that one describes and
reports on what is observed, making every effort not to blame
individuals or place a value judgment on the process. It appears
that women, perhaps because they so often find themselves in
powerless positions, are most apt to name, and call others' attention to, male dominance and privilege. In the examples above, it
was the women who detected power imbalance, diagnosed sexism
or discrimination, interpreted events to others, and sometimes
took action to intervene. While these vignettes were deliberately
chosen to make a point about rigidly stereotyped behaviors, in my
experience they typify fairly common power dynamics between
women and men, not only in families, but in other groups as well.
We will return to these scenarios again later.

As we have seen, extreme gender roles can sabotage mixed-group
process and subvert the possibility of colleagueship. Instead of con-
centrating on major issues under discussion and respectfully supporting one another, women and men are mired in gender-driven
power maneuvers: men trying to maintain power through intimidation or indifference, women trying to cope within this coercive hierarchical framework. I call these hierarchical shufflings *gender politics*.

How do men and women fall into these roles? What part does
their upbringing and socialization play in molding these extreme

behaviors? And why might a person gravitate to these polarities in an effort to control others or to cope in a group?

The Dysfunctional Collusion of Dominance and Subordinance

"Women are taught to accommodate to men," suggests therapist Michael Obsatz (1975):

> Women are taught to accommodate to men.
> Men are taught they will be accommodated to.
> Men expect to be understood.
> Women work to understand.[1]

Like Norman in the therapy session depicted in Case 1.1, men may expect others to work to understand them; they may control through detachment, expecting to be accommodated to. Like Norman's wife, Barbara, women frequently make extra effort to understand and accommodate.

What are some possible origins of men's tendency to either detach or dominate? Obsatz (1975) thinks that men are pressured to "measure up" and compete. This means they have difficulty revealing their inner doubts and vulnerabilities (which would make them appear weak) but must report "events external to themselves," such as sports, politics, their prowess with women. Because many men find it difficult to share feelings, they are difficult to know:

> Men are difficult to love. They are difficult to love because they are difficult to know. They are difficult to know because they never discuss who they are or what they feel. (pp. 2-3)

Obsatz believes that because men "project their insecurity . . . onto other men and women," they have difficulty interrelating with others, which may help explain their greater comfort in the detached mode, or what he calls "withdrawal":

> The real man is always on top of things, in command, in control, and confident. . . . He is totally independent and invincible. As a result of the pressure on men to "be men," a male never learns a vocabulary

of sharing. He is unable to share his feelings, his doubts, his wants. Revealing himself is unmasculine. *As a reaction to caring, a man responds with withdrawal.* Caring is prying. . . . "Boy Talk" involves continuous frustration because it avoids *the basic need in a relationship to share oneself with another.* (p. 2; emphasis added)

Similar ideas are represented in the psychological theory of Alfred Adler (1914/1980), who believed that our primary motivation as humans is to *connect*. However, since many men during their upbringing traditionally have not learned to connect, they feel inadequate when they try to establish intimacy, and may compensate for this inadequacy by trying to dominate (Rigby-Weinberg, 1986).

Detachment and withdrawal were the coping mechanisms that Norman used in Case 1.1; this is a function of the need to control. To Charles Niessen-Derry, who facilitates groups for men who batter women, in a system of control, detachment is a form of oppression:

Detachment and dominance seem to be at opposite ends of a continuum but they are all part of a system of control. The detached person appears helpless. He sits in the corner of the group saying nothing or is really distant in the family. People think: He's not saying anything. Poor man can't share himself—we must draw him out. Maybe he could use some assertiveness training so he can learn to share his feelings.

But he is really controlling from that position. He's letting other people in the group or the family take responsibility to interact and make decisions. It looks like he's distant and uninvolved. *But detachment is actually synonymous with oppression.* The detached person is controlling from a distance, pulling other people's strings. It's all part of the same continuum of dominance. The detached person knows others are very much preoccupied with him in his absence: What is he thinking? What is going on with him? Why isn't he involved? Why doesn't he contribute? *What the male is NOT doing becomes a preoccupation.* (personal communication, 1989)

Niessen-Derry then provides a very personal self-revelation about his own journey toward gender equity: "The problem is, after all, men and male culture. . . . The bottom line is, men don't want to give up power and privilege. . . . Part of my process in trying to become a 'feminist male' was learning how much I had to give up."[2]

Just as males have learned to control through intimidation or manipulative detachment, females—perhaps to cope from their one-down position—may resort to continuous accommodation and deference. In a group, for example, females may try to provide a balancing contrast to male dominance by being receptive and listening, or by clarifying and diagnosing. Of course, this accommodating behavior can be an asset to any group, and it is a function that women learn, says Obsatz, partly because of their nurturing role. Women have learned to be empathic and good listeners, he says, because "others are dependent upon their perceptions and hearing." What other authors (e.g., Adler, 1914/1980, in Rigby-Weinberg, 1986; Belenky et al., 1986; Desjardins, 1989a; Gilligan, 1982) might call "connecting," Obsatz (1975) terms "accommodation" and "receptivity":

> Receptivity has been termed a female trait, related to biological and physical factors. But receptivity is a socialized trait, related to accommodation. . . . Women work at clarification, explication, and expression. Women work at relationships. (p. 5)

In spite of the value of receptivity and empathy, women's tendency to defer—in its extreme form—might be interpreted not as helpful accommodation, but as maladaptive submissiveness and even manipulative obsequiousness. Also, spending one's energies diagnosing the behaviors of others instead of taking a strong position oneself can be used as a control mechanism just as much as can dominance or detachment.

Moderately deferent behavior in groups *does* have its place—it allows others to have the floor and speak their minds. It is important for both women and men to learn to yield to others in order that all voices can be heard; in this manner discussions evolve, business is transacted, decisions are made. However, deferring and accommodating persistently, refusing to state one's own opinions or to meet one's own needs, is actually irresponsible behavior because it allows others to make all the decisions. Extreme accommodation and on-the-surface passivity can also be utilized to manipulate and control others, as in: "Oh, I don't mind [sigh], you boys go and have a good time [gulp], and I'll just stay here and do the dishes [sob]." This is classic "passive/aggressive" behavior. Pierce and Page's (1990) Male/Female Continuum (see Figure 2.1) depicts this indirect aggression as *psychological punishment*: The woman is *withholding*, with *anger frozen inside*, behavior that has its counterpart in male *avoidance*.

As the Male/Female Continuum makes clear, there is a sorry synergy between the dominance of males and the deference of females. As a male *intimidates*, a female may act *helpless*; as he *devalues* her (as in the third example above: "Can't you cook without making such a mess?"), she tries even harder to *control through helping* (she will show *him*—she will cook the entire meal alone). Thus women and men do a dance around each other, and the dysfunctional system of gender politics feeds on itself. It is clear that these sorts of mixed-gender interactions fail to provide the kind of raw material out of which honest, collegial, mutually respectful relationships are forged.

Both extreme deference and extreme dominance may arise from a need to control others. When females and males exhibit these behaviors, they are perpetuating what Pierce and Page (1990) call the "collusion of dominance and subordinance." It must be reemphasized, however, that although collusion between equals implies mutual agreement, commonly understood deceit, and even mutual benefit, collusion between dominants and subordinates is not always mutually beneficial, because of the power differential. Because males retain power and privilege in our society, females hold less power and may defer simply to survive. Thus when we see a woman resorting to unhealthy extremes to accommodate, it is important that we recognize her as second-class citizen and even a victim who is trying to cope within a hierarchical system in which she is chronically underprivileged.

How Males Try to Reinforce Their Privilege

Males may attempt to maintain this hierarchy through a variety of strategies, two of which involve encroaching on common space (territorial sexism) and using language to discredit or disparage women "linguistic sexism" (Henley & Thorne, 1977, p. 202). *Territorial* sexism has to do with space: how people arrange themselves in a given area and how they take control of, or relinquish, territory.

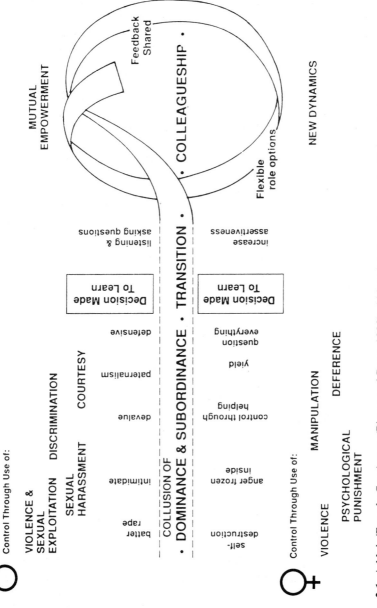

Figure 2.1. *A Male/Female Continuum* (Pierce and Page, 1990). Abbreviated version, used with permission.

37

At its most extreme, territorial sexism allows no space at all for one gender—a form of "bias by omission." Attempts to assert status can be observed as we watch who sits where in meeting rooms, lecture halls, and workshop settings. Who sits at the head and foot of the conference table? Which gender distributes itself across the back row of the lecture hall? Will it be women or men who tend to isolate themselves in a self-contained but controlling pod in a corner of the room? Will one gender be expected to accommodate to spaces designed to exclude them altogether?

Linguistic sexism is about how people use words as weapons with which to criticize, marginalize, assert status, and compete. Several forms of discouraging, disparaging sexism are evident in the examples above: "We don't want those [female] supervisors to get smarter than we are"; "I have to hurry home and beat my wife." As we explore the interface of language and bias, we will recognize how the subtle *absence* of a word is also sexist, and is yet another form of bias by omission.

Finally, we will look at what part leaders play in all of this: Do leaders condone the use of space and language as tools of discrimination, or do they intervene when some group members try to segregate, isolate, or denigrate others?

Territorial Sexism:
How Use of Space Marginalizes Women

Those who try to control others by appropriating territory reveal their motives in the ways they distribute themselves in a defined area—in other words, how they take up space. Described below are three structured educational environments with a designated leader in which males have asserted status by occupying advantageous territory. In the first two groups, someone simply describes what is bothersome (descriptive intervention). In the third scenario, however, a participant actually suggests a concrete way to restructure the situation (transformational intervention). (These and other intervention strategies are defined more thoroughly in Chapter 7.)

Example A: Graduate Class

Psychology professor Mary A. Dwyer, St. Cloud State University, notices that students are seated in a horseshoe shape, with two men at the apex. She comments: "If you were to draw this circle, the men would be in the center—they are in the *power place*" (describing).

Example B: Informal Seminar at a Large University

"We are very split in this room," comments a professor as she observes a brown-bag seminar during which a female guest presenter is very much preoccupied with, and colluding with, controlling males (see Figure 2.2). "Over here are the women; over there are the men who are doing all the talking, with lengthy speeches. There is a very strange dynamic, or lack of one, going on here" (describing).

Example C: Workshop

As a conference breakout session is about to begin, a female participant notices the segregated seating arrangement: The male facilitator sits at the center of one semicircle, surrounded by male participants, while females occupy the opposite half of the circle. She expresses concern to the facilitator: "With the males all lined up around the leader, we'll automatically be off to a bad start." She then asks him to change the arrangement (transforming) and he graciously complies.

In each of the above examples, intervention was initiated by a woman. It is important to emphasize, however, that an intervention can be implemented smoothly and effectively by anyone—female or male, group member, observer, or leader.

But what if there is no leader in sight, and we find ourselves in a less structured environment, perhaps interacting with peers, colleagues, or strangers? Who will intervene then? Consider the following informal scene.

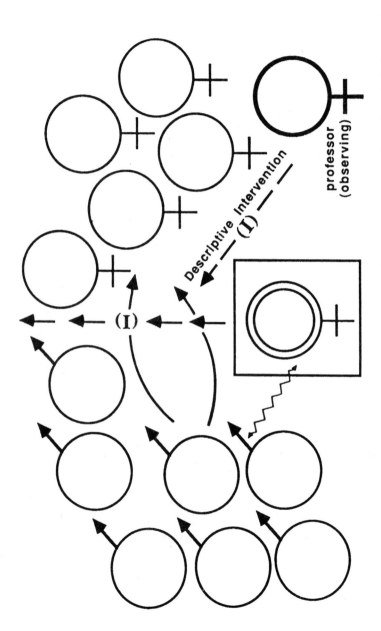

Figure 2.2. Seminar Presenter Colludes With Controlling Males: *"There is a very strange dynamic or lack of one, going on here . . ."* (Descriptive Intervention Used)

Example D: Airplane Seating

An author of books on gender issues is a frequent flier because of her national speaking engagements. She reports that whenever she is seated between two males on an airplane, they invariably take the arm rests. After numerous trips, and her repeated requests for accommodation, this author and professional speaker gave up in exasperation. She reports, "I'm tired of lecturing men about respecting women's right to personal space." (Her testimony is especially relevant. A study aboard airplanes revealed that "male chauvinism transcends gravity": Males seated next to females were more likely to use their mutual armrest on a ratio of three to one, even when the experiment was controlled for males' larger average body size; reported in H. Goodman, 1983.)

Nancy Henley and Barrie Thorne (1977), in a discussion of "womanspeak and manspeak," explain how societal expectations of femininity and masculinity may affect how each gender occupies personal space:

> Women's general bodily demeanor must be *restrained* and *restricted*; their femininity is gauged, in fact, by how little space they take up, while masculinity is judged by males' *expansiveness* and the strength of their flamboyant gestures. Males control greater territory and personal space, a property associated with dominance and high status in both human beings and animals. (p. 213; emphasis added)

When we see a woman restraining her behavior (using the airplane armrest less than one-third of the time!) or restricting herself from space she has every right to occupy (near the center of the circle), we see a female fulfilling two sets of expectations: the *external* expectation of society that she behave a certain way (Don't put your elbows there, he might think you're aggressive!) and also her *internal* self-messages about what it means to be "feminine" (If I'm a real lady, I'll keep my elbows to myself).

When we see a man assuming that a certain space is his, we see a person also fulfilling societal expectations, if he lives in a society that gauges masculinity by a man's "expansiveness." This expansiveness can go beyond thoughtlessness to extreme arrogance: One of the males in the study of airplane armrests reported, "I feel I deserve to have [the armrest]; she doesn't" (H. Goodman, 1983).

The logistics of who appropriates armrests or who deserves to claim "power places" becomes a symbol for inequity on a larger scale. To usurp common space, claiming it as one's own, may seem like an innocuous minitransgression, or microinequity,[3] yet it is part of a larger collusion of dominance and subordinance: The male *excludes, discounts, devalues*; the female *endures* and *withdraws*. These minor usurpations in the microcosms of airplanes, class-rooms, and workshops are harbingers of more devastating infractions—greater oppression in the macrocosm of society at large. The word *usurp*, which originates from the same root word as *rape*, means "to take [a position, etc.] and hold without right." Usurping certainly is not raping, but those who consider it their right to encroach arbitrarily and persistently on personal or mutual space are taking one more stitch in the fabric of an overall violent and oppressive system.

Sexism, as we have seen, is expressed in what gender sits where and how "expansive" they are when they get there. But what if women or men have no place at all to call their own? It is one thing to feel excluded from mutually shared space or a certain section of a room, but what if there is utterly no room available?

A total absence of space can also reveal an underlying bias. For example, until very recently, there was no women's toilet in the physicians' lounge of my community's only hospital, in spite of the fact that more than 19 female physicians had joined the staff in the previous three to four years (Bergquist, 1990).[4] The absence of facilities for females, although understandable considering attitudes that prevailed when the hospital was built, exposes an underlying assumption—women are not doctors, only men can be physicians, this is male territory—and even, possibly, the assumption that women's needs are not as important as men's. This sexism by omission is not peculiar to health care, as many women who have worked at construction sites will testify.

We leaders cannot do much about the placement of elbows on airplanes, and we certainly are not about to organize sledgeham-mer brigades to remodel our local hospitals. But we *can* confront, within our own learning environments, the privileged position-ings executed by some that place others at a disadvantage. We can begin by being especially observant about use of territory and language, as suggested by poet Adrienne Rich (1979): "Observe the space men allow themselves, physically and verbally, the male assumption that people will listen even when the majority of the group is female" (p. 243).

When territorial sexism is suspected, how can we remediate? We need to move beyond simply describing how males usurp territory: My, my look here—the men are all cozying up to the leader; or "We are very split in this room—the men are over there, doing all the talking." Rather, it is important that we provide practical solutions that reshuffle people and restructure the space: We're off to a bad start with this seating arrangement; let's sit in different chairs!

Throughout this text we will see leaders take similar risks to modify their own leadership patterns. Such initiative involves heightening one's awareness of space and even modifying one's body language, as suggested by English professor Richard Pearce, who offers a method for encouraging reticent, less verbal group members who are being interrupted by dominant, excessively verbal, nonlistening "over-participators": "The most important thing is to be aware of the space in the room and think about who is speaking. . . . Then you can consciously, even physically, turn away from over-participators" (quoted in Fiske, 1990, p. 5E).

The way we negotiate who sits where or who controls turf will be a reliable thermometer for measuring whether our group environments are "chilly" or "warm." Leaders (and their institutions) who are able to confront territorial sexism and solve space problems are demonstrating an important ingredient of gender-responsible leadership.

Linguistic Sexism:
Where Seldom Is Heard an Encouraging Word

Just as leaders must recognize how males may subtly appropriate certain territory in order to reinforce privilege and marginalize women, so also must we be aware how men may employ nuances of speech as an instrument of control or a way to discredit women. Researchers Zimmerman and West (1975) recorded cross-sex conversations in coffee shops and other public places, and analyzed segments for speech overlaps, interruptions, and silences. Virtually all the interruptions and overlaps originated with the male speakers. Women exhibited the most silences, and these silences tended to follow delayed minimal responses, overlaps, and interruptions by the men. According to Grady, Brannon, and Pleck (1979):

> The authors [Zimmerman & West] suggest that retarded minimal responses and interruptions function as topic *control* mechanisms. The cross-sex patterns of interaction are reminiscent of adult-child conversations and seem to represent the assertion of the male to *control* topics and to limit the rights of the female speaker to *control* the conversation. (pp. 108-109; emphasis added)

"Most of us are still largely unaware of the nuances of expression and gesture that identify and stereotype sex," explain Henley and Thorne (1977, p. 202). The work of these researchers, plus that of Elizabeth Aries (1976), is cited in *As Boys Become Men: Learning New Male Roles* (*A Curriculum for Exploring Male Role Stereotyping*) by Doug Cooper Thompson (1985). This guide enumerates certain stereotypical male communication patterns, listed in Box 2.1, that set up communication barriers and are notorious for disrupting group process.[5]

Faultfinding and other controlling, competitive behaviors, as described in Box 2.1, are the norm in many settings, and "listening to self" may become more important than listening to others. However, the communication skills of asking questions and listening are essential to healthy group function. If a group or a culture is to move toward the conditions of "colleagueship" (Pierce & Page, 1990) and "partnership" (Eisler, 1987), these consensus-building skills must be honored and cultivated. When leaders make an effort to reinforce such rapport-building behaviors as "clarification and explication," such nurturing skills as asking questions or "adding a thought," we demonstrate not only that we value "women's ways of knowing" (and learning), but that we are committed less to hierarchical, adversarial, "ranking" environments and more to egalitarian, cooperative, and "linking" climates (Eisler, 1987).

Many of the females in our examples—for instance, Sue, whom we will meet momentarily—demonstrate communication skills that promote linking. These women reach out, verbally and nonverbally, and make an effort to cultivate collegial relationships. They try to keep conversations going, add a thought, do the interaction work, nurture others and accommodate. In short, they

BOX 2.1

**Male Talk: Stereotypical Male Behaviors That May Create
Communication Barriers in Mixed Groups**

Dominance: Often the males as a group will have more airtime than women, especially if the subject is considered serious and not personal.

Problem solving: Males will tend to answer questions while females will ask questions; more specifically, males will tend to make demonstrative and declarative statements while females will offer qualifying and inquiring statements.

Self-listening: Males will tend to interrupt each other (and females) more than women do, indicating that they are not really listening. They are instead listening to the first part of the other's statement and then beginning to formulate a response in preparation for competition in the conversation.

Finding fault: Often males will find fault while females will "add a thought."

Topic selection: Most of the time, conversations will center on those topics where males feel secure or feel they are experts.

SOURCE: *As Boys Become Men: Learning New Male Roles (A Curriculum for Exploring Male Role Stereotyping)*, by Doug Cooper Thompson (New York: Irvington, 1985, pp. 31-32). Reprinted by permission of the author.

want to *connect*. Many of the men, on the other hand, seem more preoccupied with trying to achieve personal rank using "male talk." They try to control by maneuvering conversations to topics in which they are interested and turning off topics they do not care for; in the process, they discredit and depersonalize others, as we shall witness in most of the following scenarios. Unfortunately, we leaders often reward this controlling behavior. We may give more credence to demonstrative, declarative speech patterns than to qualifying, inquiring language. We pay more attention to "report talk" than to "rapport talk" (Tannen, 1990), thus placing already marginalized females at a further learning disadvantage.

Put-Downs by Men: Psychological or Political?

For whatever reason, whether it be male psychological development, sex role socialization, or a host of other factors, many males continue to use language as a vehicle for maintaining status. No matter what the personal toll on their bodies and collective psyche, many men continue to strive verbally to be the expert, seem more preoccupied with ranking than with linking, and, in the process, often invest little energy in building collegial relationships. The following exchange between two professionals, although very brief, illustrates the dichotomy in interaction styles that places a woman at a disadvantage:

> A workshop facilitator, Sue, decides to upgrade her skills by attending a seminar on personality types presented by another facilitator, Sam. As she enters the room, she is introduced to Sam by the seminar coordinator, who says, "Sam, I'd like you to meet Sue. She presents workshops and seminars just as you do."
>
> *Sue* [smiling and reaching out to shake Sam's hand]: Glad to meet you, Sam. I'm looking forward to being in your workshop.
>
> *Sam* [solemnly shaking her hand, and speaking in terms of the upcoming workshop content]: I can see that you're a "high dominant."

Using terms from the "male talk" shown in Box 2.1, we see that Sam seems to be listening to himself (*self-listening*) rather than to Sue. He does not respond reciprocally to her greeting; there is no Glad to meet you, Sue. Instead, he selects a topic, and a different one at that: He decides to analyze her personality style. In one fell swoop, Sam fails to nurture Sue, changes the subject, and labels her (*topic selection* and *finding fault*). His behavior is a prime example of projection. Sam attempts to establish status for himself (dominance), which he then proceeds to project onto Sue: "I can see that you're a 'high dominant.' "

In short, Sam feels threatened. He finds it necessary to prepare for competition rather than to connect. Because he feels insecure, he "projects [his] insecurity" (Obsatz, 1975, p. 2) onto Sue, which interferes with his ability to connect with her. He will not, or cannot, see Sue in a collegial light as another professional deserving of equal respect. He does not find words to ask, What sort of seminars do you offer, Sue? He refuses to nurture by saying something like, I look forward to having you in this workshop. No, Sam must appear to be the expert. To him, the situation must be "one up, one down." A win/win equilibrium is not possible; he sees the interaction in terms of win/lose. Sue has tried to connect, Sam needs to compete; she wants to link, he needs to rank. "He is protesting against the equality of the other sex by asserting his own superiority" (Woolf, 1929/1957, p. 105).

Carolyn Desjardins (1989a, 1989b) provides a possible psychological framework for understanding why Sam puts Sue down. Desjardins, building on concepts developed by Carol Gilligan (1982) and others, explains that females frequently function in a "relationships/care" mode; that is, they try to *synthesize and bridge,* to *cooperate and nurture.* Males, on the other hand, often feel more comfortable in a "justice/ rights" mode, preferring to interact with others through *competition and power.* Like Sue, women may spend extra effort trying to connect; since their primary need is to establish and maintain intimacy, they may feel threatened when others assert autonomy by refusing to connect. Like Sam, men may spend extra effort trying to be separate; since their primary need is to be autonomous, they may feel threatened when others try to connect or establish some level of intimacy. (Desjardins cautions that these behaviors are not gender specific: "Everyone has behaviors in both modes but will be dominant in one.") Using this framework, it appears that Sam, wanting to maintain autonomy, is threatened by intimacy and thus keeps Sue at arm's length. Or, perhaps even more than her expression of caring, he fears her assertion of professional competence and her autonomy. We see a male afraid of being "pushed around" and a female afraid of being "pushed away" (Tannen, 1991).

We could continue our therapeutic analysis of Sam's behavior and speculate: (a) Poor Sam must have a self-image problem—maybe he could use a workshop on self-esteem. (b) Sam has a problem with authority: He perceives Sue as "one up"—a threat to his status—and therefore an adversary with whom he must compete. Or (c) It's all the fault of Sam's female parent: Since Sue is female, she's seen as Mother—thus Other—and Sam must therefore push her away.

Viewing Sam from this psychological perspective, we could give him the benefit of the doubt, determining that his motives were completely unconscious and that he meant no disrespect. He was a little out of bounds, maybe, a little aggressive, but certainly not maligning on purpose. But Niessen-Derry, speaking from his experience with violent men, doesn't buy this—what he calls—"Poor Shmok" theory (personal communication, 1989). From his knowledge gleaned while leading groups of male batterers, he reasons that if we analyze oppressive male behavior solely within a psychological framework we are making excuses and missing the point. Men verbally put women down—and criticize, categorize, patronize, trivialize, marginalize, and even beat women—because men benefit politically from this exercise of power and privilege, pure and simple:

> I believe we allow men to escape from responsibility when we use a therapeutic model to define oppression. Not only is it inaccurate, but it is extremely helpful in maintaining the status quo. This is beneficial to men, of course, but it is exceedingly dangerous to women. . . .
> In naming Patriarchy, it is often put forth that men oppress women because of [deficiencies] in individual makeup: lack of self-esteem or communication skills, inability to access feelings, etc. With this type of therapeutic analysis, men then are seen as victims . . . and therefore, not responsible for the oppressive system they maintain. (If the poor guys were just "fulfilled" personally they wouldn't find the "need" to control or abuse others: the "Poor Shmok" theory.) . . . The problem *is*, after all, men and male culture. (see also Niessen-Derry, 1991a, 1991b)

Using Niessen-Derry's framework as worst-case scenario, we could then surmise that Sam's behavior is coldly and consciously calculated as a power play—a control mechanism to put Sue in her place. No matter what his motivation, our friend Sam might find it helpful to display, in some prominent spot where he can be reminded daily, a favorite slogan of the women's movement: "A man of *quality* is not threatened by a woman seeking *equality*."

The Spoken Word: Damned If She Speaks, Damned If She Doesn't

In spite of sometimes unwitting but oppressive male exercises in status seeking and leader collusion with males, many females do eventually establish themselves in mixed groups. They finally *do* get the floor (or the leader's attention) and begin to speak in their own authentic voices. When they speak, however, they are often confronted with several ironies: Others perceive them as either "too talkative" or "too opinionated" even when they are not. Women who talk one-third of the time are perceived as talking half of the time, reports Roberta Hall (1986), citing linguistics research. "If their participation level is thirty percent, it's seen as 50/50," she reports, "and if women talk more than that, they're seen as dominating."

The myth of the "gabby" woman prevails, in spite of overwhelming evidence to the contrary. According to linguistics professor Alice Freed (1985), "Studies have repeatedly shown that in identical settings, given the same question or situation (all other things being identical), men talk for a longer time than women."

Furthermore, even though women use appropriate language, when they make strong statements or requests they may be categorized as "unfeminine," "uppity," or "overachieving" by leader, participants, or both. Like Sue, an assertive woman using language to establish connection and to *link* is often perceived as an aggressive woman trying to achieve status and to *rank*. As a result of this linguistic sexism, many women choose one of two options: They retreat into even more obscure anonymity or they speak up and openly diagnose their mistreatment, which then often evokes even worse repercussions. Women are therefore damned if they do speak, and damned if they don't.

Because she is expected to be "nice," "polite," and "feminine," a woman is seen as quite normal when she sounds tentative and hesitant, when she hangs back waiting to be introduced (like the executive at the business reception, Chapter 1), when she defers to others opinions, or even when she lets herself be controlled. Since men are expected to be in charge, sure of themselves and knowledgeable, and since their oversights and even rudeness are sometimes excused ("Boys will be boys"; Miedzian, 1991; Obsatz, 1989; Schafran, 1989b), males are also seen as perfectly normal when they categorize and denigrate others (as Sam did to Sue), persist in having their way, or insist on being the "expert."

As a matter of fact, a male may respond much more readily to niceness, collusion, and even manipulation in a woman because her apparent acquiescence or deference serves to reassure him that he is really the expert he so desperately wants to convince every-one he is. This unfortunate male reinforcement of subordinate female behavior is obvious in the testimony of an ordained min-ister, the Reverend Jean Boese Dickson, who admits her collusive interaction with a punitive professor.

CASE 2.1

A Theological Tale

In divinity school I was a straight A student. I turned in a paper for a class that I began with the words "God the father is dead. . . . " The professor gave me an F on the paper.

I thought to myself: This is ridiculous. I'm a straight A student, here on full scholarship, and doing outstanding work in all of my other courses. The only reason this professor is flunking me is because he disagrees with my topic.

I decided to question him about the grade, so I went to his office. When I walked in, I felt assertive, competent, and confident. I said, "I would like you to reconsider this grade; I feel you flunked me on this paper solely because you disagreed with the content."

His response was unbending. He refused to either examine his own bias or change the grade. I didn't know what to do next, so I went for advice to another student. She said, "Oh, I know how to handle him. Just go in there and cry—you'll get what you want."

I didn't want to manipulate him by crying, but I also was afraid to have that F on my record. So I went to see him again, and did exactly as the other woman suggested: *I cried.*

This changed the power balance between us. Now, instead of seeing me as confident and assertive, or like a respected equal, he could pat me on the shoulder and imply, That's all right, little girl, everything will be all right.

I got what I wanted by playing the "traditional female" role. I did not like to be manipulative like that because I felt I was compromising my self-respect. But it seemed this was the only level at which he could hear me—a level where he was in control and still held the power. *When I tried to communicate at a level that commanded respect, he was too threatened to hear me.* Unless I played the game by his rules, I was punished.

When a woman sounds knowledgeable and sure of herself with forceful writing, clearly stated opinions, or strong requests, she may be not only negatively stigmatized as being unfeminine, but even penalized. Unless this divinity student turns herself into a diagnosing detective and figures out how to play the game by the professor's rules (reverting to a *powerless* role so he can feel *powerful*), she is punished unreasonably.

Using the Male/Female Continuum (Figure 2.1) as a guideline for analysis, we notice definite collusion in the interaction between the divinity student and her professor: The professor *intimidates*, the student eventually acts *helpless*; he *downplays women's presence*, she *yields*. She colludes with one stereotype (I should let him look important) to get what she wants: a changed grade. He reinforces another stereotype (Women who cry seem so helpless and so cute) to get what he wants: power. He uses an indirect method of control (flunking his student) and she uses an indirect method of manipulation to try to meet her needs (crying).

Many at this point will now blame the victim: Why does the divinity student play the game by the professor's rules? What causes her ultimately to defer, accommodate, and act powerless? These are valid questions to ask regarding a relationship between so-called equals—a husband and wife or two coworkers, for example. But the difference here is that the professor has the power—he holds her fate in his hands. His act is thus a form of harassment and possibly even abuse, because he uses his position as leverage. He further distorts the balance of power by refusing to evaluate her written words impartially or to take seriously her spoken words— to listen to her in an atmosphere of collegiality. Instead, he insists on a power play, and immediately elevates himself to "one up."

Both professor and student use manipulative strategies to meet their individual needs for power or consideration, but the difference here is that it is the woman who feels she must compromise her self-respect. Any educator who puts a student in this position is unethical. A goal of good education and responsible leadership is to honor diversity and try to establish a learning environment of openness, honesty, and mutual respect. This leader, however, discourages differing opinions and fosters a closed system of conformity, dishonesty, disrespect, and manipulation. The student is in an untenable position: damned if she asserts herself, damned if she doesn't. Either way, she loses.

Both the example of this divinity student and the experience of Sue described above demonstrate how women become ensnared in a Catch-22 no matter which communication style they use. The push/pull of expectations becomes debilitating. When Sue uses the more private form of speech (rapport talk) and tries to establish connection with her colleague using a supportive statement ("Glad to meet you, Sam"), she is categorized as "high dominant." When the divinity student employs the more public form of speech (report talk) and submits written beliefs and opinions using a firm, decisive statement ("God . . . is dead"), she finds herself victimized by her professor's reprisal. Whether a woman uses rapport talk to establish connection and foster intimacy or report talk to reveal competence and maintain autonomy, she is criticized.

Challenges to Women's Credibility

Personal biases about gender roles have a great deal of influence on who people will or will not perceive as credible, take seriously, pay attention to, or even pay equally. Whether in the workplace, the political sphere, or a host of other environments, females face frustratingly insidious barriers as their competence is discounted by colleagues and/or leaders. "Women are sometimes not seen as credible in my field," confesses the sales manager of a pharmaceutical company. "When one of my female salespersons stands up to talk in a meeting, the guys don't take her seriously. They yawn or look at their watches—sort of a 'ho-hum' attitude."

Even when a woman performs exactly the same task as a man, she may be perceived as less capable. For example, in some studies, essays and paintings attributed to male authors and painters were evaluated as superior to identical essays and paintings bearing female names (Goldberg, 1968; Pheterson, Kiesler, & Goldberg, 1971). When "work by a woman is perceived as inferior to the same work by a man," this is discrimination (Geis, Carter, & Butler, 1982, p. 5). In other words, it is a question of *credibility*.

Of course, if one is perceived as inferior, one is thereby "worth less" and naturally should be paid less. Although wage discrimination is still very prevalent (women earn less than 70 cents for every dollar a man makes), the bias against equal pay for equal work is usually expressed in a much less blatant manner than it was in a recent phone conversation I had with a long-standing business client:

Van Nostrand: Before we sign a contract for another in-service training series, I want you to know I'll be raising my speaking and consulting fees in the coming year.

Client: Just a minute—I'll check my files and see what we pay our other female consultants.

Such distortion in perception—seeing women as less credible, less capable, and therefore worth less—may explain why leadership status is not automatically conferred on women even when they deliberately place themselves in positions connoting status, such as at the front of a room or the head of a table: "Being seated at the head of the table in a mixed-sex group identified a man as a leader but failed to confer the same distinction on a woman" (Porter & Geis, 1981; cited in Geis et al., 1982, p. 5). This phenomenon may also help explain why, in the earlier vignette about space and sexism (Example C), female workshop participants chose not to sit at the center of the semicircle: they could easily have determined that to arrange themselves in such a power place would not make any difference.

As a matter of fact, the fear of appearing "too knowledgeable" is a constant encumbrance for most women. "The more capable [women] are, the more likely they are to be treated negatively," state Deborah Borisoff and Lisa Merrill (1985), discussing "male dominance as a barrier to change":

Women learn fear as a function of femininity, and . . . the fear women experience is isolating, confusing and debilitating. Women fear if they act in an unfeminine manner, they will be isolated, avoided and ignored. Furthermore, women are confused because they are frequently chastised or punished for the very behaviors for which males are rewarded—for speaking loudly and forcefully, for example. (p. 81)

Such confusion must have been felt by several nationally known female leaders who testified during the 1990 Senate hearings concerning the confirmation of Judge David Souter to the U.S. Supreme Court.[6] Fearing that the *Roe v. Wade* decision would be overturned were Souter appointed, these women urged senators not to confirm him. The witnesses' knowledgeable and impassioned testimony was met with what columnist Ellen Goodman

(1990) calls a "linguistic alarm" from Senator Strom Thurmond: "Mr. Chairman, we have a group of *lovely ladies* here. We thank you for your presence" (emphasis added). Recognizing that Thurmond's "courtesy" was an attempt to categorize and trivialize them rather than to take them seriously, some of the "lovely ladies" rolled their eyes. (These women could sense that, as Goodman puts it, "One man's chivalry is another woman's chauvinism.")[7]

The eye rolling was then met with the following chastisement from Senator Alan Simpson:

> *Senator* [speaking to the women]: Don't shrug. I get tired of women looking up at the ceiling. We treat you with courtesy and you shrug or cast a glance as if to say, Who are these boobs? You are behaving with tiresome arrogance.

Note that both senators, in order to discredit these capable women, throw up frustratingly covert barriers, shifting the focus from the women's testimony to the subjects of appearance (lovely), gender (ladies), and body language. They resort to stereotypical male communication devices (see Box 2.1), one of which is topic selection. Rather than attending to the issue of Judge Souter's record, Senator Simpson comments instead on what these witnesses are doing with their shoulder and eye muscles, after which he proceeds to discredit them further by labeling them "tiresomely arrogant" (finding fault).

The women find themselves categorized by gender; every physical movement is scrutinized; they are overly criticized when they react to the manipulative courtesy; their reaction is then labeled and stigmatized. All of these maneuvers depersonalize the women to the point that their important testimony is not taken seriously but is trivialized, and the women themselves are marginalized.

This denigration is accomplished in the name of *courtesy* (what Goodman terms a "liquid civility"): "We treat you with courtesy and you shrug." Courtesy combined with criticism creates a curious concoction. On the Male/Female Continuum, courtesy is just a stone's throw from *discrimination*. It is not a courtesy based on respect and caring, explain Pierce and Page (1990), but rather a "niceness [that] evaporates quickly" when a woman departs from "role prescribed responses" (p. 13). So-called courtesy can be used as an excuse to intimidate, devalue, and dismiss others. In this hearing, as women try to *acknowledge their own power* and display *assertiveness*, they are met not by true courtesy, but by *paternalism, depersonalization,* and *indiscriminate competition.* "The culture of chivalry talks to women as children and calls it polite," explains Goodman. "The culture of equality is demeaned and insulted." The words of retired Supreme Court Justice William Brennan, revived during or after one woman's testimony, seem particularly appropriate to these proceedings: "We don't put women on a pedestal, we put women in a cage."

If the witnesses had been male, would they have received similar mixed messages of courtesy and criticism, overattention and underattention? At least one female witness did not think so. Speaking to the press after the hearing, she clearly named the sexism: "Senator Simpson lectured to us women—he treated us as children. He would *never* do that to males who were testifying."

Similar condescending paternalism—attempting to discredit a woman by treating her like a child—is evident in the following excerpt from a television debate between vice presidential candidates Geraldine Ferraro and George Bush, held during the 1984 U.S. national election campaign. As we observe the subtle linguistic alarms directed at Ferraro, exacerbated partly by her own attempts to deal with them, we understand why women are often reluctant to seek public office, and why—as of this writing—no female has ever been elected vice president, much less president, of the United States. A woman's credibility is being insidiously undermined, yet the covert sexism is quite difficult for her to detect, define, or even debate against. A female might qualify for one of the highest offices in the land, but viewers would be led to discredit her—sort of a "Sure she's a lawyer, but does she know anything?" mentality.

This debate illustrates very subtle nuances of speech—including patronizing "courtesy"—used to insinuate that a woman is not competent or believable. Employing skillfully camouflaged strategies of "male talk," Bush attempts to control by dominating, while Ferraro—trying desperately not to defer—is ultimately reduced to playing the role of diagnosing detective. The excerpt also provides a sneak preview of linguistic devices sometimes used by women that can weaken their own credibility.

CASE 2.2

Geraldine or George: Who Is More Credible?

Geraldine Ferraro and George Bush are engaged in a debate that
includes, among other issues, a discussion of foreign policy in the
Middle East, the handling of the hostage crisis during the Carter
administration, and the bombing of embassies.

> **Bush:** Let me *help* you, Ms. Ferraro, with the differences between the
> embassies in Iran and Lebanon. . . .
>
> **Ferraro** [intervening]: Let me first of all say, I almost *resent*, Mr. Bush,
> your patronizing attitude—that you have to *teach* me on foreign
> policy. I've been a member of Congress for six years—I was *there*
> when the embassy was bombed. Don't categorize my answers!

Bush attempts to control the discussion by using condescension—an almost paternal, professorial posture, as if Ferraro were
his daughter or a schoolgirl ("Let me *help* you"). He uses *topic
selection* to define the parameters of the debate: the difference
between embassies. He also seems to *find fault* by trying to establish his opponent's ignorance, playing hierarchical games to make
Ferraro appear less credible and thus less competent. Bush also
discusses an issue entirely external to himself: embassies, not
emotion.

Bush's offer of "help" appears initially to be truly courteous or
chivalrous, but his language has a disturbingly familiar ring,
similar to the liquid civility of the phrase "We have a group of
lovely ladies here" heard in the Senate confirmation hearings
described above. It is exceedingly doubtful that Bush would have
used such condescending language had his opponent been male.
Ferraro detects his patronizing trivialization of her knowledge and
experience, and she intervenes to confront the sexism. As a matter of
fact, her strategy is a combined intervention because it synthesizes
three strategies: self-disclosing, fact-finding, and limit setting.

In her intervention, Ferraro, unlike Bush, *does* discuss emotion:
her resentment. She also plays, or feels obliged to play, the diagnostician. Because she feels on the defensive, she does not respond
at first to the content of Bush's remarks, but instead is preoccupied
with, and comments on, his attitude and manner—that is, his

process: "I almost resent . . . your patronizing attitude—that you have to *teach* me." For better or for worse, by reporting her emotion of resentment, Ferraro reveals an issue very *internal* to herself that could render her more vulnerable (Borisoff & Merrill, 1985, p. 12). She becomes more vulnerable because, in a system that values ranking over linking, vulnerability equals weakness; she is thus perceived as "less than," and is relegated to a position of less credibility and lower status. (Her revelation also supplies ammunition to any critic who believes a woman's "raging hormones" automatically disqualify her from higher office.) However, Ferraro's words do provide a fairly direct self-disclosing intervention: "I *almost* resent."

(Perhaps George feels he must become the faultfinding expert to avoid the "wimp factor"—being labeled as not aggressive or decisive enough. Maybe he feels compelled to establish and maintain dominance in order to dispel any possible suggestion that he is not completely knowledgeable in all areas, a pitfall that would be unthinkable, given that his opponent is a woman. But let us return to Geraldine.)

The female candidate then continues with some confidently assertive "I statements": "*I've* been a member of Congress. . . . *I* was there" (fact-finding intervention). So she has unabashedly convinced the television audience of her credibility—or has she? Note her use of the word *almost* as in "I *almost* resent . . . your patronizing attitude." This is one of many linguistic devices used predominantly by women. Although some observers feel these word patterns send a mixed signal that tends to associate women with lower status,[8] sociolinguist Tannen (1991) believes such patterns should be appreciated as essential components of rapport talk.

Perhaps Ferraro uses the qualifier *almost* in an effort to tone down (protect Bush from?) her anger and resentment. Or perhaps she is trying to link, connect, and accommodate to Bush: I will take care of you by softening my words so you won't see my full anger. Maybe she is even trying to give him the benefit of the doubt: I hope you don't intend to be as intimidating, Mr. Bush, as you sound.

Although Ferraro ends her intervention with clear limit setting ("Don't categorize my answers!"), she has exhausted some of her valuable TV time dealing with Bush's chauvinism masquerading as chivalry. Bush's "fatherly" efforts to discredit her, with subtle insinuations about her accuracy, cause her to shift attention from debating to defending herself—could this have been her opponent's unconscious intent? Like the women in the Senate hearings, Ferraro temporarily detours from important policy issues to protest the microinequities that put her in a one-down position. In the end, the American public is deprived: Instead of being enlightened by an in-depth examination of international politics, we are reduced to monitoring gender politics. The collusion of dominance and subordinance is exacerbated, communication breaks down, and the message is lost.

Women in peer interactions, graduate schools, Senate hearings, and political campaigns have every right to engage in such perfectly reasonable adult activities as shaking men's hands, submitting papers on theses that concern them, postulating opinions, or engaging in debate. However, when these seemingly normal human endeavors are reciprocated with subtle suggestions of violence (grades used as weapons or words used as barbs), it is easy to see why women shy away from more assertive or ambitious quests.

We are dealing with a double standard here: Male actions are perceived to be normal while female behavior is seen as "deviant": Why is she so uppity? Why does she come on so strong? Who does she think she is, asking me to change this grade? What does she know about foreign policy? Male behavior becomes the criterion against which all other behavior is measured; males become the "insiders" and females the "outsiders."

"We encourage small differences in speech that wind up communicating important differences about human beings," says linguist Freed (1985). Leaders who are oblivious to how these differences marginalize women not only aggravate the inequities, but support the assumption of male privilege that undergirds these destructive patterns. Such leader bias, states Freed, has a damaging effect on women's self-confidence, and hence their performance:

> If we believe that women and girls are hesitant in their speech, then we are likely to judge a woman who sounds quite sure of herself as being overly confident, "masculine" or slightly pushy.
>
> Conversely, the woman who does sound reticent, having learned her lesson well, is then passed over in matters of responsibility since she appears to lack sufficient self-esteem.

A woman is thus discouraged by the spoken word, both in the speech of others directed toward her and even through her own choice of language. She may first be discredited by the linguistic alarms and verbal flares sent her way by others who are trying to trivialize her. Then, if she departs from role-prescribed responses and replies with the merest hint of hesitancy, resentment, or anger as she tries to cope with these alarms, she is further disparaged. Liquid civility, chauvinistic chivalry, finding fault, topic selection, and other linguistic devices are subtle tactics used against women to warn them that they have strayed too from the norm.

Bias in the Written Word

Women experience sexism not only in the spoken word, but also in the written word, or absence thereof. If what we read is mostly about women, and men are scarcely mentioned (or vice versa), this is another subtle form of *bias by omission* or *sexism by default*. What appears, or does not appear, in print is a powerful tool used by insiders to maintain status and remind outsiders of their second-class position. When it happens to be men's issues that are conveniently unavailable to the reader's eye, men are thus overprotected from examination—a form of promale linguistic sexism.

Consider, for example, the index of a textbook or lists of topics offered by professional speakers. What if the category of "women" is a clearly designated topic, but the category of "men" is given no attention at all? These omissions would suggest that the textbook author's or speaker's associations assume that males are the given and females the unknown quantity to be studied: males the norm, females the deviant. Within this paradigm it is expected that women will be "other"—the object of scrutiny; since it is males who are the known quantity, then obviously they do not need to be scrutinized.

One recent textbook on communication in small groups, for instance, has a distinct index entry for "women in groups" (Bormann, 1990, p. 303). There is no parallel entry for "men in groups." This omission suggests that a group is normal only if it consists entirely of males. Should women join the group it will then become irregular and will need to be researched. Similarly, for the directories of two different professional speaking associations, members are sent a list of possible topics on which they have expertise to present, and are to check which topics they wish printed next to their names.[9] Options include—among many others—such subjects as "motivation," "relationships," "stress management," "ethics and morality," and—predictably—"women in society." The topic "men in society" is not an option.

These omissions from textbook indices and speakers' directories may seem inconsequential. However, because we understand what infinite power and potential lie in the use of (or absence of) certain words, we recognize that these omissions are of great significance. These "oversights" have broad ramifications for curriculum development, course syllabi, level of student commitment to subject matter, interest in certain workshops or presenters, audience mix at conference breakout sessions, and other challenges in education, human resource development, and related disciplines. By omitting references to men and males, an author or an organization sends the message that the behavior of men in groups or men in society does not need to be researched or discussed. What *does* need careful scrutiny and analysis, however, is how women will adapt or fit into the male norm: My goodness, we have some women in our group—I wonder how they will cope?

Of course, in some quarters, men *are* involved in the process of self-examination, the many factions of the contemporary men's movement being active arenas for this exploration (Van Nostrand, 1986, 1987a, 1987b). However, when men *do* investigate themselves, many deem it exceedingly important to keep their findings under tight security. This was made glaringly obvious to me as I listened to an experienced educator's account of her conversation with a colleague:

> During a conference lunch break I was introduced to, and seated across from, a professor. As we discussed feminism, gender issues, and related concepts, it became obvious that we were both very knowledgeable about the contemporary men's movement. He also seemed very well informed about, and supportive of, women's issues.
>
> As we got deeper into conversation, he quizzically tilted his head toward me and asked, "Why are you so interested in men's issues?" I was a bit taken aback by the question, but I responded, with a smile and a gentle challenge, "Why are you so interested in feminism?"
>
> When I saw the sheepish grin on his face, I knew immediately that he had recognized his own bias: Women's issues are open game to

be studied by both genders, but men's issues are men's business, best kept to themselves. We both laughed—it was a refreshing moment of revelation.

As leaders, we have much influence over who discusses what, who puts down whom, who will be taken seriously, and what topics will appear in conversation and in print. Our awareness of—and willingness to confront—linguistic sexism is another crucial component of gender-responsible leadership.

How Leaders Can Detect and Defuse Gender Politics

Gender-responsible leaders will create group environments that are as hospitable to women as they are to men. Achieving this goal requires that leaders (a) recognize how gender role extremes disrupt a group, (b) confront male privilege, (c) admit personal biases, and (d) tap the strengths of all participants. Let us examine each of these elements in turn.

Leaders need to recognize how extremes of dominance/detachment and deference/diagnosis will disrupt group process. Just as these gendered patterns are learned through socialization, so can they be unlearned. Men and women can be taught how either excessive domination or accommodation places one gender at a disadvantage, interferes with productive dialogue, and discourages collegial interaction. While remaining sympathetic to the fact that rigidly stereotyped patterns are partially perpetuated by deep psychological roots, the gender-fair leader needs to acknowledge that when these behaviors are used manipulatively, they may create "gender politics" in which we all too often collude.

Leaders must confront male privilege, especially when males try to enforce entitlement through misuse of space and words. How we allow people to arrange themselves, how women and men interact in discussions, and how we respond to these dynamics are barometers of our leadership effectiveness. Persons—particularly males—in our groups who are more interested in ranking than in linking will make strategic efforts to assert status by encroaching on common

space or controlling group interaction. If we condone either territorial or linguistic sexism, we solidify male privilege and continue
to disempower women.

How will we respond to these challenges? Will we choreograph
a room arrangement to facilitate smoother discussion among all
participants? Will we create a learning environment in which
put-downs are discouraged and diverse voices are honored and
heard? Most significantly, will we reinforce the female who risks
positioning herself, verbally and spatially, to assume a more visible role? The leader who can reshuffle space grabbers and shift
focus from attention seekers demonstrates the flexibility essential
to gender-fair leadership.

*Leaders must admit how our own personal biases can cause us to favor
some persons while ignoring others.* Based solely on our own inner
assumptions about gender roles, we may capitalize on men's
advantage while jeopardizing women's credibility. If we want to
provide women the same opportunity as men, which behaviors
will we reinforce? Will our responses to certain individuals reveal
deeply ingrained biases? For example, do we condone society's
message that "real women" should hide their intelligence, defer
to male opinions, and manipulate to get their way? If so, we will
reward weeping women who collude in our power games instead
of supporting those who courageously state their views.

Do we believe that "real men" can say, I am entitled to this
territory—she isn't? Or, I know the correct answers, she doesn't?
Do we assume that males can appropriate public space, categorize
women's actions, dominate conversations, or discredit women's
written and verbal opinions at will? If so, we will say nothing to
inconsiderate airplane passengers, status-seeking colleagues, vin-
dictive professors, or senators who label nationally known female
leaders as tiresomely arrogant.

Do we assume that "real women" should be primarily responsible for interpreting, diagnosing, connecting? If so, we will exploit females for this very tendency (as did the therapist with
Barbara in Chapter 1), label them "dominant" in conversations
(Sue), or put them in positions where they must diagnose their
own mistreatment (Geraldine Ferraro).

Do we believe that it is unmasculine for a "real man" to show
concern or "reveal himself" (Obsatz, 1975), and that real men have

every right to remain detached during group process and not to "take responsibility to interact and make decisions" (Niessen-Derry, personal communication, 1989)? If so, we will allow males to distance themselves, and give little support to those men who are trying to develop a concerned "vocabulary of sharing" (Obsatz, 1975). The gender-sensitive leader will examine, admit to, and be willing to modify any personal assumptions that interfere with group members' acceptance, full participation, and personal growth.

Leaders need to appreciate and tap each person's uniqueness. To avoid reinforcing shopworn stereotypes and colluding in power plays, leaders can develop appreciation for women and men as individuals rather than as mere token representatives of their gender. Our goal should be to "promote all strengths in all [participants]," as suggested by researcher Catherine Krupnick. Based on her observations of coeducational interactions at the college level, Krupnick recommends that we "encourage women to initiate comments, resist interruption, and be willing to assume the risks of a public role" (in Fiske, 1990, p. 5E). Similarly, we can encourage men to listen more, resist the temptation to find fault, and be willing to assume the risks of the self-disclosing, supportive role.

Leaders can learn to stop blaming women for their spatial reticence: Why doesn't she assume a more central position—why won't she ever take the podium? We can also stop blaming females for their verbal valor: She has such strong opinions—sometimes she even seems *brassy*! Conversely, we need to stop cultivating men's spatial expansiveness: The men have appropriated the prime seats, but I won't move them—they're entitled to sit there. We also need to stop condoning males' linguistic sexism: That man is really overcontrolling this discussion, but I won't intervene—he must know what he's talking about. Instead, we need to recognize that our leadership methods may be contributing to the very climate in which women struggle in vain for credibility; indeed, the ferocity of their struggle may correlate directly with the depth of our own bias.

Notes

1. This paper, titled *Boy Talk: How Men Avoid Sharing Themselves,* was later published informally in a "men's survival resource book." Obsatz is an associate professor of sociology at Macalester College in Saint Paul, Minnesota, and a

therapist in private practice; he presented some of these concepts in a workshop titled "Tough and Tender" at a Midwest Regional Men's Conference, Hamline University, St. Paul. (Using poetic license, I have presented the quotation as verse; in the original, it is in paragraph form.)

2. Charles Niessen-Derry is men's program coordinator of the St. Cloud (Minnesota) Intervention Project. His words are from several dialogues he had with me, plus a formal critique written in 1989 in response to a preliminary draft of this book.

3. *Microinequities* are "small behaviors [such as disparaging comments or oversights] that often occur in the course of everyday interchanges in which individuals are either singled out, ignored or discounted because of sex, race, or age" (Hall & Sandler, 1984, p. 4). The term originated with Mary P. Rowe (1977).

4. At the time Bergquist's (1990) article was written, 19 female physicians had joined the hospital staff in the previous three and a half years. As of November 1992 there were 28 female and 180 male physicians on the hospital staff, according to the Medical Staff Office, and a women's rest room has now been constructed.

5. This list of male behaviors is excerpted from a chapter in Thompson's book titled "Male Talk," which is also used here as the title for Box 2.1.

6. These women included Molly Yard, president of the National Organization for Women; Eleanor Smeal of Feminists for a Female Majority; Kate Michelman, executive director of the National Abortion Rights Action League; and Faye Wattleton, president of the Planned Parenthood Action Fund. The hearings were broadcast on National Public Radio, September 19, 1990. I did not view these hearings on television, and hence did not actually see the nonverbal interactions between Senators Thurmond, Simpson, and others and the female witnesses. My source of information, other than newspaper, was radio only, and thus purely auditory. For a related article, see Ellen Goodman's "'Ladies' Still Have Long Road to Equality," which appeared in the *St. Cloud* (Minnesota) *Times* on September 28, 1990, © 1990, The Boston Globe Newspaper Company/Washington Post Writers Group. Quotes from that article appearing here are reprinted by permission.

7. *Chivalry* is defined as "especial courtesy and high-minded disinterested consideration to women," a fitting description of the senators' treatment of the female witnesses. As mentioned in Chapter 1, similar "courtesy" in an educational setting is described by researcher Myra Sadker as "classroom chivalry"; that is, an instructor, assuming a woman cannot handle a task, might actually operate a piece of equipment instead of letting the woman do it herself. The instructor is not really interested in letting the woman learn by doing, and this disinterest "deprives women of important feedback on their intellectual endeavors" (in Griffin, 1990, p. 12). See also the discussion of chivalry as a way to *underchallenge* women in Chapter 4.

8. For discussions concerning how women's communication styles are often equated with low status and powerlessness, see Hall and Sandler (1984, p. 5) and Sandler (1986, pp. 11-12).

9. For the following directories, professional speakers may have their names listed under the category "Women in Society," but the topic "Men in Society" is not an option: *1991-1992 Who's Who in Professional Speaking* (National Speakers Association), and *1991-1992 Who's Who in Association Management* (American Society of Association Executives).

◖ 3 ◗

NEW GOALS, OLD ROLES

How Leader Favoritism Impedes
Female and Male Role Flexibility

From hierarchy to equity is not a simple journey. . . . As dominant (or subordinate) in a hierarchy it is easy to avoid sharing who I am. Personal information is part of the power game and I guard what I share and with whom. In equity I am visible in unexpected ways. I learn things about myself. . . . I find that I am compelled through equity to own more fully who I am. This means joy and pain.

(David Wagner, organizational development consultant, 1990, p. 1)[1]

Leaders in the helping professions know that women and men come to our groups for a variety of reasons. Besides hoping for informative instruction and sensitive guidance, these individuals are with us to give and receive support, to grow personally, to learn from (and affiliate with) others, and, one hopes, to make unique contributions as group members. Some are trying to break out of the gender role extremes of *dominance/detachment* and *deference/diagnosis* (Box 1.1) that have undermined their ways of relating in other settings. They want to practice new modes of behaving—more effective ways of being—but old behavior patterns, polished so well through years of conditioning, keep reemerging. And when these deeply ingrained patterns resurface in groups, they may severely disrupt process because they are essentially *controlling* behaviors.

What is the role of the leader in these circumstances? As we see individuals trying to be less manipulative and more straightforward, or less detached and more connected, how can we confirm and support these emerging behaviors? How can we create climates in which all participants feel motivated to understand, affirm, and support each other's growth away from stereotyped roles? In this chapter we will see women and men making efforts to meet individual developmental needs—trying to overcome barriers that keep them from experiencing intimacy or autonomy, yet pursuing these goals using dysfunctional behaviors. And we will observe how leaders cope with all of this.

Male/Female Developmental Tasks

Each student, client, or workshop participant brings her or his own psychological baggage and expectations into the group. Each has an agenda based on individual needs that are driven by heredity, personality, family background, life experiences, and a host of other factors, including *gender*, the factor of primary concern here.

In terms of gender, each person is on a developmental journey, explains Carolyn Desjardins (1989a) in her analysis of the implications of Carol Gilligan's theories for the learning environment. For males, the primary task may well be to learn to *connect* and *develop intimacy with others*; for females, a common task is to learn to *separate* and develop *autonomy*.

Male Developmental Task: Intimacy

While achieving separation and autonomy becomes a lifelong task for many females, many males have already learned to establish their identities through separation—making sure they are not similar to, or influenced by, females (J. B. Miller, 1976). One might even say males *define by defying*. As one middle-aged male confessed:

> As a boy grows up, he decides what he's NOT. To be "sissy" is the worst possible thing you can call a man, so while growing up he pushes himself away from anything to do with girls or women. *He has to find out who he is as someone separate and different.*

Pierce and Page's (1990) Male/Female Continuum provides a framework for our discussion of the male developmental journey. (In the following discussion, terms enclosed in quotation marks are excerpted from the Continuum, either from its abridged version, as illustrated in Figure 2.1, or from its original version, which is a pullout chart in the back of the text of the same name.)[2]

If we interpret the Continuum using a psychological framework to understand men's need to define by defying, we could say that some males push themselves away from women because of deeply embedded, unresolved childhood trauma. Using "sexual harassment" and "discrimination" to "intimidate" or "downplay women's presence" in a group, a man might make sexist jokes, change the subject while women are talking, or focus attention on himself instead of listening to others. Or he might emotionally distance himself from women who are sharing feelings, as if to say, No way am I going to open up like that; I'm not like those females! His pushing away might even manifest itself as false "courtesy": treating a woman with condescending compliments or controlling "paternalism," as if she were an inexperienced, naive child, rather than an adult on an equal plane with him.

It is important to reemphasize, however, that this type of oppression goes beyond the psychological to the political. We need to recognize that the "Poor Shmoks" who refuse to treat women as equals receive enormous political benefit for their behavior. Their maneuvers serve to keep women trivialized, marginalized, and in the position of second-class citizens, thus perpetuating male entitlement.

Many males, however, have evolved into a "transition" stage on the Continuum, when a "decision [is] made to learn." They are now trying to move beyond controlling behaviors and to leave dominance behind. These men recognize that their primary task is to *connect*, to "risk vulnerability and interdependence with other people" (Desjardins, 1989a, p. 139); to begin "listening and asking questions" and to become "increasingly introspective" (Pierce & Page, 1990).

In a group, a leader who observes a male's fledgling attempts to *connect* may find this man's new openness so refreshing that the leader may bend over backward to allow him the floor. The leader lavishes attention on him as he shares himself, thus inadvertently fostering dominant behavior. Conversely, if the male's discomfort at risking vulnerability causes him to try to *disconnect* by retreating further into detachment and aloofness, a leader may also collude with this excursion into anonymity, making all the necessary arrangements to allow him to escape fully into hiding. In either case, the leader overprotects this man by enabling him to revert to stereotypical roles of *dominance* or *detachment*, both of which interfere with his developmental task of experiencing intimacy.

Female Developmental Task: Autonomy

Like males, females are also on a developmental journey. Many women have learned to establish their identities largely by *affiliation*, suggests Jean Baker Miller (1976, p. 89), and often "the only forms of affiliation that have been available to women are subservient affiliations" (Rigby-Weinberg, 1986, p. 199). As a matter of fact, many women have learned all too well how to "connect": They may connect so efficiently that they repeatedly put the needs of others before their own. Because so much of women's identities have been developed through relationships, their greatest fear may be that they will be abandoned. Thus the task of many females becomes learning to *separate*, to be *autonomous*, to stand on their own two feet.

Management expert Rosabeth M. Kanter (1977c), recommending skills women need in order to cope in organizations, suggests that females learn "the experience of power, task orientation, intellectualizing . . . addressing large groups and invulnerability to feedback" (p. 383). However, the journey toward acknowledging and activating their own agency and autonomy is not an easy one for many women. The Male/Female Continuum illustrates how women may be stalemated in a stage when they act "helpless" with "anger frozen inside," may allow themselves to be intimidated, or may use "psychological punishment." In a group, for example, a female might sit in stony silence during a male-dominated discussion, complaining later to the leader (or her peers) that she found the verbose men to be insufferable. Then, in order to meet her needs, she might move to a stage of "manipulation" in which she appears to *defer*, but may actually be trying to "control through helping." In other words, she tries to take charge of others rather than being in charge of herself, taking responsibility for her own behaviors, making her own decisions. Subsequently, after cycling back through more periods of "deference," she may leap to a stage in which her "anger [is] surfacing": She "question[s] everything" and "compete[s] indiscriminately," an example of which we will see in Case 7.1, in Chapter 7.

In discussing female behaviors, it is important to place women's actions in the context of an overall oppressive and patriarchal society in which males hold economic and political power. Many of the so-called subservient female patterns are therefore not so much efforts to control others as simply efforts at self-preservation. For example, when a single parent who receives no child support is being sexually harassed by her boss, and she knows there are very few other jobs available at her skill level, she may decide not to report him, but to play the game by his rules in order to feed her children.

Women's chief developmental task, then, to return to Desjardin's model, is to "assert their needs—even if doing so leaves them alone" (p. 139). On the Continuum this developmental stage is evident when a woman begins to "acknowledge [her] own power" and "increase assertiveness." When a woman at this stage opens up in a group, the leader might be so delighted at her emerging autonomy and ability to express herself that the leader unwittingly exploits her newfound straightforwardness, perhaps allowing her to express explosive anger inappropriately by maligning others. As a result, this woman would not only fail to connect with other group members, she would also be left underprotected.

Leaders have an ethical responsibility to recognize that when we encourage women to assert themselves and speak their own truth in their own unique voices, we foster a mode of risk taking that could have severe repercussions: Women who confront punitive professors, harassing bosses, or insensitive colleagues may thereby lose grades, jobs, and friends. Fear of such retaliation may cause many women to remain silent even though they experience persistent sexual harassment. For example, law professor Anita Hill, who testified during the 1991 Senate Judiciary Committee confirmation hearings that she had been sexually harassed by U.S. Supreme Court nominee Judge Clarence Thomas, was extremely hesitant to testify publicly about the alleged incidents. She rightly suspected that victims are frequently turned into villains; their sanity and credibility are so severely challenged during the interrogation process that they become doubly punished—once at the time of the harassment and again at the time they speak up about it. For many a woman faced with the choice of whether to maintain her job and professional connections or to say what *really* happened to her and risk "burning bridges," there is only one option: She will abandon attempts at self-assertion in order that she herself not be abandoned, and that she not lose the hard-earned ground for which she has fought so diligently.

Common Group Task: Development of "Social Interest"

Thus, while many men are learning to connect with others so they can be more open to feedback and develop intimacy, many women are learning to stand on their own two feet so they can be more autonomous. In spite of these divergent paths, women and men have in common a primary social need—the need to belong, to "contribute to and participate in communal life," explains Dorothe Rigby-Weinberg (1986). To meet this need to belong, humans must learn to relate effectively with others—to develop what Alfred Adler called a "social interest" (*Gemeinschaftsgefühl* or "communal feeling"). Social interest means we cooperate with others "toward furthering the common good." The central issue in psychological development, according to Adlerians, is the "development and quality of our connectedness and cooperation with others" (Rigby-Weinberg, 1986, pp. 196-197).

In the corporate world, for example, Kanter (1989a) suggests connectedness as a desirable direction toward which organizations can strive. Organizations can foster more "connecting" environments, with emphasis on "team incentives," "employee networking," and "kinder, more cooperative" policy, all of which enhance productivity. The company or institution that adheres to such a collaborative ethic, says Kanter (1989b), will ask itself such questions as, "Does each part contribute to the whole?" "Do we give bonus points to the department which shares innovative ideas with another department?"

These caring, connected, egalitarian conditions, which emphasize the "common good," are exemplified in the states of "colleagueship" (Pierce & Page, 1990) and "partnership" (Eisler, 1987) discussed earlier. When women and men achieve colleagueship

(Figure 2.1), they are capable of more "flexible role options," and are able to give and receive emotional input and feedback. Members of both genders place a value on being both connected and autonomous. In Eisler's (1987) state of partnership, because relationships are built on the principle of linking rather than of ranking, "neither half of humanity is ranked over the other and diversity is not equated with inferiority or superiority." Power is seen as *responsibility* that can be used to the benefit of all persons; this is preferable to power as *privilege* that commands obedience through oppression or fear (p. 28).

The concepts of colleagueship, partnership, and kinder, more cooperative organizations and relationships are not always well understood or appreciated by those who reap benefits within the patriarchal culture. Indeed, most males raised in our society have been socialized in a very different direction. Therapist Michael Obsatz (1975) states this clearly: "Men work at getting ahead of others, not communicating or empathizing with them. To be sure, communication and empathy might penalize success. In a competitive venture, too much concern may be distracting" (p. 6).

If it is true that a primary need of human beings is the need to belong, and if connectedness to and cooperation with others is such a strong human desire, why is it that participants in our groups so often fall into dysfunctional behaviors that inhibit or block this connectedness? Moreover, when we leaders notice that a group seems thrown off balance by this gender role rigidity, what must we do to provide environments that stimulate colleagueship and partnership?

Part of our leadership task is to help participants recognize that their enculturation into certain roles may interfere with both their individual needs for intimacy or autonomy and the common good of the group. We can help them understand that persons who try to establish themselves as protected or privileged (and thereby powerful) will have difficulty connecting, because their focus on maintaining rank and status interferes with their development of intimacy. Conversely, we can explain that those who feel underprotected and disenfranchised (and therefore powerless) will have difficulty individuating because their struggle to receive approval and to stay connected—or their struggle merely to survive—interferes with their manifestation of autonomy. Through our guidance we can create settings in which participants find enough latitude to meet their own needs appropriately, yet still feel responsible for the well-being of the group as a whole—climates in which all persons honor diversity enough to respect each other's autonomy, yet stay connected.

Roadblocks on Developmental Journeys

Controlling Behaviors Impede Personal Growth

Males use direct strategies. In pursuing their social need of belonging, explains Rigby-Weinberg (1986), humans act from a position of helplessness and vulnerability learned from their families or communities of origin, in which "power and privilege [were] unequally distributed" (p. 198). To compensate for the resulting feelings of powerlessness and low self-esteem, they may try to control others, using either direct or indirect strategies. The "male" strategy may involve an "open exercise of power":

> The higher value placed on all things masculine burdens the man from childhood "with the obligation to prove his superiority over women" [Adler, 1914/1980, p. 27] [and also other men, which] prevents men from developing the *social interest* and cooperation which would yield a secure sense of connectedness with others. Instead, an emphasis on competition, dominance, and open exercise of power become part of the life style of many men, in a vain effort to compensate for feelings of inferiority (Mosak and Schneider, 1977). (Rigby-Weinberg, 1986, p. 199)

Females use indirect strategies. Females, on the other hand, may be more apt to use *indirect* strategies to meet their needs for recognition and belonging, but these strategies are also "distorted in the direction of power seeking":

> Women tend to develop one of two approaches in attempting to insure their social significance—the "male" strategy of openly attempting to dominate and defeat others and prove themselves "as good as or better than men" or, more frequently, indirect techniques such as attempting to demonstrate "moral superiority" or "superiority through goodness and self-sacrifice." (Rigby-Weinberg, 1986, pp. 199-200)

Thus, in the view of Adlerians, both females and males are trying to function in the world from a position of inadequacy that they perpetually try to overcome by using controlling, self-defeating patterns in a desperate attempt to ensure that they are socially significant. Yet none of us can ever *really* control others, and in our attempts we perpetuate the destructive "collusion of dominance and subordinance" (Pierce & Page, 1990).

Gender Role Expectations

Internal expectations. As females and males develop psychologically, they learn to internalize specific gender role expectations placed upon them by society. However, when individuals attempt to move ahead in their developmental journeys beyond these stereotyped behaviors, they may find their paths blocked by *internal* psychological conflict. For example, a male may feel a deep need to connect, to be respected for his efforts at affiliation, but his internal message to himself may sound like this: "In order to belong in this world I must always be in control" (Rigby-Weinberg, 1986, p. 198); or, I'm a male in this group—I'd better not show my feelings too much or people won't think I'm "masculine" enough. This internal self-talk might cause him to try either to *dominate* a discussion or to *detach* himself from it, and either behavior can sabotage his need for intimacy.

A female may feel a deep need to be respected as an autonomous individual, but she may be so withdrawn that she does not say who she is or what she wants; therefore, nobody gets a chance to know her as an independent, decisive person. Like the executive in the refreshment line in Chapter 1, her internal message may be, I can't take the initiative or those men will think I'm too aggressive. Or she may say to herself, "To be accepted as a woman I must always put the needs of others first" (Rigby-Weinberg, 1986, p. 198); or, I'm a female in this group—I'd better not state my opinions too strongly or people won't think I'm "feminine" enough. This internal self-talk might cause her to *defer* excessively in discussion, or turn into a *diagnosing detective,* self-righteously pointing out deficiencies in the behavior of others, which sabotages her own efforts at autonomy because it keeps her focused on them rather than on developing her own skills.

So both persons, in spite of their need to develop autonomy or intimacy (and still to be accepted and belong), may allow old behaviors to detour them from new journeys. They throw roadblocks into their own pathways toward developing social interest and learning to link and connect—skills necessary for colleagueship and partnership.

External expectations. In addition to these internal roadblocks, individuals who are changing their ways of relating may also face obstacles in the form of *externally imposed* sanctions. Suppose that a previously dominating person has made the decision to relinquish some privilege and become less controlling. This person wants to stop "discounting" and "depersonalizing" others and to instead begin "listening and asking questions," becoming "increasingly introspective" (all descriptors found on the Male/Female Continuum). If this individual happens to be male, other participants may say: Isn't he charming! Look how vulnerable he appears—he's trying to open himself to others! How delightful—he's actually trying to connect! However, welcome as this modification may be to those who have been feeling discounted and ignored, his new behavior begins to disrupt the balance of power. Other group members are no longer having decisions made for them, and are no longer being trivialized and marginalized. They now must find ways to speak for themselves, which places more responsibility on their shoulders. In the paradigm of partnership and colleagueship, power equates with responsibility, so when power is being shared, responsibility is also being shared.

A similar disruption in power balance might occur when a group member who previously had constantly deferred to others now decides to become more autonomous. This person no longer wants to be dominated, is tired of "controlling through helping" or "yielding" to others, and decides to stop letting "introspection freeze actions," to use the Continuum's terminology. Naturally, this unexpected turn of events is confusing to those accustomed to being in the driver's seat. Such confusion was described by one of my students, who worked for a very unreasonable boss. She strongly disagreed with both his policies and procedures, but had never summoned the courage to confront him until she took an assertiveness training class:

> It used to be, when I was mad at my boss, I would just stomp my
> foot and act exasperated. (He used to say I looked "cute" when I was
> mad.) But I never really told him what was on my mind. Now that
> I've had a few sessions of this class, I speak out at work and clearly
> state to my boss what I'm angry about. He wants to know what this
> "assertiveness stuff" is all about—*he says he liked me better before.*

This student's testimony illustrates how, when previously deferring individuals stop trying to meet their needs by the indirect
exercise of power (stomping the foot or acting exasperated) others
are temporarily taken aback. If the newly assertive person is
female, some may remark: How delightful! She was always such
a doormat—now just look how she stands up for herself! Others
may react negatively, not only because they have been benefiting
enormously from her previous halfhearted attempts at autonomy,
but because her new assertive behavior challenges their expectations about how women should behave. In our example above, the
boss might have assumed about his employee: She's a female; I
can probably expect her to comply with my policies and go along
with just about anything I say. And meanwhile, although she
disagreed with his unreasonable policies, she may have acqui-
esced to his dominance because her internal expectation was: He's
a male; he must know what he's talking about, so I'd better keep
quiet. (Of course, since we have a power differential here, we must
also acknowledge that she may have complied with his policies
simply to hold on to her job.)

Human interactions go along fairly swimmingly as long as
everybody's behaviors stay predictably mainstream and nobody
tries to rock the boat or navigate against the current. However,
what if one is leading a group, and a new male joins. He is hurting
emotionally, and when he begins to share his feelings, revealing
painful experiences, he seems almost to *plead* for support from
others. Many may see his vulnerability as "charming." Yet, to
others, his needs are unacceptable. They react with a strong bias:
This fellow seems out of control. Men should be able to cope; what
is this guy, some kind of wimp? This vulnerable male is thus
labeled as unnecessarily "needy," maybe even "dependent" or
"weak." Because he appears to deviate so far from the expected
gender role of "the guy who has it all together," his neediness
provokes overreaction from others—a new strain of the virus of

sexism. Medical sociologist Patricia Rieker explains that this reaction exemplifies a "more subtle level of sexism than the traditional bias," and it is important that we professionals understand its subtlety:

> [This new sexism is] directed against men or women who deviate greatly from conventional standards of behavior for their sex. [Those] who deviate from traditional roles often are seen as suffering a mental illness. . . . People don't really realize the extent to which an implicit sexism permeates notions of how normal men and women ought to behave. (quoted in Goleman, 1990, pp. 1E, 2E)[3]

If we perceive that this suffering male in our workshop "deviates greatly" from the conventional male role, we may quickly label him: Males are supposed to be autonomous and in charge; how come he's acting so helpless? By the same token, if a woman in our group seems rather dispassionate and not particularly empathic, or she acts assertive and independent, we may also label her: She seems rather disconnected from this whole process—even a bit self-centered; how come she's such a cold fish?

In an effort to extricate themselves from the confusion of conflicting expectations, individuals who are striving toward more versatility in gender role behaviors may inadvertently fall back on old restrictive patterns. For example, a male might profess great commitment to "toning down" his overbearing communication style, yet continue to be aggressive. A female might profess great commitment to "tuning up" her assertiveness, yet continue to let others use her as a doormat.

A Leader's Implicit Sexism
Discourages Personal Development

As if it were not enough for group members to be struggling with their own internalized gender role expectations and fending off expectations from others, we leaders add fuel to the fire by continuing to display our own biases. For example, a therapist, social worker, or other professional who believes strongly that the male in a family should be the primary breadwinner might say to a client who has chosen to express connection to his family by being a househusband, "Where did you get your ideas about what it means to be a man?" (in Goleman, 1990). Similarly, the professor who believes strongly that females belong in more "womanly" occupations may subtly suggest to a woman who has chosen to express her autonomy by studying law or engineering that she "try nursing instead."

Each of us elaborately structures "role slots" (Pierce & Page, 1990)—arbitrary categories into which we believe "normal" men and women ought to fit: He brings home the bacon, she should forget her law degree; he makes all the decisions, she should be docile and comply. We may unquestioningly reinforce these categories, subtly insinuating that there is something deviant about individuals who do not fit into them. Unless we become aware of just how limiting and stultifying our preconceived notions can be, we leaders may miss opportunities to empower participants who are ready to extricate themselves from the gender-restrictive, self-defeating patterns in which they feel "stuck"—patterns that preclude the development of intimacy or autonomy, and that inhibit the "mutual empowerment" and "new dynamics" of colleagueship.

As leaders, our response must be to "cultivate the observer" in ourselves—to watch our own behaviors, plus the behaviors of our group members toward us and toward each other. We can be constantly alert to the fact that our perceptions will be clouded not only by our own implicit sexism, but by our lack of understanding about where each person is on her or his developmental journey. We also need to admit that we may be oblivious about the extent to which some individuals will go to meet their own needs, and that it is very probable these needs will differ and clash in our sessions.

When Developmental Needs Clash in Groups

Next, I present the story of an assertiveness training workshop that I led, which was attended by a lone male, Ted, who was Desperately Seeking Symbiosis. Ted, like the solitary females we met earlier at the business reception and committee meeting (Chapter 1), is one of a kind—a "solo" (Kanter, 1977b, p. 966). We will witness how Ted's behaviors are received by his female peers, one of whom, Theresa, is Desperately Seeking Separateness. After discussing the assertiveness group's dynamics and suggesting an appropriate intervention, we will then visit an "addictions anonymous" support group attended by a man named Ralph; this group is also composed almost entirely of women.

Skewed Groups and Tokens

Because the proportion of females is uniquely high in the groups in the following examples, they are considered *skewed groups*; that is, groups in which one type or category of person vastly outnumbers the other. In skewed groups, the person or persons in the minority are called "tokens" and those in the majority are called "dominants" (Kanter, 1977b, p. 966). Tokens are categorized on the basis of easily recognizable characteristics—sex, race, ethnic group, age—that carry with them a set of assumptions.

Solos and tokens, rather than being treated as individuals, are treated as representatives of their categories, and are apt to experience three phenomena: performance pressure, boundary heightening, and role encapsulation (Kanter, 1977a, 1977b; cited in Powell, 1988, pp. 112-114). *Performance pressure* means that tokens react to being highly visible and singled out by trying to overachieve or call further attention to themselves in other ways. Tokens also experience *boundary heightening*: The differences between tokens and dominants becomes even more exaggerated, and the tokens may be treated as outsiders. In the third phenomenon, *role encapsulation,* the token is classified according to a stereotype, whether or not that stereotype fits the particular person. Increasingly, as people move into fields that are nontraditional for their sex (male paralegals, female engineers), men as well as women will be placed in the role of token, and the groups in which they try to function will be skewed groups.

In the following case study, we have a token male who has registered for a series of my evening assertiveness classes. His interest in this topic is significant, because assertiveness training is usually considered a "women's subject." As facilitator, because I am so gratified at his presence and so pleased that he is sharing himself during the first session, I find myself making unnecessary allowances and granting him privileges not given the female participants. (As evident in Figure 3.1, the controlling energy comes from this male, and it is he with whom I collude.) Already I am condoning his "encapsulation" into his male role; already the boundaries are becoming "heightened" between him and the women.

CASE 3.1

Token Male Dominates: *"If you can't get that guy to shut up, I'm dropping the workshop"*

I am leading the first session of an assertiveness training series. Participants include eight females, one of whom I will call Theresa, and one male, whom I will call Ted. Since I am committed to offering the subject coeducationally, I am pleased about Ted's presence (even though I am acutely aware that he is a token male), and I admire what courage he must have summoned to enroll in the workshop. Unfortunately, my enthusiasm backfires, as we shall see.

Because of the nature of the topic, I urge participants to begin expressing their needs, opinions, and differences right during the session; the workshop then becomes a microcosm for rehearsing self-assertion techniques that they can use later in the real world.

Ted is going through a painful divorce and is really "unloading" on the rest of us, calling attention to himself and his problems. He is using language to maintain status (Tannen, 1990) and to determine the "parameters of the talk" (Spender, 1980). Ted carries on at length while all of the females, including myself, patiently listen—we don't respond, intervene, or change the subject.

I begin to sense that the other women are becoming not only restless, but downright hostile. Although I have given myself and the group permission to ask questions and assert our needs at any time, I don't practice what I preach, and neither do they. Theresa's silence, I notice, is particularly palpable.

We are all in complicity with Ted's *dominance*: The poor guy is hurting, our issues can wait. What men have to say is more important. We can't confront him—he might get alienated. Good girls listen. As though we are afraid he will abandon us, we women try to take care of Ted. And, although assertiveness training certainly is *not* therapy, some of the same dynamics observed in the marriage counseling scenario in Chapter 1, and that were delineated by Goldner (1985), also obtain in this workshop setting. Others in the room with the male detect his "relative helplessness" and may pick up another message as well: "If I am not protected here, I'm not coming back" (Goldner, 1985, p. 40).

What I had not sensed at the time, but what has become glaringly obvious in retrospect, is that Ted's needs are being met at everyone else's expense. This is not a warm climate in which both genders can thrive equally. As leader, I have been caught between my professional role of Dispassionate Facilitator, trying to keep a balanced discussion going, and my socialized role of Doting Damsel, performing what Pamela Fishman has indelicately termed the "shitwork" in conversation. (Shitwork, according to one interpretation of Fishman's concept, means that women "feed men the lines, draw them out, respond to the topics that men determine, and act as their audience" [in J. L. Thompson, 1983, p. 117]. Based on her observations of college classrooms, Catherine Krupnick has a more benign way of describing this sort of imbalance: "In a normal coeducational world, boys act like boys, and girls act hospitable" [quoted in Kelly, 1990].)[4]

At any rate, during this assertiveness workshop, I have no interventions up my sleeve; neither Theresa nor any of the other women in the class state their needs, and Ted carries on with his monologue. After the session, Theresa, using an abrupt but delayed intervention, telephones me to complain: "Unless you get that guy to quit talking, I'm not coming to the next session. I work in a nursing home all day and listen to people's problems; I don't need to come to a group at night and listen to some man go on and on about his troubles. I'm a caretaker on the job—I don't need to be a caretaker in the workshop too. *If you can't get that guy to shut up, I'm dropping the workshop.*"

I assure Theresa that I will speak to Ted, but I also remind her that she was given permission to express her own needs and opinions in the group. I tell her that as facilitator I am willing to accept *part* of the responsibility for the imbalance, but that she was also empowered to speak up during class. I then phone Ted and explain the situation. Ted drops the workshop.

Restriction of Women in Mixed Groups

In terms of the previous discussion of the Four D's of gender role extremes (see Box 1.1), everyone in the room seems to be playing an extreme role, including Ted, the female participants, and me. This one man embodies the whole continuum of the stereotyped male role, from dominance to detachment. If he cannot be dominating, he will go to the other extreme: He will distance himself completely and detach. In other words, he will quit the group.

The women, meanwhile, stay in the deference mode, with Theresa striving to meet her needs for autonomy by playing diagnostician:

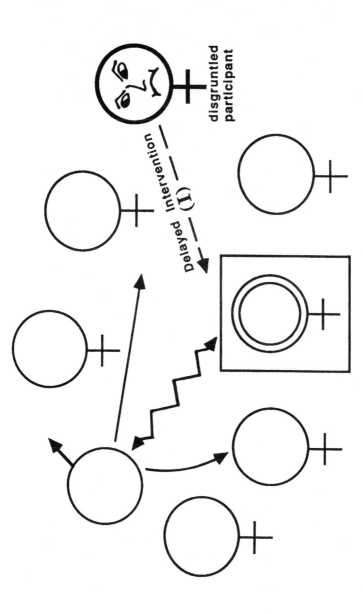

Figure 3.1. Participant Confronts Leader Who Overprotects "Token" Male: *"If you can't get that guy to shut up, I'm dropping the workshop . . . "* (Delayed/Abrupt Intervention Used)

81

"I don't need to . . . listen to some guy go on and on about his troubles."

The events here may have been predictable, given the state of affairs in many mixed-sex settings. Women, as well as men, may leave a group out of dissatisfaction because their needs are not being met. Folkins et al. (1982) describe a leaderless couples group that the women abandoned, protesting lack of intimacy, but that the men thought was just fine. Supporting their empirical observations with some of the research in psychology, these authors conclude that "mixed-gender groups appear to offer more to men than to women" because

> men become more personal and self-revealing and are less aggressive and competitive. . . . Women, however, decrease self-disclosure, tend to talk less than in female-only settings . . . and are reluctant to assume leadership roles. . . . It appears, therefore, that, compared with one-gender groups, mixed-gender groups allow men more variation in their interpersonal styles, but women experience greater restriction. Also, women probably experience less power and diminished self-esteem in mixed-gender groups. (p. 369)[5]

It *does* appear that the women in this workshop experienced less power than Ted. Whether or not they experienced diminished self-esteem is also of great importance, because there is a strong correlation between positive self-esteem and success in most situations.

It is possible that Theresa's implicit sexism caused her to complain about Ted's dominance, and that she was blowing the situation out of proportion partly because of her biased expectations. Because females are not used to males who display emotion, they may "scapegoat" a man who steps out of his gender role to express "dependency or distress," just as males may scapegoat the female who is assertive or expresses anger, labeling her "hysteric" or "bitchy" (Folkins et al., 1982). That women may be taken aback by men's newfound expressiveness was documented on a television program about the male role in which one male panelist stated:

> Women are not used to hearing us men complain about ourselves. The women's movement gave us mixed signals: Women want men to be more sensitive, but *if a man opens up, he'll get stomped on.*

Nevertheless, the assertiveness workshop was clearly out of balance, and as leader, I wish I had intervened at a much earlier stage, because one person's needs were being met to the exclusion of others' needs. I was so pleased to have a living, breathing male in the group, so delighted that Ted wanted to learn about assertiveness, so receptive while he was sharing himself and trying to connect, and so hopeful that he would feel encouraged on his journey that I allowed him privileges not assumed by the other participants—all of whom happened to be women. My collusion with Ted was absolute: Ted was *overprotected* and *underchallenged* in this setting while the women were *underprotected* and *overchallenged*.

What would have been an appropriate way to restore balance, to nip the situation in the bud at the moment Ted's controlling neediness was detected? If you had been facilitator of this skewed group, how would you have handled our acceptance-seeking friend? When I presented this case on a panel titled "Gender-Linked Communication: Breaking the Barriers" (Van Nostrand, 1988), the following combined intervention was suggested by an audience member who was an experienced facilitator:

> I've been in a situation like the one with Ted, where there's one male, the rest women, we're discussing issues we all share, and he's talking—we're all listening. I *did* intervene: I let him know that I was supportive of his talking out ("Thank you very much for sharing") and then I said, *"We all need to be sensitive to one another as well as [to] ourselves."* I left it there and let people take it where they wanted to. He finished up what he had to say—on his own—and then the women were able to open up more.

This leader combines two strategies: She first supports the overly verbal participant and shows understanding (nurturing/empathic intervention). She then suggests behavioral boundaries (limit-setting intervention). She affirms his "new" need for connection and intimacy, yet lets him know how his "old" emphasis on self- centeredness is antithetical to the group's social interest. She shows him how he can shed nonproductive behaviors and step into more collegial patterns; such guidance would have been very helpful to Ted.

New Goals, Old Roles

Ted is trying to reach new goals, but he falls instead into old roles. His new goal is to be the sensitive, connecting male, capable of listening to, and developing empathy with, others. Instead, he reverts into the old role of insensitive, dominating male, who uses report talk and calls attention to himself. Although he wants to connect, he is not able to communicate in a way to establish rapport and compensates for his feelings of alienation by trying to control the group discussion.

Similarly, we see Theresa, who wants to be the assertive, autonomous female, capable of stating her needs and standing up for herself, reverting instead to the role of dependent, deferring female, who keeps her anger frozen inside and blows up later. She compensates for her feelings of alienation by trying to control the leader. Theresa's efforts are quite understandable, given that the leader seems hardly aware of the female participants, being so preoccupied with trying to make sure Ted feels comfortable. Thus a climate is established that further exacerbates Theresa's feeling of marginalization and alienation.

Neither Ted nor Theresa behaves in a way that fosters affiliation, intimacy, or collaborative group spirit (Adler's "social interest"). Ted could empower others and himself by saying, "I would like to accept feedback and learn from all of you"; however, his need to control—first by dominance and finally by detachment—stands in his way. Theresa could empower others and herself by saying, "I have some suggestions that might improve our group dynamics," but her efforts to meet her needs—first by deference and ultimately by diagnosis—consume most of her energy.

Nudging Women and Men out of Restrictive Roles

The task of the leader in such cases is to replicate the techniques suggested above in the combined intervention: First we *nurture,* then we *set limits.* Initially we affirm and support those who take risks to break away from old patterns, then we define the group's parameters *on our own terms* rather than allowing a dominant faction to determine boundaries. In the case of men like Ted, who claim they want to be the new sensitive male, we first support their willingness to be vulnerable, and then deliberately nudge them away from restrictive male patterns that cause alienation and interfere with the group's cohesiveness.

In like manner, we must decisively nudge the Theresas who claim they want to be the new assertive woman, but who instead tenaciously insist on being accommodating and hospitable (see Kelly, 1990). In reminding Theresa that all group members had been given permission to express individual needs, I was giving her permission to step out of the restrictive role of caretaker who put the needs of others first. However, since I myself was playing "colluding caretaker," my words probably fell on deaf ears. As leader, I was not practicing what I preached, not "walking the talk," not really *mentoring* what I *mouthed*. We leaders who ask our followers to change a behavior that we ourselves are unwilling to change are not authentic—we are not credible or responsible leaders.

An essential leadership ingredient here is that all group members must feel empowered. When a leader announces to a group that their feedback is welcome—I urge each of you to get involved in our discussions; Feel free to assert your needs here; I welcome your critical feedback at any time—then she or he must create a climate in which this can happen. In short, we can be the kinds of leaders who guide women and men away from the collusion of dominance and subordinance toward more gender role flexibility. Table 3.1 provides techniques for helping others reach new flexible goals by modifying old roles.

A word of caution is in order. The sequential strategies for effective leadership shown in Table 3.1 and the encouraging intervention suggested above for dealing with people like Ted are not meant as foolproof remedies. Remedial measures raised during leadership training sessions (and in manuals such as this) have a way of sounding coolly professional, polished, and poised. However, in the heat of actual group process, our best intentions sometimes fly out the window as we cope with the pressures of content, time constraints, room environment, diverse personalities, and numerous other factors. Dealing with gender bias may be the *last* thing on our minds.

And even when we make efforts to be gender responsible, we may find ourselves confounded, caught between power factions in a classic double bind. For example, if a female leader colludes with controlling males, as I did with Ted, she can be accused of

Table 3.1 New Goals, Old Roles: How Leaders Can Delineate Female/ Male Developmental Tasks and Encourage Gender Role Flexibility

Females and males have different developmental tasks. The task of many females is to achieve *autonomy*, to learn "the experience of power" (Kanter, 1977c, p. 383) and to "assert their needs—even if doing so leaves them alone" (Desjardins, 1989a, p. 139). The task of many males, on the other hand, may be to develop connection and *intimacy*—to listen to, get feedback from, and learn to feel empathy for others, even if doing so means relinquishing some autonomy and separateness. Women and men who master these skills have a greater repetoire of behaviors available to them, and a better chance of attaining "colleagueship" (Pierce & Page, 1990). However, learning new behaviors requires willingness to leave behind familiar, comfortable, and often stereotypically gendered patterns.

Using a sequence of three techniques, leaders can enhance the progress of women and men on their individual developmental journeys. Leaders must first *define the stereotyped behavior*, then *encourage greater role flexibility* and *provide behavioral guidelines*. For example, if an overly defensive male is just learning to share himself, but fears that further self-disclosure will cause him to lose status or appear "soft" or "unmasculine," the leader can name his need to connect and affirm him for his efforts at reaching toward others. Similarly, if an unassertive female has difficulty voicing her opinions because she is afraid that by speaking forcefully she will invite criticism as "unsympathetic," "pushy," or "unfeminine," the leader can *define* her need for empowerment and *encourage* her to speak her mind.

However, as individuals try to break out of old patterns and experiment with new roles, their fledgling transitional behaviors may either disrupt group process or cause it to stagnate altogether. The leader must then move to the third step, which involves showing women and men how to balance their newfound quests toward autonomy or intimacy with the welfare of the group as a whole.

As you follow the sequence of the three techniques below, note that the leadership language applies to Theresa and Ted, who participated in the assertiveness workshop (Case 3.1) during which both experimented with modes of self-expression atypical for their gender.

To develop a group atmosphere in which females and males have an equal voice, and in which gender role extremes don't control process, the responsible leader will take the following steps:

(1) *Define stereotypes and provide examples of gender role rigidity that inhibits personal growth or contributes to imbalanced participation.* The leader could say something like the following:

Some behaviors lock women and men even more tightly into stereotyped roles and throw the group off balance. For example, because males are expected to be the "expert" or to "keep a stiff upper lip," men may be either consistently deferred to as authority figures or criticized for showing emotion. Or because females are sometimes perceived as "less knowledgeable," or are expected to be "nice" and defer to others, women's opinions may not be taken as seriously as those of men. When I notice that these patterns seem to have a negative effect on group process, I will call your attention to them.

(2) *Encourage and affirm particular individuals who demonstrate flexibility by breaking out of traditional patterns and taking risks to deviate from expected roles.*

　(a) To reward a dominant or detached male for trying to connect with others (thereby affirming his efforts to develop intimacy): Ted, I want to support how you shared your experiences and feelings with us today.

　(b) To encourage a reticent female to express her opinions (thereby helping her to develop autonomy and individuality): Theresa, I am so pleased that you telephoned me about your dissatisfaction with the assertiveness workshop. I appreciate your risk taking and honesty.

(3) *Provide guidelines for more appropriate behavior if old roles get in the way of new goals.* Set limits and guide group members to see how extremely stereotyped behaviors of dominance, detachment, or deference may not only impede the completion of a successful gender role journey, but also prohibit the equitable distribution of opportunity, responsibility, and power in a group. Show them how they can develop autonomy or intimacy and simultaneously practice behaviors that promote the "social interest."

　(a) Ted, part of your job as a sensitive group member learning to connect with others is to listen to, and affirm, their contributions.

　(b) Theresa, feel free to speak to me any time alone; but, since each of us acquires new assertiveness skills by rehearsing them first in the group, I urge you to verbalize your opinions during the session so we may all learn from you.

During each of the above stages, the leader continues to demonstrate respect for participants and their individual and collective processes. The leader also monitors her or his own attitudes and methods to assure that

continued

Table 3.1   Continued

there is no favoritism toward, or collusion with, one individual or gender
more than the another.

> (a) I notice that in my effort to help the token male in this group
> to feel comfortable, I have been ignoring the females. Did
> anyone else notice that?
> (b) I'm going to stop the discussion right here; I feel my chivalry
> toward the females is unnecessarily protecting them and is
> overemphasizing the contributions of the males. I need to
> check this out with the group.

---

favoritism or—worse—seduction (Wow! Is she ever thick with
him!). If she stops colluding, plays diagnosing detective, and confronts male dominance, she can be accused of being pushy or—
worse—castrating (How can she be so unsympathetic to men?).

If a male leader overprotects women and allows them continually to defer or take a backseat in the group, he can be accused of
underchallenging, discounting, or being condescendingly chivalrous. If the leader colludes with females, letting them control the
group process, he could be accused of being a "wimp" who is
"henpecked" because he allows women to "take over" (Look!
Those women have him in the palms of their hands!). If the leader
stops colluding and confronts women about why they are either
under- or overinvolved, he could be labeled as either heavy-
handed or unsympathetic to women's reality.

Thus leaders can be accused of sexist favoritism no matter
which gender they seem to acknowledge more. As we saw in the
scenario above, and as we will observe in the support group
depicted in the next case study, it is all too easy for any leader to
slip into the role of colluding caretaker. When I facilitated the
assertiveness session, I was more concerned with taking care of
Ted than with being a gender-fair leader. I modeled a traditional
female role of deference that the other women imitated, although
not without anger, until eventually there was a petition for remediation from Theresa. Her communication was not particularly timely
and not exactly "assertive," probably an indication of her extreme
frustration at trying to function within this male-privileged environment. However, it is precisely this kind of plea that awakens a

leader to the need for more appropriate and forceful interventions—in short, for more gender-fair leadership.

Our task as leaders, then, is to be alert to the ways in which women and men may use rigid gender role behaviors to meet their own needs—behaviors that are exercised in an effort to control group process. Of course, it is not humanly possible for us to recognize and meet everyone's expectations, particularly if individuals don't bring themselves to express them. However, we can develop techniques for affirming women and men in their gender roles if they *do* feel comfortable in these roles, and learn strategies for empowering them to change behaviors if they *do not*. It is also helpful if we can be sensitive about where participants are on their individual developmental journeys. Simultaneous with all of this, we need to monitor our own biased assumptions about what we think is appropriate gender role behavior. This is a tall order for any leader, but essential to a principle suggested by feminist therapist Goldner (1985), that of "retriev[ing] gender as a category of . . . observation" (p. 45).

If we are able to cultivate the observer in ourselves, as recommended in Chapter 1, we will catch our bias earlier and not have to wait until the group falls into disarray to be shocked into sensitivity. Subsequent chapters will suggest concrete steps that leaders can take toward developing a more gender-sensitive stance.

We facilitators may find ourselves frustrated not only in class or workshop environments, such as the one above, but in a variety of other settings as well. A hypothetical support group provides the setting for the next case study. The skewed gender distribution in this group is similar to that of the workshop above: Men are again vastly outnumbered. However, now, instead of a female facilitator, the leader is male. How will he reveal his bias? Will his expectations about appropriate gendered behavior contaminate his leadership? If so, how will this affect group dynamics?

CASE 3.2

Token Male Detaches: *Isn't He Smart!*

Imagine yourself a male therapist facilitating a support group consisting of 11 women and 2 men. The group's purpose is to help members deal with issues of addiction, that is, how one can learn to change behavior in regard to chemicals, food, and other substances and habits. Your job as facilitator is to create a climate in which members feel encouraged to be vulnerable and to share their trials and errors in overcoming addiction. Through such sharing it is hoped that all participants will gain affirmation and support that will then motivate them to continue being disciplined in their personal habits.

One male member has already dropped out of the group, and you don't want to lose any more men. Of the remaining males, one is a highly educated professional, Ralph, who is about 10 years your senior. In no uncertain terms, Ralph has informed you privately that you are *exceptionately fortunate* to have him in your group because of his advanced professional training. However, he says that, in spite of his sophistication and expertise, he will probably be able to trust you anyway because you have *nearly* as much education as he. Ralph also informs you that he would not have accepted just *any* leader; he especially wanted to be in *your* group. Here we have the early seeds of the old boy network; in fact, Ralph may already have you exactly where he wants you.

During weekly support group sessions, Ralph, in order to establish and solidify his status, remains emotionally detached and aloof. The women go on at length, talking about how difficult it has been to let go of old habits, how their spouses or significant others are reacting to their changed life-styles, how they are coping with emotional highs and lows. Although somewhat reluctantly, the other male participant also shares events in his journey away from addiction. Ralph, however, admits to no ignorance, temptations, emotional upheavals, dependencies, or any need for personal behavioral change. He also does not nurture or support others who share information about their addictions, vulnerabilities, or struggles to change. In short, Ralph contributes to the discussion only when he can engage in "report talk," discussing facts external to himself and spouting considered judgments and knowledgeable pronouncements from his self-appointed position as resident authority.

Male Is Overprotected and Underchallenged

Ostensibly, the purpose of this group is to help members to be open to giving and receiving feedback, to learn more about themselves and others, to practice new patterns of behavior. Ralph may even have joined the group with every intention of following that agenda. However, because of his deep need for self-protection and status maintenance, which is perhaps a function of his insecurity, Ralph falls into old defensive behaviors. He may have new goals, but he plays an old role.

Ralph emotionally distances himself, and you the friendly facilitator allow it. You find yourself seeking his input only for his calculated technical advice, but never asking him how he *feels* or whether he is struggling with his addiction. Certainly you never challenge his carefully cloaked defensiveness or his lack of emotional connection with the others. You do, however, begin to wonder at the group's overall lack of cohesiveness. You notice that very few people appear to be close to Ralph or to talk to him during breaks. But it does not occur to you that part of the reason for the group's failure to establish an optimal level of connectedness might have something to do with your leadership.

Ralph is playing the classic male role discussed earlier, that of the dominator who controls by detachment, and you, the experienced facilitator, are letting him get away with it. Both of you are well on your way down the slippery slope of collusion. Ralph has hooked you into becoming his caretaker, helping him to construct an impervious bubble of immunity around himself, a subtle ego boundary of privilege that both of you keep in good repair. In effect, you two are engaged in a "covert operation," each tacitly agreeing: You and I are the experts here, but we'll keep our little agreement from the others to reinforce and maintain our status. I have nearly as much education as you, and you are almost as smart as I. No man of such standing should have to reveal himself in front of *all these women!* What we know won't hurt them.

Because you and Ralph are functioning within a hierarchical framework, both of you are preoccupied with status. After all, status was the premise upon which Ralph joined your group. If Ralph were to become vulnerable, his position of prominence might begin to deteriorate. You, with great empathy for this tenuous state, collude with Ralph's fear that if he discloses any weakness he will temporarily lose standing with other participants. It would be totally unthinkable for him to appear as less than "the expert." He is allowed to continue controlling through detachment, and you are unwilling to challenge him to become more involved.

Were we to have a moment to interview privately first Ralph, then you the facilitator, the other male participant, and the women, we might hear these comments:

> *Ralph:* Quiet? Well, yes, I'm quiet. But the reason I don't talk much is I don't want to steal the leader's thunder; I don't want to appear to compete with him. After all, I've got even more education than he.

> *Friendly facilitator:* Quiet? Oh yes, Ralph is quiet in the group. But that's *good* for him. It's good for him to sit there and listen to the women.

> *Other male participant:* There's something fishy going on here.

> *Female participants:* Ralph is pulling rank.

Earlier in this chapter, we saw how the developmental task of many men is to learn to be *less* separate, not *more* separate: Many males need to learn to be less defiant, and to move *toward* others rather than pushing others *away*. If Ralph's task is to potentiate some latent social interest in himself, to learn to "contribute to and participate in communal life," to grow in ability to connect with others as an equal group member, his task will not be accomplished unless you, the leader, alter your modus operandi.

You are in the leader's classic double bind. If you don't side with Ralph, you are breaking the rules of the old boy network. If you take the women's part, you risk being labeled a "woman pleaser," an "Uncle Tom" to the male cause, or a "male basher." If you confront Ralph, he may feel you are unsympathetic or "unbrotherly"; he might even interpret your action as male-to-male competitiveness, and respond with fight or flight. Then you would either have a battle on your hands or he would leave the group, as did the previous male member, thus undermining your credibility as leader.

By your conscious or unconscious connivings, you and Ralph are both trying to cover potential losses: You want to avoid losing credibility as leader, and he wants to avoid showing his soft underbelly, thus losing face. Each of you also wants to avoid what may be the worst pitfall of all for a male—appearing incompetent or vulnerable in front of a preponderance of females. If you appear incompetent you risk losing the power of your position as leader; if Ralph appears vulnerable, he risks losing the status of his position as privileged professional. But Ralph loses even more:

Because he doesn't share himself, he loses the chance to be affirmed and supported by his fellow participants. The primary losers, however, are the other group members, who are deprived for three reasons:

(1) Participants see, by your collusion, a model of weak leadership. You are not being gender fair and are not promoting all strengths in all participants.

(2) Group members do not get to know Ralph because he never really opens up to them. They miss the opportunity to dialogue and interact with all parts of his personality, to accept his weaknesses as well as his strengths. His controlling detachment and dominance preclude intimacy.

(3) Participants have become victims of a hierarchical system that perpetuates male privilege.

This system has allowed Ralph, and you the leader right along with him, to be "above it all" and to speak from a position of male entitlement: There's nothing wrong with us; it's you others who need to do the changing. Just look at how much you've said about your addictions. Obviously you folks have *real problems*. Have we disclosed any such frailties? If must be clear to you that we've *arrived* and have all the answers.

In *The Power to Communicate,* Borisoff and Merrill (1985) suggest that group participants who reveal themselves are vulnerable and have lower status:

> Males have been taught to be logical, objective and impersonal; while women have been encouraged to be subjective, self-disclosing and personal. Always, however, the "masculine" traits have been afforded greater status. Women render themselves vulnerable by their self-disclosure; men derive power from sounding authoritative and communicating facts rather than emotions. (p. 12)

Henley and Thorne (1977) discuss how self-disclosure, or the lack of it, can aggravate power differentials: "Women disclose more personal information to others than men do; subordinates . . . are also more likely to self-disclose than superiors. People in positions of power do not have to reveal information about themselves" (p. 209).

In a competitive paradigm, vulnerability connotes a "one-down" position. Since being "emotional" or "self-disclosing and personal" is a position most often taken by women, the dynamics of the support group above have served to make women feel like second-class citizens. The leader who allows the male to "sound authoritative" and "communicate facts rather than emotions" attributes power to that person and enforces male entitlement. By allowing Ralph his detached distance, the leader guarantees his dominance.

What was needed in Ralph's group was a revaluing of the word consensus. We usually take this word to mean "reaching agreement," but it can also mean a "feeling or sensing together" that produces in groups a "crossing of the barrier between ego and ego" (Holland, 1975, p. 291; cited in Belenky et al., 1986, p. 223).

A Connected Group: Fostering Community

Applying these concepts in the educational setting would give us *connected teaching* or a *connected classroom* (Noddings, 1984), to be discussed further in Chapter 5. Since support groups qualify as an educational experience, these concepts apply to Ralph's addictions group. Perhaps what Ralph needed all along was for the facilitator to find a way to help him and the others to cross ego barriers and be able to "feel and sense together" so that Ralph would know he could be accepted, warts and all, accepted for his internal vulnerabilities and insecurities as well as for his knowledge of external facts. Had the leader created a warm climate of acceptance, letting Ralph know that appearing extra smart or having it all together was not a criterion for belonging, Ralph might have been able to receive and accept affirmation and even honest negative feedback from others in the support group.

When a leader empowers followers to be a connected group, "emphasis is placed on the development of a sense of community in which each person knows all the others so well that criticism can be not only tolerated but accepted and built upon" (McClelland, 1988, p. 4).[6] Had some of Ralph's ego boundaries been permeated, the group could have seen the real Ralph. Had the therapist said no to Ralph's behavior, the group might have had a better chance to know him. This is where true intimacy begins.

How Gender, Power, and
Collusion Contaminate Leadership

In the two groups above, participants Ted and Ralph represent the stereotypical male who either dominates or detaches to meet personal needs. In Case 3.1, Ted dominates the assertiveness workshop by playing "Mr. Victim," reporting on how "oppressed" he is, distancing himself from others by his insensitivity. In the support group depicted in Case 3.2, Ralph dominates by playing "Mr. Expert," distancing himself through his preoccupation with status. Neither male is able to connect, yet each manages to control group process and subvert the social interest.

These men are aided and abetted in their controlling maneuvers by their facilitators, whose implicit sexism perpetuates male privilege. Not much is required of either Ted or Ralph; neither is expected to be sensitive to the group climate to monitor whether his behavior contributes toward furthering the common good. No interventions are used: Nobody asks Ted to listen more and talk less; nobody confronts Ralph about his privileged detachment from the issues at hand. Because of their personal biases and intensely collusive leadership, neither facilitator functions as a gender-neutral professional, and thus neither is able to empower all participants fully.

Also, in both these cases, the uncomfortable position of token male is aggravated, not alleviated, by the leader. Both Ted and Ralph become more encapsulated in roles; the boundaries between them and others are heightened, and they appear even more pressured to "perform."

The examples in this chapter illustrate the full impact of gender, power, and collusion on the leadership function. We have observed how internalized expectations of one's own behavior and that of others can make it exceedingly difficult for group members to support one another and for the facilitator to be gender neutral, much less gender fair. We have seen how, in a desperate attempt to meet psychological needs, participants may throw group dynamics off balance.

We have also seen how being a token person in a group can exaggerate one's gender role, causing performance pressures, boundary heightening, and role encapsulation. Here males were the tokens, and partly because they were outnumbered (but mostly because of their entitlement), they were *overprotected*. In Chapter 4 we will observe females who are also outnumbered. However, rather than being overprotected, they meet with a much different fate: They are categorized, ostracized, and definitely *underprotected*. Thus the irony: While one gender is often handled as an endangered species, the other may be treated as a threatening one.

Notes

1. The "equity experience" is described as a condition in groups "where power equity is assumed and diversity is valued and achieved" (Wagner, 1990, p. 1; see also Pierce & Page, 1990).

2. In its original, unabridged version, the Male/Female Continuum is illustrated by a pullout chart in the back of the text of the same name (Pierce & Page, 1990); however, it is also the subject of a wall chart, available separately. For information, contact New Dynamics Publications, 21 Shore Drive, Laconia, NH 03246.

3. This and all subsequent quotes citing Goleman are from his article "'Mr. Moms' Affected by New Sexism," which appeared in the Minneapolis *Star Tribune* on April 16, 1990. Copyright © 1990 by The New York Times Company. Reprinted by permission.

4. This quote is from Kelly's article "Will Finances Foreclose Tradition?" which appeared in *USA Today* on April 30, 1990. Copyright 1990, Gannett Co., Inc. Reprinted by permission.

5. Folkins et al. (1982) reach the conclusion that "mixed-gender groups appear to offer more to men than to women" (p. 369) based partly on the work of Aries (1976), Bernardez and Stein (1979), Megargee (1969), and Wright and Gould (1977).

6. The "development of a sense of community" is one of numerous criteria necessary for establishing a "connected" learning environment, as determined by students and faculty during a workshop on connected education at Kent State University (as reported in McClelland, 1988). These concepts of "connected knowing" are based on the work of Nel Noddings (1984). For further discussion, see Belenky et al. (1986) and Goldberger (1989).

◀ 4 ▶

OVERCHALLENGED AND UNDERRATED

Women's Struggle in Traditionally Male Spheres

Women face maddeningly ephemeral barriers . . . largely having to do with male[s] . . . being uncomfortable dealing with female colleagues. Thus, a woman cannot be too aggressive for fear of setting the boss' teeth on edge. And she can't be too feminine lest she be accused of being flirtatious or—worse— being regarded as not strong enough to be taken seriously. . . . It is a balancing act that comes close to being a no-win situation in many instances. And I don't blame the women who have given up in disgust.

(Dick Youngblood, columnist, commenting on two studies about the paucity of women in top levels of management, 1990a)[1]

When I took a coed sailing course, hoping to become a qualified "skipper," I knew it would be an uphill battle to become certified. Even though I had once been a sailing instructor at a camp, I suspected that I might fail to pass this particular course—the fate of many female students before me. This success gap between female and male students had partly to do with the fact that, while growing up, most of us females had not experienced motors, compasses, winches, and lines. We probably needed some remediation. However, it also had to do, I discovered, with bias-driven collusion on the part of the male instructor, as well as collusion of dominance and subordinance among students.

97

Our course began in a classroom, with theoretical lectures on points of sail, weather, and navigation. We then divided into crews for our practicum in 40-foot sailboats on Lake Superior. In spite of the fact that my particular crew contained an equal number of women and men, when the instructor would call, "Man the lines," "Man the sails," or "Man the motor," the male students literally *did* the maneuver.

These men were not advantaged just because the instructor used noninclusive, sexist language (the accepted parlance among yachtspersons); their primary privilege was that they seized the initiative, got their hands on the equipment first, and the instructor let them get away with it. Although the instructor tried to assign tasks equally to each gender (e.g., John, take the mainsail; Mary, take the jib), he did not intervene if males appropriated most tasks. Nor did he try to involve females who sat by, waiting to be asked, deferring to men's dominance. The instructor seemed oblivious to women's invisibility on two fronts: initially, how women were being marginalized by male peers; and, ultimately, how he as educator reinforced this marginalization by perpetually favoring the men.

This teacher knew his subject matter well; he was thoroughly prepared and related comfortably with us all. I learned a great deal and—perhaps as a function of my previous sailing experience—even passed the course, although many of the other women did not. However, even though the instructor had established excellent rapport in our class, a bias existed, and it was the *covert* kind of favoritism that was extremely hard to pinpoint. No one was overtly suggesting to the women: You can't handle this. But the inference was: Oh, you haven't had a turn? Well, maybe next time. Or, Whoever gets there first will have priority.

The sailing instructor must have sensed the gender gap in learning opportunity, because when I chanced to meet him a few months later he asked, "Catharine, do you think this course should be taught to women and men separately?" After expressing my appreciation for his sensitivity, nondefensiveness, and openness to feedback (nurturing intervention), I found myself agreeing with his idea and encouraging him to follow through on it: "Yes," I said, "males had the advantage and were allowed to *maintain* that advantage. It was difficult for us women to get our hands on the equipment often enough, and long enough, to develop skills. Yes, for more women to become certified, it would be helpful if females were taught separately."

To this sailing saga one might be tempted to apply the old saw, "A woman must be twice as good to get half as far as a man" (Hall & Sandler, 1984, p. 3), also sometimes stated as, "A woman must try twice as hard as a man to be thought half as good." No matter how we word this misogynist myth, it conveniently places blame for lack of achievement on the woman, rather than examining the environment in which she is expected to "be better," "try harder," or "get further." It is much less embarrassing to blame the female sailing students for lack of initiative (Why don't the women just jump right up and grab those lines? Why are females complaining—they know where the motor is!) than to examine the instructor's apparent favoritism, which smacks suspiciously of an old boy network.

"Unassertive" Participant
or Unresponsive Leader?

Perhaps it is time, instead of blaming participants for not taking initiative, we should suspect that learning climates are repressive; instead of criticizing women for "lack of aptitude," we should criticize our own leadership methods. Sandra Keith (1987), who has developed strategies for encouraging female mathematics students, states the problem clearly: "Rather than [teaching] students to be more *assertive,* a more productive approach might be . . . for teachers to learn to be more *responsive*" (p. 95; emphasis added).

The sailing instructor demonstrated, although belatedly, a very positive awareness of his promale bias and a refreshing responsiveness to criticism. As leaders, it is our charge to develop this kind of *responsiveness* in ourselves so we may become more *responsible* to our followers. We must be sure our leadership methods are as empowering for women as they are for men (Van Nostrand, 1990b, 1993b).

It is also up to us to detect whether our subliminal favoritism may cause us to underchallenge participants or to overchallenge them. As discussed in Chapter 1, to *underchallenge* means we do not expect much; we chivalrously overprotect, or we place the person on a pedestal: I really think you're too delicate to haul in this sail or to turn that winch handle; here—let someone else do it for you! Such condescending overprotection—another example of the "classroom chivalry" mentioned earlier—is very damaging to women because it "deprives [them] of a chance to learn by doing" (Sadker, in Griffin, 1990, p. 12).

Conversely, when we *overchallenge* someone, we expect too much; we measure a person by a more rigorous standard than others, or we create an atmosphere in which some persons are excluded and ignored while others are granted automatic privilege and entitlement: Oh, you wanted a turn at the helm? Sorry, I didn't see you sitting there.

The female sailors were simultaneously underchallenged and overchallenged: Since crewmates and instructor assumed that women were less capable, less was therefore expected of them (underchallenge). They consequently accomplished fewer tasks, presumably learned less, and many failed the course. In order to become visible, gain recognition, and actually handle the boat, they had to overcome many barriers (overchallenge).

It is difficult enough for a woman to experience bias in an informal experience like sailing, but what if she encounters discrimination in her chosen life's work? And what if her career is in a male-dominated profession such as medicine, law, engineering, insurance, or a host of other fields in which she may be even more outnumbered by men? Our arena of analysis here is precisely these traditionally male spheres: How will women be treated when men see them treading on what is considered "male" turf? What is *male privilege,* and how will women feel its ramifications as they attempt to establish themselves in so-called men's territory?

Throughout this analysis, the focus remains on our own leadership: When women are a minority in our groups, we may be tempted to overprotect them as if they are an endangered species, or to isolate them as if they are a threatening one. Either treatment amounts to a "denial of ordinary status" (Schaper, 1990), a very subtle form of sexism that is difficult to detect yet powerful in its impact.

In this chapter I want to broaden the meaning of the word *leader* to refer not only to a person who facilitates a group, but to any person who lives with, works with, or interacts with others. Whether partner, peer, or parent, we are *all* leaders, and we are constantly influencing others. We set examples all the time; somebody, somewhere, can be either hindered or helped by our words and actions.

Like a Fish Out of Water:
Women in Male-Dominated Professions

At this time in history, women are still a minority in many traditionally male fields. For example, women represented only 17% of physicians in 1989 (American Medical Association, 1990), and only 20% of lawyers are women (Minnesota Bar Association, personal communication, March 1991).[2] "Girls still *perceive* their options as limited; . . . though women were 53 percent of all college students in 1987, they received less than 15 percent of all engineering degrees" (Griffin, 1990, p. 11). Women are no better represented in mathematics. According to the Minnesota Women's Fund (n.d.), "65% of boys have enough math to enroll in college calculus, the gateway to science and technology careers, compared to 45% of girls—a 20% gender gap."[3]

Preparation in math is essential for job success in the twenty-first century, as Marsha Matyas, keynote speaker at the 1989 National Conference on Women in Mathematics and the Sciences, has pointed out. Matyas (1990), director of the Women in Science Program, American Association for the Advancement of Science, reports that 4 in 10 new jobs will be in the fields of science and engineering (p. 7), yet women are not prepared to fill these jobs. Skills for the 1990s include mathematics and problem solving, and if students do not take elective math in high school, they may be excluded from many college majors and thus later, "certainly, they eliminate many possible jobs" (p. 8).

Some women do study nontraditional subjects and enter male-dominated careers, but will they stay there and advance? Or will they continue to face the "maddeningly ephemeral barriers" described by Dick Youngblood (1990a) and "give up in disgust"? Some of these barriers were evident during the interchange between Sue and Sam (Chapter 2) in the form of "male talk"—self-listening, finding fault, and topic selection—which often precludes meaningful intergender dialogue. That these barriers are subtle and difficult to detect has been established in other case studies: Women are devalued by barely detectable but treacherous courtesy, paternalism, and intimidation, as senators discredit "lovely" witnesses; Bush patronizingly "helps" Ferraro, and an unjust theology professor flunks a student in reprisal.

On the Male/Female Continuum (Figure 2.1), the behaviors of *courtesy, paternalism,* and *intimidation* are discouragingly distant from the desired state of colleagueship. And at the more violent end of the continuum we encounter the ultimate devaluation of women: *battering, rape,* and even *murder.* Needless to say, any one of these manifestations of oppression discourages hospitable learning and working environments. Yet collegial climates are essential if women are to gain the skills they need to enter and succeed in male-dominated careers, and for women and men to develop the kinds of physical, psychological, and political partnerships necessary for survival in the twenty-first century. Unless leaders confront even the most rudimentary expressions of male privilege, they will give the green light to the whole spectrum of more devastating behaviors that serve to keep women disenfranchised. Such leader intervention is crucial not only in male-dominated fields, but in all environments.

Sexism Among Colleagues and Parents

We may insist that we really hope our daughters will become engineers, scientists, doctors, and lawyers, and that we prefer our female friends to serve us as accountants and insurance agents rather than as waitresses and clerks. We may claim that we actively support women in nontraditional careers, and that we have begun to take measures to prevent the brain drain of competent women leaving our organizations because they have hit the glass ceiling of discrimination. Yet the evidence shows that good intentions are not enough, and that women continue to face overwhelming roadblocks to success, as evidenced by the subtly condescending treatment described by this female insurance agent:

> I'm in the worst field you could possibly be in as far as discrimination goes—it's so *male dominated*! When I first became an insurance agent, I hit the bias head on—like a brick wall.
>
> I don't like dealing with the stratosphere of the corporate structure and I don't like going to meetings, because when I *do* go, the men's first comment is "Gee, you look so nice today." They don't say that to any of the *male* agents present, just to me. It's a pat on the head—it puts you in your place and sets you apart. Right away my teeth grind, and I'm done. . . .

> I ask myself: Do I want to turn into a table pounder? I've decided
> to save my energy for the big fights. . . . How do I survive? I went
> into business for myself.

On the job, this woman is singled out with a trivializing courtesy that feels to her like devaluation: We will discuss your appearance rather than your competence—your gender rather than
your job; you are different, therefore not one of us. She sees that
no other persons present receive such overattention, and because
of this differential treatment she feels set apart and stigmatized.
The condescending paternalism puts her in her place and makes
her feel ostracized. Note that on the Male/Female Continuum the
behaviors of *devaluing* and *paternalism* are not as extreme as *harassment* or *sexual exploitation,* but certainly fall under the rubric of
discrimination. In any case, this agent feels uncomfortable enough
that she eventually decides to set up her own business.

In the insurance field, as in numerous other professions, a
female may be seen as "out of her territory" or "in over her head."
Translated, this means less proficient, less knowledgeable, or less
of an authority than her male counterparts. And since everyone
treats her as if she is less capable, she may begin to believe that
she must try harder to measure up (to males). This concept is
operant in many settings where we assume a woman is less able
because she is female, and it follows that only if she is exceptional
will she be adequate to compete with the average male: She must
be twice as good to get half as far.

For example, a father reported to me, "My 10-year-old daughter
is gifted; she won't have any trouble in life—she'll be able to stand
up to any *guy.*" Again, we see the basic underlying supposition of
male superiority: Only the most talented female will be able to
cope—it requires a Superwoman to deal with Averageman. What
message is this parent sending to the rest of his daughters and
sons, who in this case were within earshot? That his other "average" daughters will not be able to stand up to men? That his sons
can function merely at par and still be assured of success? This
father's attitude is blatantly paternalistic; as a matter of fact, he
provides us with an example of paternalism in its most literal and
negative form.

When we treat a girl or woman as *less* capable, or suggest that
she will survive only if she is *more* capable, she soon begins to feel

pressure to measure up. Ironically, if she internalizes this pressure—believes it, acts on it, and puts forth extra effort—she then runs the risk of being labeled an "overachiever." This double standard is evident in the following comments from a conversation I had with an ordained minister, aided and abetted by his wife, concerning a colleague who is not only ordained but also serves as an official in his denomination:

> *Pastor* [describing a clergyperson of greater status]: She is really an overachiever; she's trying too hard. I suppose she feels she has to overachieve to prove her competence; after all, she's trying to make it in a world of men. But she's so *rigid* about it—trying so hard! She'd be a lot better if she would just relax a little.

> *Pastor's wife:* She can't preach a sermon either. She simply *refuses* to use any "male" words. So every time she comes to a pronoun [that would define the gender of the deity], she just avoids it and keeps saying "God, God" [as in "God is in *God's* temple" instead of "The Lord is in *his* temple"]. It's so awkward!

> *Pastor:* Well, she's so young; I mean, she's only [he states her age]. Maybe she'll learn.

The pronouncements of this couple present a mixed bag of expectations. Lurking behind the supposition that the woman they are discussing has to "prove her competence" in order to "make it in a world of men" is the assumption of female incompetence and *imperfection*: Since the world of men commands such a high standard, and her skills are supposedly so far from adequate, she has a long way to go.

On the other hand, beneath the confusing expectation that she "relax a little" and not be so "rigid" (meanwhile managing to summon enough inspired energy to deliver an ideal sermon) is the unreasonable standard of female *perfection*: If she could just get it right, maybe she would be more successful. This mixture of expectations—You have a long way to go baby, but why don't you relax along the way? (or, Try hard, but not *too* hard)—is enough to make even the most even-keeled woman feel schizophrenic.

Like the insurance agents who focus on their coworker's appearance rather than her competence, this couple view their colleague through a biased lens: She's a woman—she's in a separate category; we will measure her by a more stringent standard and scrutinize her even more closely for the way she looks, what she does, and how she does it. The clergywoman is criticized not only for what she says (her avoidance of gendered pronouns), but for her manner of speaking ("rigid"; "awkward"). As in the case of the divinity student described earlier, her choice of language becomes the very vehicle by which she is discredited.

Note that besides the pastor's excessive criticism, we have the added dimension of his wife's disapproval. Why this unsisterly move? Why would a woman join so eagerly in the disparagement of another woman? It is a function of her own sense of disempowerment within the system of male privilege, asserts Rita Johnson (1991), a consultant who designs and presents workshops on the topic of "women versus women." "Women buy into male values and mindset, and they cut off parts of themselves in order to curry favor with men," says Johnson. In other words, when men put down women and other men, they do it to maintain status, whereas when women disparage each other, they do it because they have no access to this status. It is easier for the pastor's wife to join her husband in casting stones than to question why she herself feels disempowered, why he feels his position is threatened, or why he initiates the stone throwing in the first place.

This clergy couple should be aware that their words carry much weight, made even weightier by the prominence of the husband's profession. Others take heed of what they say, even if they communicate outside of a formal church setting. The pastor could take one small step for man and one giant leap for womankind by declaring: "We're so fortunate to have a person of this woman's ability serving as an official in our denomination, and I wish her well." With such supportive language, these leaders could demonstrate that they measure women and men by the same standard, and will not contribute to an environment in which females are overchallenged and underrated.

Bias Potentiated by Peer Pressure

A mature professional who has finished her training and is active in her profession may be able to brush off disparaging remarks from biased colleagues. After a woman has worked in an organization long enough, she usually develops some street smarts and is probably not quite as vulnerable to discouraging words as she may have been earlier in her career. But what if she is young—perhaps still a graduate student, trainee, or intern—and is discounted, overchallenged, or trivialized by classmates or coworkers? In this case, her reaction to the treatment may be intensified because her relative youth renders her more vulnerable to being ignored or marginalized by her peers. I gained a new appreciation for the far-reaching consequences of this marginalization from Julie, a woman in her early 20s who is a graduate student in the department of materials science and engineering at a large university:

> In my lab there are 13 researchers (students and Ph.D.s). I'm the only woman in my lab, and also the only woman in my immediate research group of 7 students. The way we learn in this smaller group is that each lab partner studies the mechanics of a piece of apparatus or a new computer technique, and then is supposed to teach what she or he has learned to the other students in the group. If I need help, I go to the male students, but if I try to explain to them how to do something, some of them don't listen. It's not blatant or overt, but it's there.
>
> For example, we were using CAD, computer-aided design, and I was supposed to be explaining the software to this male student, Jack. He had previously said, "Yes, I want you to show me the program." So he sat at the computer while I looked over his shoulder. But as I explained the program, Jack was very short with me—"Yeah, yeah, I get it." *He was not comfortable with my instructing him.* This has happened with some other male students too: When I showed them a process, instead of listening, they interrupted me. They didn't let me finish instructing.

Jack and some of the other students are revealing negative aspects of "male talk": They are trying to control and dominate—they refuse to listen and want to decide what will be talked about. These characteristics seem somewhat similar to Tannen's (1990) category of "report talk": For males, talk is a public "display"—a way to "maintain status" and to "keep attention on self." Our culture expects males to report and to "show their intelligence." Conversely, we expect that when women use language, they use a more private style of "rapport talk" to develop intimacy, to cultivate relationships, and to establish rapport. In other words, as Linda Witt (1990) puts Tannen's findings, "men lecture—they view their roles as providers of information. Women listen and tend to share, ping-pong information and confirm others' roles" (p. 8A).

Because males use talk as a way to "negotiate status," they may interpret someone who is attempting to report to them as trying to be one up. "Men have a gut-level resistance to doing what they're told, to doing what someone expects them to do"; what men fear is being "pushed around," Tannen explains. Women, on the other hand, because they use talk as a way to "negotiate closeness and intimacy," may experience not being listened to as a form of rejection. What women fear is being "pushed away" (in Taylor, 1990, pp. 62-63).

What happens, then, when a woman is placed in the position of having to provide information and display her intelligence, as Julie was? As she tries to teach others, this student steps outside the expected female role of purveyor of support and negotiator of intimacy. Now, instead of being the developer of rapport, she has become a reporter. As she assumes this new role, she departs temporarily from the accustomed and expected behavior of listening, sharing, and confirming others. She even begins to use some of the strategies of "male talk": She temporarily takes charge, selects the topic for discussion, and helps others learn to solve problems.

But who will now play the supportive role? Naturally, a few of the regular reporters will be upset: They are uncomfortable with a female who, instead of performing her nurturing task of listening and cultivating relationships, has taken on "their" reporting role (and in a male-talk style to boot). Some of the men may perceive her as trying to be one up; they may feel pushed around. And, to make matters worse, she is fairly good at reporting, and is telling them something they don't know much about. This means they must temporarily admit lack of knowledge, become learners, and start attending to—and thereby confirming—her. Many males may feel that being placed in this learner position cuts threatening inroads into their privileged function as displayers of intelligence and providers of information.

Were there a teaching assistant or other designated leader in this engineering lab, she or he could subtly facilitate more gender role flexibility in each of these researchers, an intervention appropriate not only to this highly male-dominated setting but to other fields as well (Van Nostrand, 1990a). For example, the leader could reinforce the female student's instructional role by saying, "Julie, your research seems quite thorough; I also noticed that you provided clear and concise information to Jack and the rest of your group." The leader could then test the male student's listening habits while also fulfilling his need to be a reporter: "Jack, could you share with the rest of us what you learned by listening to Julie?"

The suspicion, however, that turnabout is *not* fair play in these educational settings, and that some males may indeed resist being put in the learner position, is confirmed by Sally Gregory Kohlstedt, associate dean of the Department of Technology, University of Minnesota. Dean Kohlstedt describes gender politics that parallel almost exactly the research lab interaction:

> In recently talking with a group of female engineering students, I asked them whether they had difficulty in dealing with their male peers in class. They initially responded that there were no problems, but then one student paused and reflected, "I am a B+ student, quite good at what I do, and the guys are willing to study with me and answer questions when I ask. But, you know, they never ask *me* for help."
>
> This female student identified a situation that has fundamental implications for education and employment: Women lose ground because they are not part of operating networks and not viewed as particularly competent. (personal communication, January 6, 1990)

It must be emphasized that the skills of problem solving and topic selection are often crucial to keeping a group on track, and that the characteristics of male talk or report talk are not negative per se. These characteristics become destructive only when they are used to discount, exclude, or coerce others, or to manipulate a situation to one's own advantage. At that point they become roadblocks to mutually respectful communication, and barriers to colleagueship.

As gender-responsible leaders, we can work to create learning climates in which the more positive characteristics of both male and female communication styles are encouraged and cultivated. Just as many women could benefit by learning how to take more "airtime," how to make "demonstrative and declarative statements," and how to solve problems decisively, so many men could benefit by learning to refrain from using these same behaviors when they impede women's full participation. Leaders can praise men who inquire and listen, who "add a thought," or who allow others to solve problems. Additional communication skills helpful to those men wishing to connect with each other and with women are enumerated in the essay "Overcoming Masculine Oppression in Mixed Groups," by Bill Moyer and Alan Tuttle (1983): "not interrupting people who are speaking," "getting and giving support," and similar sensitive behaviors. When a man feels that he is about to attack or "one up" another person, Moyer and Tuttle suggest he stop and ask himself, "Why am I doing this? What am I feeling? What do I need?" (p. 27).

Women in "Male" Territory: A Threat?

The preceding examples demonstrate how both leaders and peers may discourage a woman by not giving her enough to do, by criticizing her because she is doing too much, or because she is doing it the wrong way. This reluctance to measure women by the same standard with which we measure men, and hesitancy to treat them as equal colleagues, has shown itself in subtly oppressive ways: males refusing to network with, listen to, and learn from women. Perhaps these males feel insecure or threatened by some females' intelligence. Perhaps they even feel that females have somehow invaded "male" territory or are treading on "their" turf.

Or perhaps men isolate or even bully women because of a much deeper fear, suggests Edward Gondolf, a researcher on male violence who created a rehabilitation program for batterers. Perhaps, deep down, men may actually fear the mysterious "feminine nature": "It's something we don't grasp, so we degrade it, and resist it, and try to contain it," he explains, in an effort not to condone male violence but to look into—and beyond—the cultural values and social conditioning of males (quoted in Mason, 1990, p. 19A).[4]

Even though we try to understand and appreciate what motivates men psychologically, we should not forget the political benefit males receive when they degrade, resist, and try to contain females. Women, too, may find the masculine nature mysterious and difficult to grasp, and many women have good reason deep down to fear men, much less their nature. But most females do not use bullying or violence in order to discover this male mystery.

It may seem innocuous enough when a man isolates or refuses to network with a woman. However, because we understand the continuum of subtle increments by which violence expresses itself, we know that male insecurities about territory can escalate to much greater oppression and even to such violent acts as battering

and murder. This violence may be partly the result of male conditioning, because some in our culture condone the mistaken idea
that to be considered "macho" one must act like a bully. "Men are
raised," says Gondolf, "with a sense of entitlement, privilege and
expectation that women can and should do what we want them to
do. And if they don't, we resolve the problem with aggression and
force" (quoted in Mason, 1990, p. 19A).

The ultimate degradation of women in order to contain them
and preserve male entitlement may have been the motivation
behind the mass murder of 14 female engineering students at the
University of Montreal. Committed by Marc Lepine with a semi-
automatic rifle, this act has been described as *femicide*:

> [The students] were murdered by a man who felt humiliated by
> women. . . . Lepine targeted young women who had attempted to
> enter male territory—the very territory that Lepine himself was
> unable to enter; he failed to complete his application for the graduate
> engineering program at Montreal. . . . The goal of femicide—
> whether conscious or not—is to preserve male supremacy. (Russell
> & Caputi, 1990, p. 17)[5]

Although this incident is an extreme example, I use it here to
heighten awareness of the full spectrum of dominance and subordinance. This act is an example of a "hate crime," a crime
perpetrated against members of a certain group simply because
they belong to that group. In this case, it was a crime perpetrated
against women simply because they were women. The murderer's
logic was that "engineering . . . was a *masculine* occupation, from
which women *must* be excluded" (Levin, 1991).

When Leaders Condone Male Privilege

What is the leadership issue here? What does it matter if a
woman is told she "looks nice today"? Why is it a sign of bias if a
woman is labeled an "overachiever"? Aren't we stretching the
imagination a bit to assume that just because male students do not
seek a peer's advice, she is therefore automatically shut out of
operating networks? Or that when a researcher happens to be
ignored in her lab group this incident is somehow distantly related
to campus violence? Our leadership task—indeed, our mandate—
is to recognize that when we blink at these minor transgressions

and put up with these put-downs, we are actually condoning an elemental form of oppression: We are exacerbating and perpetuating male entitlement and privilege.

What is *male privilege,* and how do we recognize it? Therapist John H. Driggs (1990) offers an example: A single mother stands up in a town meeting, makes a suggestion, and nobody takes her seriously; a local businessman stands up, makes essentially the same statement, and his suggestion is applauded. Driggs's definition of male privilege is very workable for our purposes here:

> Male privilege is the social system of views and behaviors that encourages men and women to believe that men are entitled to special treatment simply because they are men. In this system, men are not obliged to be as responsible for their behaviors (but women are) and [men] act as if they are deserving of respect without having to earn it. The judgement, work and authority of women are seen by both men and women as lesser than that of men. Men obtain male privilege simply by virtue of their being born male. Lacking accomplishments or status doesn't lessen their entitlement to male privilege. (p. 9)

A prime example of a man acting as if he is "deserving of respect without having to earn it" is the student Jack in the engineering lab described above. As required by their research assignment, Julie takes on the role of teaching Jack, yet he feels it is his prerogative to be as abrupt, short, and unresponsive as he wishes—"Yeah, yeah, I get it." Julie's judgment, work, and—especially—authority are seen by Jack as lesser than his own. Were Jack to be more respectful, he would afford Julie the same measure of attention he commands (or demands) for himself. But this is not what he values—he expects "special treatment." He will not do her the honor of receiving her help and instruction.

The engineering students' stories demonstrate clearly how those whose expertise is ignored or unsolicited are viewed as less competent. When this happens to women, they are thereby excluded from operating networks, all of which serves to solidify and intensify males' advantage. Like the female sailors, these students are overlooked and marginalized; like the insurance agent, they are undervalued.

As leaders, we need to recognize that this system of male entitlement is an ever-present reality that we ignore at our peril. Partly because of the way females and males are socialized, and partly because of deficiencies in our leadership, women may not only be victimized by male privilege but even encouraged to collude with oppressive tactics. Under our supposedly unbiased tutelage, women may actually begin to internalize the belief that their judgment, work, and authority are lesser than that of men. The oppression women experience ranges all the way from being chivalrously excused from tasks, to not being taken seriously, to being stigmatized for their efforts (She's an overachiever)—and worse.

As a woman tries to cope in a climate where she is disrespected, discounted, ignored, excluded, degraded, contained, or resisted, she begins to feel that her very survival is at stake—emotionally, if not physically. Miniassault after miniassault, the oppressive tactics contaminate her space, exhausting her energies. She may flounder like a fish out of water, trying to find breathing space, her existence threatened in an alien environment.

Discrimination Against Women Among Educators and Other Leaders

When women are outnumbered by men, women's feeling of isolation and alienation may be aggravated by a paucity of female role models. In educational settings, for instance, very few instructors of traditionally male subjects may be women. One explanation for this scarcity could be exclusionary tactics used by male faculty against potential female teachers. For example, a male industrial arts teacher was overheard to remark about a student teacher in his high school: "Any lady who wants to teach industrial arts ain't no lady."

Instructors may not only resist having women as colleagues, they may also resist even having female students in their classes. A science teacher told me about his experience 30 years ago, when there was only one woman in his university biology class: The male professor came over to this young student's chair, stood looking down at her, and said, "What in the hell are you doing here?"

But we are about to enter the twenty-first century, you insist; surely the present era is more enlightened and such misogyny has by now died a natural death! Sadly, contemporary examples abound. One of the most blatant horror stories about faculty bias is recounted by educator Myra Sadker: A professor announced, on the first day of an agriculture class, that "anyone with ovaries" should drop the course (quoted in Griffin, 1990, p. 10).

Most educators would be reluctant to admit that they had ever taught the female students described in *Women's Ways of Knowing*, who "left school as soon as they legally could 'so that we wouldn't have to put up with being put down every day' " (Belenky et al., 1986, pp. 227-228). Yet, in our roles as colleagues, parents, counselors, and teachers of females, do we ever display some of these discouraging behaviors? Is it possible that the low percentages of women in these fields could have anything to do with our leadership?

One reason women are sometimes loath to enroll in male-dominated subjects may be bias on the part of instructors, other students, or both. Indeed, one of the reasons Dean Kohlstedt was brought into the University of Minnesota's Institute of Technology, according to a newspaper editorial supporting her appointment, was to "break down faculty resistance to female students" ("Getting More Women Into Science," 1990). Bias may be extremely blatant (such as sexual harassment or direct threats), but usually common decency prevents such overt displays. The bias then assumes a much more innocuous and insidious form, such as this remark made by a male professor at a southern university to his female student in a male-dominated subject: "Since you're pulling only a C+ in this course, you might like to consider secretarial school instead."

This professor's suggestion appears to be "helpful," and he utters the words without evident antagonism. However, his patronizing chivalry is thinly veiled chauvinism—the kind that derails women from their career goals. The net effect of his remark is clearly a discounting of the woman's skills and a stereotyping of her interests. He is trying to put her in her place; to push her onto a career path that fits *his* definition of female-appropriate work, but not necessarily *her* definition. His condescending remark appears to be an underchallenge because he is suggesting that she cannot handle the subject matter. However, she could also interpret his "helping" as an overchallenge, because if she stays in his course she is going to feel pressured to excel just to prove him wrong.

The professor's remark shows the devastating long-term effects that a leader's "implicit sexism" (Chapter 3) could have on a follower. It also fits the definition of a *microinequity*: a small slight that singles out a person or that makes assumptions about someone's capabilities. Microinequities are especially dangerous because the bias is usually barely detectable at the time, and only later does the recipient recognize the full impact of the sexism. Leaders committed to women's advancement should pay special attention to how they respond to female students, how often they encourage women to take initiative, whether they ever discount women's skills, and whether or not they treat females as credible. By cultivating the observer in themselves, leaders can avoid such inequities as those described by Lida Barrett, president of the Mathematics Association of America: "If you assume women can't do mathematics, the professors don't expect as much; they don't pay attention to the student in class; they don't encourage women to go on" (quoted in Turner, 1989, p. A14).

When Faculty Display Hubris

The tragedy about such bias held by those of us in education or similar professions is that we may become deeply defensive if anyone even *hints* that our leadership methods are substandard or that we are showing favoritism. After all, our workplace or classroom is *our turf*—what right does any outsider have to evaluate us! This defensiveness about turf may be exhibited in arrogance, even insolence, as described to me by a female administrator in a large university:

> Faculty members don't think they have a problem in their classes; for example, they think sexual harassment is a joke. There is much hubris. Even mentioning possible gender bias in a department makes some male faculty angry and defensive. They say such things as: "You're making our department look inhospitable to women," or "You're painting the picture with a black brush that colors all of us."

Unfortunate incidents of discrimination against female students (and faculty defensiveness about their own possible bias) may be alleviated as more women move into administrative positions. However, at this time, there is still a scarcity of female administrators in these male-dominated fields. Dr. Shirley Johnston, associate dean of the College of Veterinary Medicine at the University of Minnesota, is interested in how gender-responsible leadership strategies could "help women move into leadership positions in the health sciences." She expresses the problem clearly:

> Women are enrolling in health sciences professional schools such as veterinary medicine and dentistry and are moving into careers in these areas at a rate equal with men. Women enter these fields, but are not moving into administrative positions in health sciences academic units in numbers commensurate with the pool of women available. (personal communication, August 21, 1990)

Although our focus here is on the field of education, we know that women experience discrimination and even harassment in every arena. The over- and underchallenging of females, aggravated by male privilege and exacerbated by leaders, promale bias, is a universal phenomenon.

Sexual Harassment: You Had to Be There!

The climates in which women try to study and work are made intimidating by sexual harassment that is both overt and covert. Remarks such as "Any lady who wants to teach [this subject] ain't no lady" and "Anyone with ovaries should drop this course" are obviously and blatantly hostile. The biology professor's threat, "What in the hell are you doing here?" is so offensive that it is hard to believe he was ever hired in the first place. These comments are a direct (and illegal) method used by some men to degrade, contain, and try to exclude women from male turf.

Direct and indirect requests for sexual favors are also harassment, and when a woman refuses to comply, her career aspirations can be severely curtailed. This was the experience of a vocalist who performed as lead singer with bands in New York City. Her mother describes how this young musician's career was cut short: "The band members wanted sex, she said no, so they reduced her parts. Every band she sang with was a battle. She finally quit—now she's just a backup singer."

The examples above reveal harassment in its more overt and blatant form. But sometimes the coercion is much more ambiguous, covert, and subtle; on these occasions a person must rely on her "gut feeling" about the incident even as her credibility is challenged. The following dialogue, which occurred in a group of academic mathematicians and scientists, illustrates this point:

> *Woman A:* I experience harassment in my department. My boss makes suggestive remarks about my clothing and appearance. . . .
>
> *Woman B* [interrupting]: I think we women ought to lighten up a little. There needs to be room for some normal healthy banter between women and men in the workplace. For example if a man says to a woman, "That's a nice outfit," he's not necessarily harassing her. She could reply with equal sincerity, "Thanks—I really like that weave in your tie"; or, "You don't look so bad yourself!" [When they converse this way] they are in repartee as equals.
>
> *Woman A* [insisting]: *You had to be there! That isn't the way it was at all!* There's an element of intimidation or coercion when my boss makes these remarks. First of all, he's this big tall guy and I'm small; I'm also new in the department. He lays his hand on my shoulder and says, "You just look so *sweet* in that cute little dress." I feel trivialized—he's paying more attention to my appearance than to my capabilities.
>
> *Woman B* [beginning to empathize]: It is a confusing time for women and men—so much depends on language and the way it's interpreted. In the midst of all this talk about harassment, we *still* need to keep a sense of humor, to celebrate "vive la difference" and to be able to play a little.

This dialogue reveals that women themselves are sometimes in disagreement and confusion about how to interpret male solicitousness. Is it intimidation, harassment, thoughtful attention, or something else? And how does one respond?

As we try to sort out issues of language, gesture, proxemics, and use of touch, we must remember, as discussed earlier, that in the terminology of the Male/Female Continuum, *courtesy* can be found in disturbing proximity to *sexual harassment* and *discrimination*. When a male's hidden agenda is to control and dominate others, he may display courtesy that a female initially interprets as kindness— even gentleness. Yet his underlying motivation is chauvinistic: to *discount* and *devalue* women and to *downplay women's presence* with *paternalism*. As researcher on male violence Edward Gondolf reminds us, a man does not have to behave like a macho bully to be oppressive: "Some macho men are very protective, paternal toward women. They are very kind. They may be unconsciously oppressing women in a kind and gentle way" (quoted in Mason, 1990, p. 19A).

To make an accurate diagnosis about whether a comment or gesture is merely collegial banter, an underchallenging trivialization, or outright coercion and harassment, a woman must listen to her gut feeling, trust her perceptions, and clearly name the inequity, as did the victim above.

In the same vein, the sensitive male—to be sure he is not misunderstood—must acknowledge that his gender, size, seniority, privilege, and status connote power to others and therefore responsible behavior is demanded of him. If he feels the need to "connect" and "link" with a woman, and still wants to be perceived as professional, respectful, and gender fair, he must be straightforward and nonmanipulative, offering a sincere affirmation of her professional competencies (You did a great job on that report; Thanks for arranging the meeting; We welcome these capable witnesses) without reference to her appearance, and definitely without the seductively paternalistic hand on the shoulder.

Mentored or Maligned?

Because women so frequently experience a wide range of oppression, from outright hostility to ambiguous and often coercive flattery, it is understandable that they may be wary when genuine help is offered. However, to advance in their careers, women need to be receptive to such guidance and mentoring. How can a woman discern whether she is being treated with caring or condescension—whether she is being mentored or maligned?

Women as well as men need to learn that when an episode feels like exploitation it probably is, and an intervention should definitely be considered. On the other hand, we also need to learn to recognize genuinely supportive gestures, and be open to them as ways to build the collegial networks so essential to alleviating women's isolation.

"Give credit where credit is due," urges Minnesota District Court Judge Elizabeth Hayden (1990), describing how she was encouraged by certain male lawyers and judges, after whom she modeled her career. Hayden admits that she definitely felt isolated in her law school class (only 20% of which was female) and had to develop a "thick skin" to survive. However, she also found very supportive male mentors.

"It's important not to blame or label men, or say men don't appreciate women's talents," says Hayden. She also feels it is crucial, especially in this era when we are becoming more concerned about sexual harassment and abuse both in and out of the workplace, not to misinterpret men's efforts to encourage women. She recalls her first day on the bench:

> Donning my judge's robe, I realized I was a bit anxious, so I called this attorney into my chambers and let him know I wasn't quite sure how to proceed on his particular case. The entire time, I was trying to *exude* confidence, but he could tell I was nervous.
>
> About a year later, this attorney said to me "I just wanted to *hug* you that day." Had he hugged me then, I would have misinterpreted his effort to nurture me as a sign of *my* weakness, as in: Do I really look so helpless that I need a hug; after all, you wouldn't treat a *man* that way! I would not have seen his gesture as helping, but as belittling me.
>
> Although this attorney did *not* hug me, I realize in retrospect that his hug would have been meant as a supportive gesture, as in: You can do it—go get 'em! (1990)

Judge Hayden explains how she has modified her perceptions and her position regarding female-male working relationships: "I realize now that this attorney's gesture would have shown how pleased and excited he was for me to succeed," she says. "Had he hugged me, I could have judged it as a put-down or as condescension. *I have since softened my views; I am not so quick to judge and label men.*" This professional, whose business is justice and truth, is warning us to "weigh the evidence" in any given situation.

We have had a glimpse into the lives of women trying to survive like fish out of water in several male-dominated professions. We have seen how males may consider certain arenas "their" turf, and how, when women are outnumbered by men, the paucity of female role models—combined with male intransigence and leader collusion—creates even chillier environments. We have also observed how females experience bias from parents, educators, bosses, and others who may consider themselves paragons of fairness.

Both in school and on the job, a woman may have no critical mass of other females on whom to lean for support. This isolation may cause her to become discouraged and to drop a course or leave an organization. The Project on the Status and Education of Women reports that "in traditionally male fields, many women lose their self-confidence and academic ambition, often transfer into other fields, or drop out altogether" (Association of American Colleges, n.d.; cited in Association of American Colleges, 1988, p. 12).[6] Institutions can little afford this brain drain, but we who call ourselves mentors may unwittingly add more layers to the already formidable glass ceiling, thus further inhibiting women's aspirations and contributing to their exodus from these fields. Fortunately, as Judge Hayden's experience confirms, there are colleagues who are willing to mentor, support, encourage, and network with women uncompetitively.

Must a Woman Be "Outstanding" to "Make Her Mark"?

Clearly, women often have their hands full trying to cope with the system of male privilege constructed by their peers—from fellow students who freeze them out of networks to coworkers who want sexual favors. This old boy network becomes even more formidable when leaders either refuse to confront it or completely buy into it.

The following testimony from a young music composer, as well as the professor's story told in the next case study, reveals the devastating effects of male privilege on women, devastation that is further aggravated by leaders' collusion in that system. These stories also demonstrate leader defensiveness and hubris in its more nonproductive incarnations. As the composer related:

> I am the only woman in a music ensemble, and I brought in one of my original compositions to be rehearsed. This guy in the ensemble, who is also a composer, looks at his part and says, "What is this . . . shit?" [He names the title of her composition.] Then we play the piece and he can see it is good music. So he comes up to me after we're finished playing and says, jokingly: "Hey! Can I put my name on this music?"

I felt very angered and definitely *harassed* by his behavior. He is sleazy and I don't trust him. He could easily steal my music, copy it, and actually put his own name on it. Most other musicians wouldn't even *imply* that they would do such a thing.

Unlike some of the other men in the ensemble, this guy could not bring himself to be supportive and to give me a direct compliment like, Good composition! I like the way you write! Instead, he chose to give me a compliment by patting *himself* on the back, as if he were saying: If her music is *that* good, maybe *my* name should be on it. He was actually admitting, Hey, she can write after all! But I felt angry and harassed by the way he said it.

This fledgling musician must certainly feel like a fish out of water. Trying to swim with the current in an area of music performance traditionally dominated by males, she is buffeted against the rocks of discrimination, marginalized by jealousy, and detoured to the backwaters of invisibility.

She also reports that as a college music major, she felt discouraged and marginalized by faculty. In her words, "A male student would have a built-in support system when he got to the university; everyone would just *expect* him to succeed." She did not want to become just another in a long chain of "women composers throughout history who have been ignored; they've been there all along, but just ignored." Upon verbalizing some of these frustrations to both female and male professors, she was advised: "*Don't talk about how unfair things are*; just work hard and be disciplined— people will see how talented you are by your product." Apparently, these professors found it easier to urge her to try harder than to ask themselves to be more responsive.

Are Women Commonly Expected to "Just Try Harder"?

Is it true that males have a "built-in support system"? Is this admonition to "just work hard" (meanwhile trying to ignore unfairness, peer harassment, and leader bias) frequently expected of females? How diligently is a young woman expected to strive in order to receive the support, recognition, and credibility she deserves? A dialogue I had with a professor at a West Coast university, presented in Case 4.1, raises some of these issues.

CASE 4.1

"Women today tend to be more achievement oriented than men"

A professor in a dental school describes presenting an after-lunch lecture in a large hall to a class that is 40% female and 60% male. The back row of the room is occupied by males, some of whom sit there so they can sleep, which they proceed to do, as depicted in Figure 4.1. (Female students, according to this professor, almost *never* sleep in class.)

> *Van Nostrand:* Do you consider it a problem that the male students are sleeping and the females are not?

> *Professor:* No, we do not perceive it as a problem.

> *Van Nostrand:* Does it seem to you as though the women have to "try twice as hard as a man to be thought half as good?"

> *Professor* [playing the devil's advocate]: Yes, that possibly fits. . . . We are in an era in which, in order to make their mark, women make their way by being outstanding. [The female students don't sleep] because they place greater emphasis on achievement; they don't take anything for granted.

> *Van Nostrand:* Do you perceive the males' behavior as privileged?

> *Professor:* The men *do* act like they've "got it made"—like they're "hot stuff." The men tend to accept their . . . position, the women don't. . . . It's not my job as instructor to interfere in this. We're in a professional school here; if students need to sleep, they need to sleep.

> *Van Nostrand* [persisting]: But do you perceive the males' behavior as privileged?

> *Professor:* No, I perceive it as sloppy and inattentive; I do not respect the male students for it. However, they could have been on a rotation where they had to work late with patients, or they could have been working at an outside job.

> *Van Nostrand:* Could the women *also* have been working late with patients or at an outside job?

> *Professor:* Yes, and if a woman were to fall asleep in class, she would receive the same treatment; she would not be awakened.

Van Nostrand: But the woman aren't sleeping. Isn't it a form of bias to assume that women "in order to make their mark, make their way by being outstanding"?

Professor [growing increasingly uncomfortable and defensive]: I don't *assume* that; my observation is that women today tend to be more achievement oriented than men. I don't perceive women falling asleep with frequency. . . . My scientific observation is that many women perform at a level equal to men. . . . I don't feel women *must* be outstanding to make their mark. . . . It's simply that the women aren't sleeping because they're trying harder; they're saying, I'm in here getting this material!

[The professor's agitation and defensiveness increase, and he finally explodes with this remark]:

Professor: Your overall paradigm is biased! You assume faculty grant males special privilege. . . . DON'T BE ON A WITCH-HUNT!

Maintaining this professor's anonymity, I seek understanding and clarification from two professionals: one a dentist in private practice, and the other a university administrator. The dentist, recalling his days in graduate school, sees the lecture hall seating arrangement and students' behaviors as not necessarily the professor's problem, but a "societal issue":

When I was in dental school, the back two rows of students were also 99% male, and it was that way in college biology and chemistry classes too. I think it's a *societal problem*: Women are the minority in these classes, and they have *more to prove*. When I was in school, the women had to concentrate very hard, and wanted to be very good. They sat in the front rows so they wouldn't miss anything. Girls [*sic*] tried extra hard, as if they were saying, Look! I'm doing this!

After receiving this input from a practicing dentist, I then describe the lecture hall scenario (and my dialogue with the professor) to a university administrator in a different part of the country. She expresses concern about the subtle form of bias:

It's scary to hear about people like that dental school profes-sor. . . . Women frequently get gratuitous comments [such as that they "make their way by being outstanding" or that they "tend to be more achievement oriented" or that they have "more to prove"]

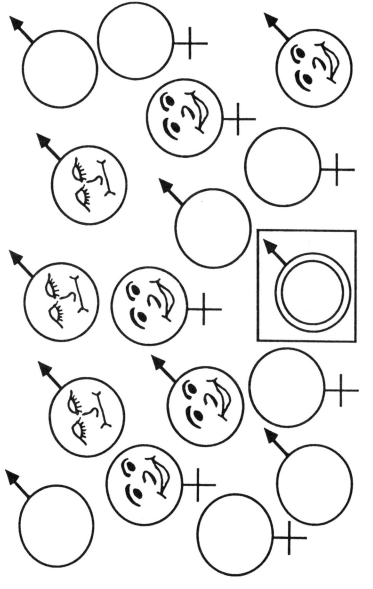

Figure 4.1. Professor Condones Privileged Male Behavior: *"Women . . . tend to be more achievement oriented . . ."*

about themselves and their futures; *women's egos are challenged constantly.* Males are not willing to change their perception that a woman must be outstanding to make it, thereby perpetuating the prejudice that sexism is an intractable problem.

This administrator, naming these gratuitous attitudes as examples of subtle bias, continues in her analysis to say that for any leader to assume that women/girls have more to prove is another way to perpetuate the status quo.

Women Cannot Afford to Be "Ordinary"

The professor of dentistry, by admitting that the female students are *not* taking anything for granted, seems to suggest that the male students *are*. While he denies that this is a gender issue, he acknowledges that the males "tend to accept their [back row] position" and act as though they have "got it made." He condones the behavior of the male students, and it is against this norm that he seems to measure the females: "Many women perform at a level equal to men."

However, the females cannot afford to conform to this male standard: Women refuse either to sit in the back row or to sleep. They apparently feel that, in this learning environment, they dare not allow themselves the ordinary, human behaviors of inattention or "taking things for granted." Although the average male might be able to "make it" at this level, a female student does not feel she can; if she were to lapse into inattention (or—in a worst-case scenario—to fall asleep), she might be judged as incompetent. In this setting she cannot afford that judgment.

Like the clergywoman criticized for "overachievement," these female students must measure themselves by a different yardstick. It is as if they are saying to themselves: Some of the men may be able to sleep, but I can't afford to; there's already enough bias against me without my appearing to be "average."

John Driggs's (1990) definition of male privilege seems especially apropos in this case: The sleeping men apparently do not feel as obliged to be responsible for their behaviors as do the wakeful women. Here we have a double standard based on an underlying assumption of inequality: Members of one gender can be very ordinary and still feel fairly confident that they are performing at a level acceptable to peers and group leader alike, whereas members of the other gender have no such guarantee.

This is a "denial of ordinary status," explains Donna Schaper (1990), and it is perhaps a new form of sexism, as it is of racism. Schaper, pastor of a church in Riverhead, New York, provides examples: We're in a department store during the holidays, and we see an adult, who happens to be African American, purchasing an expensive toy. We mutter, "How can that person afford to spend money on a toy, with *their* income?" We make instant assumptions based on race, rather than seeing the individual as an everyday parent choosing a gift for an everyday child. In our prejudice, explains this clergyperson, "Ordinary status is denied; race is added to the encounter."

Many of us are becoming more sophisticated about recognizing our own racism, but we may still have trouble recognizing our own sexism. For example, as we sit in a church or synagogue, we might assume the person speaking from the pulpit is less credible because she is a "lady minister" or a "woman rabbi." The person's gender suddenly becomes her most salient feature. In the classroom, we may perceive the human being in the front row not as just another student trying to master a subject, but as a "female student" who naturally must stay awake because she has "more to prove." Our leadership task is to recognize the basic aura of inequality hovering around any environment in which one gender expects to succeed by *mediocrity*, while the other feels it can succeed only by being *extraordinary*.

Building Leadership Awareness

At this point, whatever our discipline, we can reflect on what sort of leadership example we ourselves are setting, especially in groups in which women are a minority. Do we unwittingly assume that women are less capable? If so, do we demonstrate our prejudice by either underestimating their abilities or overestimating the amount of effort that will be required for them to succeed?

As we reflect on our own leadership using the Leader Awareness Checklist presented in Table 4.1, we can recognize whether we ever hold attitudes or display behaviors that set either unreasonably low or disproportionately high standards for women. Many of us who are educators, committee chairs, or supervisors may feel we already have a handle on our leadership, that we are equitable, and that we would never say something like "Women

Table 4.1 Leader Awareness Checklist: Do You Underchallenge or Overchallenge Females? (a personal self-audit or a tool for evaluating other leaders)

Suggestions to leader: Recall a group you formerly belonged to in which females were outnumbered or out of their element. For example, envision a highway construction crew, a city council meeting, a corporate board of directors, or perhaps a class in veterinary medicine or auto mechanics. How did the group's leader treat this female minority? Were women acknowledged as equally capable and encouraged to participate fully? Or, instead, were intangible, unreasonable barriers placed in their way?

Now imagine yourself or a colleague in a contemporary professional setting, actually leading a group. Monitor your leadership behaviors, or those of your colleague. Does the leader either *underchallenge* or *overchallenge* women? Try to get a feeling for the learning climate—what atmosphere do you sense? Has the leader established an environment in which the strengths of both genders are appreciated? Or is this unfortunately a climate in which women's talents are either insufficiently utilized or overly criticized?

How to use this checklist: This assessment can be implemented either as a self-audit or as a tool for critiquing other leaders. Although the following descriptions of biased behaviors can apply to any mixed group, the checklist might be most helpful for male-dominated organizations that want to examine whether or not they are creating a female-friendly environment.

With slight modification in language, every item here could be used to evaluate a leader's assumptions about men. To revise the list, simply reword the initial question to read: "This leader treats a *male* as though he . . . " and then change all gender-specific terms and stereotypes.

Directions: Using the following scale, rate each leader behavior that applies to you, or to the colleague you are critiquing. (The language of most sample phrases is excerpted directly from case studies found in this volume.)

(1) Leader NEVER treats women this way.

(2) Leader RARELY treats women this way.

(3) Leader SOMETIMES or occasionally does this.

(4) Leader FREQUENTLY or OFTEN demonstrates this attitude toward women.

(5) Leader seems to almost always or CONSTANTLY behave in this manner toward women.

Underchallenging Females

Leader has excessively LOW expectations of females. Leader assumes a girl or woman needs extra protection or lacks the ability to handle a certain task.

Rating

This leader treats a female as though she . . .

__ is too delicate or ladylike for the job, or the task "undermines her womanliness." (Examples: I hope none of that chemical spills on your pretty outfit. Are you sure you can maneuver that sailboat?)

___ needs protection or extra guidance, especially from males. (Example: Bonnie, if you have any trouble with the lab experiment, I'm sure Ben or Bob can guide you.) (This attitude is known as "classroom chivalry.")

___ requires extraordinary praise or effusive compliments for completing a customary task. (Example: You've been very helpful; you're such a nice girl.) (Note how the compliment is negated by the use of condescending, trivializing language.)

__ doesn't belong where she is, or should try a more "feminine" occupation (Examples: Any lady who wants to teach this course ain't no lady. Maybe you should consider nursing as a career alternative.)

Overchallenging Females

Leader has excessively HIGH expectations of females. Leader assumes a girl or woman will succeed only if she exerts extraordinary effort: She must be "outstanding" to make it.

Rating

This leader treats a female as though she . . .

__ must "try harder" or has "more to prove" than her male colleagues. (Examples: You can make it in this plumbing class if you just try harder. I suppose you'll have to put forth more effort if you want to make it in a world of men.)

__ cannot be "average" and still succeed; must be extraordinary to cope. (Example: My daughter is gifted—she'll be able to stand up to any guy.) (This remark not only discourages the average woman, but suggests that a female must be nearly perfect to achieve ordinary success.)

___ lacks so many skills or requires so much remediation that she is practically ineducable. (Examples: Why don't you get it? Why can't you catch on?)

___ is behaving or performing a task the wrong way. (Examples: She is so brassy and aggressive! She's such an overachiever!)

continued

Table 4.1   Continued

Note: There is a fine line between *underchallenging* and *overchallenging* an individual. What may first appear to be a trivializing underchallenge (We're so fortunate to have a *lovely lady* at our meeting today) may actually be an overchallenge. The woman feels pressured because, even though the leader seems to have low expectations of her, the remark is really a put-down, and thus she exerts extra effort to overcome the perceived barrier. In either case, these over- and underchallenges create inhospitable climates that discourage healthy self-esteem and inhibit productive group process, effective learning, conjoint decision making, and collegial relationships between women and men.

When this assessment is revised to apply to assumptions about males, it could be used to critique leaders in traditionally "female" settings such as nursing, the paralegal profession, and child care. For example, among child-care workers (the majority of whom are usually female), the leader might harbor the sexist belief that males are hopeless at nurturing, and would require extensive rehabilitation to even *begin* to function as caregivers (Why do you handle the kid that way—don't you know any better?). To assume—because of gender—that someone is ineducable is to discount, marginalize, and underchallenge that person. In this case, the comment reveals a definite antimale bias that could also be interpreted as an overchallenge.

All of the remarks here are based on the same prejudiced premise: Solely because of gender, the person is judged less knowledgeable and less capable, and the individual's performance is automatically assumed to be substandard.

have more to prove." Yet, because most of the undesirable leader behaviors described in Table 4.1 are driven by our socialized assumptions regarding gender role behavior, they are somewhat unconscious. In order to change our behaviors, we need to modify our perceptions. We need to stamp a clear picture of responsible leadership in our awareness; we need to know what a gender-responsible leader looks like.

Presented below are profiles of two leaders who have developed and implemented proactive strategies in order to maneuver through the everyday tangle of sexism in their organizations. The profiles trace how these leaders initiate, activate, and expedite fair treatment for themselves and others. These leaders are decision makers who determine policy in communities and institutions: One is an elected official and community activist whom we first met in Chapter 1; the other is an academic administrator at a large midwestern university.

LEADER PROFILE 4.1

"Your confrontational style doesn't move us forward"

A woman is the only female serving on a government commission, as depicted in Figure 4.2. While attempting to understand thoroughly a controversial issue raised during a public meeting, she asks for clarification. Although her questions are reasonable, she is insulted by one of the male members, who proceeds to "explain" the "obvious" to her in an exasperated tone, and then throws his pencil on the table, uttering the remark: "What's the big deal? It's easy to understand!"

Feeling, in her words, "embarrassed, devalued, frozen, and disempowered" by the Pencil Packin' Papa, this official later takes her concerns to the chairperson and other commission members, all of whom agree that they too are frustrated by this male's actions, and have been for some time. She therefore requests that the issue of the group's dynamics be placed on the next month's agenda. (By mobilizing her peers and helping to formulate this agenda, she activates a consensus intervention.) At that next meeting—having gained peer support—the woman addresses the offender:

> *Female commission member:* I did not appreciate the way you spoke to me at the public meeting. I felt put down and devalued. We must deal with our conflict. We're not getting our business done because of the group dynamics [combined self-disclosing/consensus intervention].

> *Pencil Packin' Papa* [volunteering unsolicited information about his previous behavior]: I know I was a jerk at that last meeting, but I can't promise I'll be more respectful. *It's just the way I am.*

> *Female member:* As a woman, I was raised to be "nice." I was docile and ladylike at that meeting, but I can't promise I'd handle the situation that way again [self-disclosing]. Your behavior is inappropriate; it gets in the way of doing business and it doesn't look good to the public [limit setting]. *Your confrontational style doesn't move us forward*—it's not task-oriented behavior [abrupt].

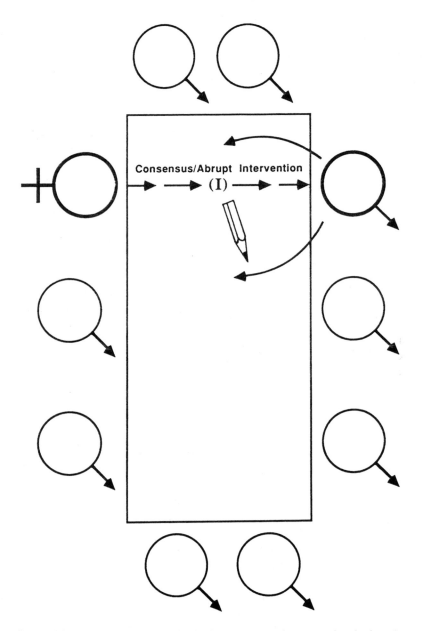

Figure 4.2. Responsible Leader in Action:*"Your confrontational style doesn't move us forward . . ."* (Combined Intervention Used)

Notice how this woman uses a very creative strategy—leadership at its best. She first checks her perceptions with others and gathers group support. Then, through self-disclosure, she makes clear her own boundaries and shares her own metamorphosis from the restrictive chrysalis of female socialization to a stage of greater gender role flexibility. She acknowledges the limitations of her conditioning and asks her peer to recognize his. She is aware of her own lack of assertiveness, yet demonstrates her willingness to risk a more autonomous role. Through frequent use of "I messages," she identifies her own behavior and demonstrates that she is responsible for her own actions. In this manner she reduces the defensiveness of others: She is naming, rather than blaming.

Refusing to collude with the stereotype of the out-of-control, irresponsible, boys-will-be-boys male, she also makes it clear that she herself won't play the role of the overcontrolled, deferring, girls-should-be-nice female. She is willing to deemphasize temporarily the usual female need for *connection* and to risk criticism in order to emphasize her *autonomy*. Her behavior change is consistent with the female developmental task delineated in Chapter 3, and also indicative of the state of colleagueship in which "being both connected and autonomous [are] valued." She is asking this inconsiderate man to set aside his apparent male needs for *dominance* and *autonomy*, which interfere not only with the group's cohesiveness, but with his own gender role journey. Instead, she suggests he behave in a manner that is more empathic and collegial. By setting an example of androgynous effectiveness, she prods her counterpart also to examine new ways of relating.

Using the four strategies of self-disclosure, consensus building, limit setting, and abruptness, this woman demonstrates that she will not be victimized by someone who creates a climate in which any person feels embarrassed, devalued, frozen, and disempowered. She refuses to buy into a system of male privilege, described above, in which "men are not obliged to be as responsible for their behaviors (but women are)"; she will not give credence to men who "act as if they are deserving of respect without having to earn it" (Driggs, 1990).

Because of boundary heightening and other group factors noted earlier, many persons in her minority position might not as readily trust, much less express, their own perceptions as does this token woman. They might resign themselves to mistreatment because they fear even more severe categorization and criticism if they speak up. However, in spite of being a solo—who surely must feel like a fish out of water—this woman trusts herself and takes appropriate action. She realizes it is healthier to name her peer's nonproductively aggressive challenges clearly than to allow him to continue disrupting group process. In Belenky et al.'s (1986) view, most women do not have a "powerful and positive learning experience" when their notions are "aggressively challenged" (p. 227). Of course, few of us do. But it is crucial, when our goal is the empowerment of women in groups, to realize how much talent and potential are lost when women must deal with dominance, self-listening, topic control, and other communication barriers of male talk.

Leaders who want to be effective catalysts for organizational change can follow the example of this community activist. By commanding respect on her *own* behalf, she gains more respect for *all* women. She is *aware,* she is *authentic,* and she *acts.* In other words, she "walks the talk," mentors what she mouths, and is congruent: She models the behavior she expects of others. As she initiates interventions, she follows two criteria that we will further explore in Chapter 6: (a) The intervenor honors the group's process, and (b) the intervenor intercedes at a minimal level, using very few words.

Power Differentials Make Intervention Risky

As embarrassing and painful as it is for a woman to intervene in a community setting such as the public meeting above, when she confronts bias in her own workplace the stakes are much higher. If she is vocal about her mistreatment she may jeopardize her career, particularly if the person who is mistreating her will also be evaluating her or serving as a reference for future employment. Like Anita Hill, who knew she might need a future job recommendation from Clarence Thomas, women fear speaking out because they know they will bear the brunt of public humiliation and reprisal.

Such a dilemma was related to me by the university administrator profiled below. She explained how she recognized biased treatment, why she could not take immediate action, and how she decided to intervene later.

LEADER PROFILE 4.2

"A person with his insensitivity should not serve on accreditation teams"

Jane Downey, then chairperson of the Department of Technology, St. Cloud State University, is concerned about microinequities—the everyday slights that disparage, discourage, and dishearten women. She describes these indignities as she and I join a cluster of women who have just attended one of my seminars. Our heated discussion is about the mistreatment of females in their own workplaces.

Downey: An accreditation team was coming to campus to evaluate our department. As department head, it was my role to make all the arrangements for their visit. This all-male team had a chairperson whom we'll call Charles. Charles repeatedly called me "girl," both in phone calls before and during the day of the team's visit. He said things like, "You've been very helpful setting up this meeting; you're such a nice *girl*"; or he said, taking me by the arm, "I'll walk this nice girl back to her office" (where we had a previously scheduled meeting). I was really bothered by this trivialization of my position. Here I am, chairperson of my department, and he is treating me like this—as if I'm so insignificant! But how could I say anything? How could I confront him? *He had the power*; the decisions he had to make were somewhat subjective. If I had objected to his language or his behavior, he might have given us a bad evaluation.

Another woman in group: Maybe he is the kind of man who feels threatened by competent, assertive women. Maybe because he perceived you as competent, he felt he must call you "girl" to keep you in your place.

Downey [continuing]: Then it came time for our exit interview, when we would hear the initial findings and recommendations of the accreditation team. In the room with me were two other female administrators—one of whom Charles hadn't met yet—plus the president of the university, another male administrator, and Charles and his team.

As we were ready to proceed, Charles announced: "Before we start this meeting, I want you all to know we're not allowed to have professional stenographers at these sessions." As he said that, he turned in his swivel chair and looked directly at the female administrator whom he hadn't met yet. He didn't look at any of the men, who could *also* have been secretaries, he just looked at her. He hesitated as if to get assurance that there were no stenographers, although we had previously assured him of that fact. He then proceeded with the meeting.

[Jane Downey's testimony is interrupted here as the seminar attendees disperse. However, she agrees to explore her feelings about the incident in a subsequent phone interview.]

Downey: I wish to emphasize that I don't believe it was Charles's intention to slight me in any way. He seemed to be totally unaware of his behavior.

Van Nostrand: How did the episode make you feel?

Downey: My overall feeling was anger. I felt powerless to intervene, either when I sensed him trivializing me by calling me "girl" or when I saw him stereotyping and demeaning the administrator by assuming she was a stenographer. Because of his comments I was on the defensive; I felt I had to be constantly proving myself, which you would anyway, given the situation. I felt he had lack of respect for my knowledge. I was offended by his use of the word "girl" and his discounting of the other female administrator in the room.

[At this point, Downey shifts her testimony from identifying and naming bias to a more proactive stance in which she verbalizes strategies she will use to deal with the demeaning treatment.]

Downey: I also have a major concern about this man's incompetence. I will be receiving a form on which I'm supposed to rate his competence—to "evaluate the evaluator" as it were. *I think a person with his insensitivity should NOT be serving on accreditation teams.* I have already verbalized these concerns at another meeting of all men; they agreed with me that his behavior and insensitivity were inappropriate, and that people like him should not be on accrediting teams.

Van Nostrand: So you're already getting peer support?

Downey: Yes. I'm getting my perceptions validated, and I intend to follow through on this incident.

Although the team's visit was very unpleasant at the time, Ms. Downey now reports to me the good news: Not only did her department receive accreditation, but Charles has been removed from the team—he will not function in this capacity in the future. She confirms that other professionals with whom she spoke were also deeply concerned about Charles's sexist conduct.

Jane Downey's experience illustrates how power differentials make it exceedingly risky for a woman to stand up for her own rights, much less to confront others about their insensitive behavior. She is in a Catch-22: If she keeps quiet and does not complain, Charles stays in a position where he can continue to degrade her and other women. If she confronts Charles (as the divinity student in Chapter 2 confronted her professor), he can penalize her with a "low grade"; that is, he can refuse to accredit her department. A woman is thus compromised by either silence or protest. It is easy to understand why women do not act in the heat of these situations—they fear losing even more ground. Wisely, this administrator waited until she could get her perceptions validated by peers. Her responsible leadership then came to the fore as she gave Charles negative evaluations, both verbal and written.

Microinequities such as Charles's excessive courtesy and trivializing language frequently "do the most harm," as Hall and Sandler (1984) remind us, "because they occur without the full awareness of those involved" (p. 4). The entire episode was aggravated by the fact that even if Ms. Downey *had* spoken up, Charles may not have known what she was talking about, since he seemed quite oblivious to his own oppressive behavior. Like the senators who labeled prominent women "lovely ladies," Charles may have assumed that addressing a woman as "girl" would be received as a compliment. Little did he know that through the patina of chivalry his chauvinism shone bright and clear.

The powerless must continually face, and waste valuable energy trying to make sense of, this quandary: Is a particular offender trivializing me out of *willful malice* or *pure ignorance*? Deliberate malice demands that one assert one's rights and even issue an indignant rebuttal, yet oblivious ignorance calls for patient explaining and educating. Which tack does one pursue? Does one take the time to decipher the motive behind the offensive maneuver? Does one patiently explain why one feels so demeaned? Or is it necessary even to *try* to analyze the perpetrator's motives when one is so totally preoccupied with just trying to cope with the degradation?

To return to the accreditation team's visit: Had Jane Downey confronted Charles at any time during the visit or exit interview, she would have faced the doubly demanding task of raising Charles's consciousness and simultaneously asking him to change his misogynist behavior—a tall order, especially when he held the status of her department in his hands. It seems too much to expect that at the very moment one is obliged to assert one's competence, one must also be on guard to defend oneself against an assault on this very competence. Yet many women daily find themselves in this position.

Also of great significance here is that *not one* of the other men present during the accreditation visit took it upon himself to challenge Charles. Gender-responsible leadership requires that men also increase their sensitivity about sexism and equip themselves to intervene when they see either women or other men being victimized by bias. Males need to interrupt "a brother who is exhibiting behavior which is oppressive to others and prohibits his own growth" (Moyer & Tuttle, 1983, p. 25). To ameliorate male privilege requires not only increased awareness, but authentic commitment to action on the part of men as well as women.

Note that in her testimony Downey admits that she would have to be "constantly proving" herself anyway, given the anxiety-provoking evaluation of her whole department. (We can assume that in similar circumstances most males would also experience anxiety, and would feel they too had to prove themselves in some way.) The important issue here is that an extra burden of proof is added when the environment is hostile. When women are trivialized and categorized, a workplace climate quickly turns from "chilly" to a "deep freeze." Women must put forth a great deal more effort just to survive, and an already anxious situation becomes nearly intolerable.

Progress is being made, however. Downey reports that many of the men in her profession seem quite open to receiving feedback about their possible sexism: "When I talk to men at engineering and technology conferences," she says, "they say such things as 'What do we need to do to make women feel more welcome in our department?' or, 'What am I doing that I shouldn't be doing?'" (personal communication, March 8, 1991). Her colleagues' requests signify good news and bad news: The good news is that these men seem quite receptive to changing both institutional and personal attitudes; however, the bad news is that they seem to be relying on a woman to play "diagnosing detective" and to determine parameters of propriety—yet another way to categorize and overchallenge her.

Like the proactive leaders profiled above, each of us needs to document incidents and protect ourselves—and others—from the perpetuation of biased treatment. Pressure from Downey, together with her colleagues, was an important influence in Charles's being removed from the accreditation team. She, like the committee member who confronted her pencil-throwing peer, is sending a strong message: Humiliating remarks, sexist language, and stereotyped assumptions about women's roles have no place in academic environments, public meetings, or—for that matter—any other setting.

In this chapter we have seen how a woman trying to survive in a "man's world" may be *itemized* by those who wish to set her apart and put her in her place; *trivialized* by those who assume she cannot accomplish a task; *scrutinized* by those who may covet her position; *criticized* by those who envy her talent; *categorized* by those who feel she is functioning in the wrong place; and *stigmatized, marginalized, and ostracized* by those who feel she is functioning in the wrong way for a woman. Hand in hand with this differential treatment comes the compendium of mixed messages. She should let someone else do it, try hard to prove her competence, relax a little, behave differently, go someplace else. The cumulative effect of these expectations can be mind-boggling; it causes women to become even more discouraged, especially if they want to attain leadership in, and make a significant contribution to, their chosen careers.

Women's efforts to achieve parity are already confounded by discrimination of peers and even parents; it is crucial that we leaders not also lend our blessing to male entitlement. We need to admit not only our possible biases against women, but also our defensiveness and even arrogance when anyone questions that bias. Our leadership mandate is clear: Following the example of the two leaders profiled above, we can learn to recognize women's mistreatment before it escalates—to name early symptoms of male privilege before old boy networks become firmly entrenched. To be responsible to women and to assure that we do not limit their options, leaders—that's all of us—need to be more responsive to women's reality.

Notes

1. Youngblood (1990a) cites two studies: One, by *Fortune* magazine, examined the proxy statements of 799 of the nation's industrial and service corporations and found that among the 4,012 highest-paid officers and directors of these companies, only 19 were women. In another study conducted by Catalyst, a group that researches women in the workplace, 80% of respondents reported that there are "identifiable barriers that keep [women] out of the executive dining room." All quotes from Youngblood's work, both here and in Chapter 7, are reprinted here by permission of the Minneapolis *Star Tribune*.

2. According to the 1988 edition of *Physician Supply and Utilization by Specialty: Trends and Projections,* cited in an American Medical Association (1990) pamphlet, women will represent nearly 30% of physicians by the year 2010. (For a discussion about sexism in physicians and other health care professionals, see Van Nostrand, 1992b; in press a.) According to U.S. Department of Labor Statistics, approximately 20% of practicing lawyers are women; a hopeful note is that, in 1991, 40% of law school students were female. (Sexism in the legal profession is mentioned frequently in this volume; see also Minnesota State Bar Association (1990), Minnesota Supreme Court Task Force (1989), and other sources in the Reference section.)

3. See also the Minnesota Women's Fund study, *Reflections of Risk* (1990). The purpose of the Minnesota Women's Fund is to "assist in removing barriers to the economic, educational, physical, emotional, social, artistic, and personal growth of women and girls."

4. This and subsequent quotes citing Mason are from her article "The Men Who Abuse Women: Their Credo Spawns Violence," which appeared in the Minneapolis *Star Tribune* on November 2, 1990. Diane Mason is a writer for the *St. Petersburg* (Florida) *Times*; the quotes used here are reprinted with her permission.

5. This quote is reprinted by permission of *New Directions for Women*, 108 W. Palisade Avenue, Englewood, NJ 07631.

6. This report is a description of the publication *Looking for More Than a Few Good Women in Traditionally Male Fields* (Association of American Colleges, n.d.). Both publications are available from the Association of American Colleges, Project on the Status and Education of Women, 1818 R Street, NW, Washington, DC 20009.

◀ 5 ▶

PEACOCK OR MIDWIFE

Do You Lead by Telling or by Asking?

Classrooms are often dominated by the most extroverted, least sensitive, shallowest voices—one of which may be the teacher's.

(Mary Rose O'Reilley, 1989, p. 29)

While passive group members yawn, the ill-prepared presenter drones on. What the leader is saying does not seem to relate to group members' personal experiences. Most would appreciate some discussion, and a few have already begun to formulate concepts in their heads, ready to contribute to such a hoped-for, but most unlikely, event. However, there is precious little breathing space in the session for asking questions or interjecting comments. As the presenter's head remains buried in notes, the session draws to a close. Finally a raised hand is acknowledged, a query is given a cursory answer. Unfortunately, there is no opportunity to integrate this new idea into the overall proceedings, as the brief remaining question-and-answer period is filibustered by a group member, grandstanding about tangential research he thinks the presenter missed.

The so-called participants file out of the room. Voices have not been heard, differences have not been acknowledged, experiences have not been validated. There is little feeling of shared community, an absence of opportunity to relate to and learn from others, and minimal chance to weave concepts into one's own frame of reference. Group members feel they have been talked *at* rather than *with* because there has been more emphasis on the *what* of the topic than on *who* is in the room. Is this learning? Not according to the student depicted in Case 5.1.

CASE 5.1

"The outcome . . . would never be the same . . . "

I'm completing a master's degree in a department of urban planning. A few of us students met with a professor in a kind of "summit" to request several changes—changes in course content as well as in some of the department professors' methods.

First of all, we asked that a particular course be added to the curriculum that would teach us skills in negotiation, communication, and mediation. We need such a course because when we become city planners and designers, we will frequently find ourselves in decision-making groups, such as city councils, that will require us to be facilitators or mediators. Sometimes there is conflict in these settings, so we need to learn negotiation and conflict resolution techniques *before* we get out in the job market. We said to the professor, "If we don't learn and practice these skills in a safe place like our local classrooms, how will we be able to use them in our future employment?"

The other change we asked for was a change in teachers' methods. The profs should refine their lectures; many are not well prepared, and some are not even *clear*. As a matter of fact, at the end of one lecture a student said to the professor, "What were you trying to *tell* us?" Many students are frustrated because class sessions are conducted in such a traditional way: Sometimes the classes are boring and unchallenging, with very little discussion or interaction. There should be much more student-led discussion, a chance to hear your own voice in a safe setting and to have other students respond supportively. If all we do is write down what the professor says, or take a test on the professor's lecture, this has nothing to do with what the other students are thinking.

The way we graduate students see it, if students could help lead discussions and be more involved in the classroom process, the outcome of the class would never be the same, even if the professor's lecture were always the same.

This student and her peers have voiced significant concerns. How can we leaders change our methods to accommodate the needs of group members? What can we do to assure that participants' ideas are incorporated into the process so the "outcome will never be the same"? And how can we structure *time* so all of this can happen?

In this chapter, these issues are examined from several perspectives. First, a discussion is presented about how feminist theory and feminist pedagogy (feminist education) can enrich group process. We will then contrast the *peacock mode* with the *midwife mode* of leadership, and critique the leadership styles of three conference presenters. The chapter ends with a discussion of how *silence*, when properly utilized, can be a powerful tool for stimulating the participation of women—indeed, of all group members.

Feminist Theory and Group Process

Dialogue

By our manner of presentation, we leaders can exert a subtle form of control over our groups. If we read from prepared remarks, move quickly from one topic to another, minimize participant input, or are threatened by doubting inquiries, we cut off dialogue. "Dialogue is one of the best ways that women learn," asserts Sudie Hofmann, an instructor in human relations. "Learning *is* dialogue; dialogue cannot happen when women [or men] are silenced" (personal communication, December 1987). Patricia Samuel, director of a university women's studies program, states:

> Dialogue is important for learning because it enables the student (workshop participant, etc.) to process the information, to relate it to one's own experience, *to shape the material and make it an integral part of one's self* [emphasis added]. . . . It is *not* an educational philosophy obvious to, or accepted by, many. (personal communication, October 1988)

When we leaders try to overcontrol group process by being so preoccupied with *what* we are saying that we ignore *who* is in the room with us, we create a milieu that is predictably comfortable for ourselves, but that does not allow for dialogue that would make the experience exciting and meaningful for participants. In attempting to manipulate the environment to our personal comfort level, we are really trying to fulfill our own needs or dispel our own fears: our needs to be the "expert," to maintain status, to be the center of attention; our fears that if we stop talking and invite discussion, the group members may either refuse to participate or jump in and steal leadership away from us. When we inhibit inquiry, neglect to solicit diverse opinions, refuse to acknowledge questions, or expound at length without dealing with the personalities in our midst, we perpetuate a chilly climate—one inimical to learning.

Discouraging questions and challenges from group members seems quite convenient for us, but not for those "participants" who feel discounted and invisible. We are convenienced because process is more regulated, protocol is established, we can simply *orate* while listeners absorb like sponges. Since the group members make minimal contributions, and their thoughts are not *evoked*, there are few surprises. Their ideas are not given much credence and their personalities do not help "shape the material." The outcome may be "the same," but, as the graduate student says, it has "nothing to do with what the other students are thinking."

Process: As Important as Content

The leader who focuses on *content* represents a "teacher-centered" model:

> In this model the student is too often passive and merely notes, but hopefully absorbs, what the teacher delivers. Emphasis is placed on student listening with little opportunity for evaluating content and formulating opinions, some of which may run counter to those held by the teacher. Pedagogy is defined as the art and science of teaching; in a sense, it may more correctly be labeled as the art and science of delivering or telling. (Hill, 1988, p. 137)

On the other hand, the leader who chooses to focus on *process* exemplifies a more "learner-centered" model: The emphasis is on the participants. This model adheres to some basic tenets of adult learning, which include the following:

- The learning environment must be physically and psychologically comfortable.
- Increasing or maintaining one's sense of self-esteem and pleasure are strong secondary motivators for engaging in learning experiences.
- There seem to be "teachable moments" in the lives of adults (and maybe in all ages). (Zemke & Zemke, 1981; in Hill, 1988, pp. 137-138)

These concepts of learner-centered process are congruent with the concepts of feminist pedagogy or feminist education. Here I use the term *feminist pedagogy* to mean leading or instructing others in an unbiased, learner-empowering, diversity-respecting, woman-affirming way.

Feminist pedagogy gives participants a chance to learn about and discuss what others are thinking, to shape the material, and to have an actual influence on outcome. Focus is on *who* as well as on *what*: on who is in our particular group and how we will all interrelate (*process*), as well as on our *content*—what we are going to say to them.

"Orator" leaders tend to overemphasize the *what*, neglecting the *who* sitting right in front of them. These oversights may occur in the most unlikely settings. Consider, for example, a class in the newly emerging field of gender studies, the new gender scholarship, or gender in the curriculum. Let us imagine that we are observing a high school women's studies class that is discussing the unsung, behind-the-scenes work women have accomplished down through history, and the value of this effort even though it may not be highly visible. The instructor, being very preoccupied with the subject of female and male roles during wartime, is asking the students such questions as, "During World War II, while the men were off fighting, what do you suppose the women on the homefront were doing?"

While a few male students contribute their thoughts on this question, the instructor chooses to ignore the fact that for nearly 15 minutes no female students have been involved in the discussion. Meanwhile, in the back of the room, a handful of other males are casting disparaging glances, occasionally sparring with one another, and carrying on a covert operation all their own—a gender issue with which the instructor is very annoyed but at a loss to cope. The classroom has thus become a microcosm of the subject at hand: the marginalization of females. How can females become more visible, less marginal? The curriculum is concerned with why the ideas and talents of women are often unnoticed and devalued and how students can become more appreciative of women's contributions and the unheralded roles women play. Yet, these issues are not being dealt with effectively because the old stereotyped gender roles—male as distracting dominator, female as deferring accommodator—get in the way. The extreme roles are no longer just theory—they are being played out. Process is aggravating and superseding content, but only content is being addressed.

Next, let us imagine that we are observing a support group at the local men's center that is exploring such issues as how males have been narrowly socialized, why some men have difficulty showing emotion, why boys need male mentors as they grow up, and why some men feel distant from their fathers.[1] The facilitator is expounding at length about a famous author's painful relationship to his father, meanwhile failing to notice that, at the opposite side of the circle, tears make their way down one man's cheeks as he silently relives the abuse and neglect he received at the hands of *his* father.

As we can see, we leaders may be very well versed in the *theory* of an issue, but still not be able to deal with that issue in the flesh. In our urgency to expound on issues while we facilitate a group, chair a meeting, or manage a department, we may neglect the embodiments of that concept in our immediate circle. For example, the city human rights commissioner might refuse to meet with the gays and lesbians who wait patiently outside the city council chambers, or the supposedly enlightened vice president for personnel may be presenting training sessions on respectful treatment of women while winking at sexual harassment in her or his own department. When our process is not congruent with our content, we have not integrated the *human* into the *hypothetical,* and we are not credible, authentic leaders.

A recent conversation I had with an academic administrator at a Minnesota college put these issues into a nutshell. She was describing how members of her department had given lip service to the state's new "Multicultural Gender-Fair Curriculum Rule."[2] Her colleagues had agreed they would need to purchase textbooks that were not so sexist, but, she said, there were more pressing problems to be reckoned with first. These problems lay in relationships between educators: "We must first face some very vulnerable intradepartmental issues, mainly the sexism among our own faculty members." As educator/administrator, she felt it made no sense to buy new books or to plan highly theoretical workshops about "gender-fair curriculum" when so much discrimination and misunderstanding existed among faculty. Only after some of these human conflicts had been addressed could these educators then move on to critique the actual content of their courses.

She noted that still another hurdle would remain after these issues of intradepartmental conflict and curricular reform had been investigated and, she hoped, resolved. That hurdle would be to convince faculty to "use teaching methods that would make women more comfortable" in the classroom:

> My sense is that it's hard for male professors to admit that certain pedagogical styles might not be helpful to women. We must find an appropriate time to introduce gender issues; if we bring them up too often, male faculty get turned off.

Hearing All Our Voices

How does all of this apply to our everyday experiences in other professional settings, such as workshops, conference breakout sessions, or group meetings? Lee Bell (1987), in a discussion about applying feminist pedagogy to groups, recommends techniques for stimulating greater involvement and empowerment of all members. Bell suggests that leaders, rather than dishing out prepared remarks, should try to learn what participants' needs are, and how they can learn from these people. An effective leader tries to motivate each person to use her or his voice as early in a session as possible; for example, even in a large auditorium, conference participants could turn to a neighbor and discuss their reactions to a particular topic (p. 76). In this manner, diversity of opinion is both solicited and respected, and there is a "legitimizing of multiple perspectives that feels quite liberating" (p. 75). Leader and group members alike can benefit from this less structured format because more time is allowed for the unexpected to happen—what I call *planned disarray* or *anticipated messiness*.

Although the focus here is mostly within the arena of classroom, training series, conference session, or interactive workshop, the basic tenets of feminist education can apply in *any* group situation, whether it be supervisor trying to motivate employees, chairperson acknowledging committee members, therapist drawing out client, or parent trying to evoke feelings from a child. A parent, for example, may insist that she or he runs a tight-knit, "loving" family in which teenaged daughters and sons "willingly" cooperate and obey. Yet this parent insists on laying down highly rigid, unrealistic rules and regulations without listening to the teens' side of the story. The offspring become more and more withdrawn and uncommunicative—eventually acting out in rebellion—and the family finally goes into therapy. The counselor, having elicited the youths' anger about not being respected and listened to, suggests that the parent initiate regular family meetings during which the young people have "equal time" to give legitimate input and help develop family policy. After a few months of these meetings, this parent gains a new appreciation for the words *diversity* and *cooperation.*

As leaders cultivate multiple perspectives, we create climates that foster dialogue—environments in which widely diverse needs and opinions are not only seen as credible, but are actively sought out and supported. In these safe environments, women (but also men) will find the empowerment they need to enter into dialogue, speaking in their own authentic voices.

Being able to speak in one's own voice and to hear the voice of another is essential for "an awareness of one's own thought process," assert Belenky et al. (1986) in their discussion of the "development of self, voice, and mind." Interviews with a wide variety of women convinced these authors that females learn much more readily in an atmosphere of mutuality, where "real talk" or real conversation is going on:

> "Real talk" reaches deep into the experience of each participant [and] includes discourse and exploration, talking and listening, questions, argument, speculation and sharing. . . . [It involves] the capacity for speaking with and listening to others while simultaneously speaking with and listening to the self. (pp. 144-145)

The process of "real talk" involves a "reciprocal drawing out of the other," explains Nancy Goldberger (1989). Women traditionally use this "drawing-out" mode, and it is frequently devalued in favor of a more competitive mode. In a group situation, such competitiveness can be on the part of the leader/presenter who insists on doing all the talking, shutting off debate. Or participants, imitating the presenter's oratorical style, may vie with each other for the limelight. When women enter the fray and try to get a word in edgewise, they may be criticized:

> Women who do speak up have been perceived as "cold, unfeminine, aggressive, abrasive, and arrogant" although the same behavior by men [is] described as "objective, efficient, ambitious, decisive, and self-confident." . . . Why don't women speak up and insist on being heard? . . . The . . . woman's dilemma is often between being undervalued if she remains polite and accommodating and being punished if she does not. (Geis et al., 1982, p. 7)

A woman may say to herself: I'd like to interject a comment now, but what if it sounds stupid? Besides, women aren't supposed to appear as if they know too much. I might be perceived as aggressive if I interrupt the instructor or another participant. I think I'll choose to be *silent*: It's good for a woman to look interested in what others are saying; it's better to defer and draw others out. As a result, this woman's chance to initiate or interact in dialogue is delayed or forever lost.

Yet being able to express one's opinions in the public sphere is essential to advancement, according to researcher Catherine Krupnick, who studied female and male behaviors in coeducational classrooms. Krupnick states that "the cost of not becoming proficient in holding an audience can be high" (quoted in Fiske, 1990, p. 5E). But too often women fall silent. "Our desire for approval stifles us," explains Jesseli Moen (1990), a chemical dependency counselor who works with women:

> Because women put such a high value on relationships, we fear losing connection, or being "too far to the edge." So we shift our voices to gain public approval. Self-esteem is a problem for *all* women, and our low self-esteem causes us to mistrust ourselves and rely on outside authority, usually male. Our poor self-image also causes us to mistrust the voices of other women. We figure, "If *I'm* not worth much, how can *she* be worth much?" Each woman must trust that her voice has merit and will be heard; she must also speak out when she sees other women disrespected.

As we know from the work of Carol Gilligan (1982), it is frequently problematic for a woman to feel empowered enough to speak in her own voice. In Gilligan's view, a woman's reticence and deference to others may be in reaction to the prevalence of male values in our culture: "Women come to question the normality of their feelings and to alter their judgements in deference to the opinions of others" (p. 16).

This deference may be coupled with women's tendency to learn in a more collaborative way, preferring attachment and connection over detachment and objectivity. Goldberger, referring to the work of Noddings (1984), contrasts these modes of learning as *connected knowing* versus *separate knowing*, concepts we began to explore in Chapter 3. Separate knowing is "normative in western culture," says Goldberger, and it places emphasis on objectively "trying to prove, disprove, or convince" rather than trying to create an atmosphere of mutual understanding. However, "many women are deeply ambivalent about detachment and objectivity," she continues; women seem to learn better when they are seeking to "understand or be understood."

Thus the conundrum: Because women "come to question the normality of their feelings," they may alter their judgments; because they mistrust the merit of their own voices, they withhold self-expression; because criticism seems to sever connection, they remain silent rather than risk separation. These deeply ingrained patterns make it quite difficult for many women to proceed with their developmental task: learning to be more autonomous.

This quandary provides a real challenge to any leader. Because women may fear being "too far to the edge," they may more heavily weigh the consequences of their actions. This tendency, coupled with the fact that women spend a lot of time paying attention to verbal and nonverbal cues of others in discourse, may mean females are a bit "slower on the draw" when it comes to becoming involved in group dialogue. The challenge to the leader is to help both women and men to keep a balance between the modes of separate knowing and connected knowing in order that all voices may be heard.

Women have been socialized to connect with and nurture others, to put others' needs before their own, to listen more and interrupt less; thus females may be on an entirely different wavelength from those who are working in the competitive mode.

Favoring connection over detachment and competition has great merit in any group, but in a competitive culture that values "ranking," women's more collaborative "linking" (Eisler, 1987) behavior is frequently ignored, discounted, and undervalued. "Connected knowing," explains Goldberger (1989), "is not honored or encouraged in our culture."

Cooperative Learning as a Key to Empowerment

One method that seems to foster an atmosphere of classroom mutuality was developed at the Cooperative Learning Center, University of Minnesota. "Cooperation is working together to accomplish shared goals," say brothers David and Roger Johnson, who developed this method. "Cooperative Learning is the instructional use of small groups so that students work together to maximize their own and each other's learning" (Johnson & Johnson, 1988). Students develop a sink-or-swim *interdependence* on each other; for example, in a math drill, they all share a combined score. In a spelling lesson students make up a story to which each contributes; as one young person put it, "We all thought of a different story and made it into one story" (quoted in Smetanka, 1990).[3] Students are assigned such roles as "encourager," whose task it is to encourage "in a friendly way all members of the group to participate in the discussion, sharing their ideas and feelings" (Johnson & Johnson, 1988, p. 4). These methods would probably be wholeheartedly embraced by the graduate student in urban planning (Case 5.1). Certainly, were these techniques to be implemented in her classes, she and her peers might discover "what other students are thinking."

Of course, we cannot expect our group members to spend all their time being friendly encouragers. It is not practical to have dialogue, discussion, or "real talk" going on constantly. As leaders, we are expected to provide well-organized content and a certain amount of "meaty" material. There are syllabi, lectures, agendas, and organizational goals or policies that must be adhered to—after all, we are there to *lead*. However, we realize that to lead does not have to mean to establish total control. We can lead by integrating process with content to ensure that all participants are absorbing the material, that the subject fits with the personal experiences and relates to the lives of individuals, and that everyone feels comfortable challenging the subject matter and the leader. In short, we can adopt the characteristics of a "midwife" leader as profiled in the dialectic that follows.

Leader as Peacock or Midwife: An Educational Dialectic

Peacock Mode

When leaders are obsessed with their own brilliance—the importance of their position and what they have to say—they are like peacocks who "strut their stuff" in front of the hens (the group), suggests Nancy Miller (1980), writing in the context of the feminist teacher in the classroom. In an educational setting, for example, "peacock professors" or "peacock teachers" may hand down the subject matter from on high; the end result is that students find out how much teachers know, but teachers learn precious little from (or about) their students. Transmission of knowledge becomes a one-way street and dialogue is not encouraged. As the innovative educator Paolo Freire (1971) describes it, educators become like "bankers," making deposits in students' empty heads (cited in Belenky et al., 1986, p. 214ff).

If a student does try to raise a controversial issue during discussion, or if the student actually challenges the teacher and is discounted for it, the experience can be shameful and emotionally draining for the student:

> As a graduate student and teacher's assistant I have been working with a male professor who is not only "always right," but condescendingly (and completely insensitively) so. I spent the first semester of my assignment smiling and swallowing hard when he displayed his insensitive and chauvinistic behavior. I tried to ignore the nausea I felt when he preached that his way was not only the best, but the only way.
>
> By the second semester I knew the nausea was real, and my distaste for him was mixed with the shame I felt for acquiescing to his methods and mannerisms. So, I began to challenge them. I was then accused by him of having a "bad attitude" and of being "disruptive" and "negative." It has been a difficult, confusing, and emotionally draining semester. (MacVeigh, 1988)

Since the goal of this manual is to help create group milieus in which both women and men can reach their full potential, and since we are especially concerned with helping women to find their voices, it is important to recognize that some women will actually *leave* school as a result of the sort of condescending treatment recounted above. Belenky et al. found that "several women said they and their friends left school as soon as they legally could . . . so that 'we wouldn't have to put up with being put down every day' " (pp. 227-228). These authors of *Women's Ways of Knowing* also determined that "none of the women we interviewed wanted a system in which knowledge flowed in only one direction, from teacher to student" (p. 217). Because females are interrupted often (Zimmerman & West, 1975), and frequently have their ideas challenged in mixed groups (Geis et al., 1982, p. 7), they often feel discounted; consequently their self-confidence may suffer. Having an opportunity to voice opinions in an accepting, noncompetitive environment seems essential to the identity and self-worth of women, and—one would assume—to men also.

Too often, however, those of us in positions of leadership succumb to the "seduction" of "mastery" (N. K. Miller, 1980): trying to impress those we lead with how much *we* know. In this competitive mode, we strut our stuff, and those around us may feel forced to follow suit, with everyone displaying feathers to dazzle each other. (As a participant remarked to me after a professor filibustered one-third of a 15-minute question and answer period following one of my interactive seminars: "People pay *homage* to those displaying *plumage*.")

The peacock position is similar to an "adversarial mode" or one of "advocacy" as delineated by Sandra Keith (1987), who suggests innovative methods for integrating female students into math classrooms. The *advocacy mode* is one of "power, intimidation and contest, . . . a mode that women have traditionally felt uncomfortable in and have been unaccepted in" (p. 88). It is one of "claims and assertions, which generally ignores its audience, is not generally interactive, and competition runs high" (pp. 91-92). A noninteractive, competitive mode is deleterious to women, say Belenky et al. (1986): "Only a handful of women described a powerful and positive learning experience in which a teacher aggressively challenged their notions" (p. 227).

Midwife Mode

As an antidote to the adversarial mode, Keith recommends a *response mode* that "enables students to reconstruct ideas presented from the context of their own experiences" (p. 94). This mode is focused on process, and when a leader focuses on process, she or he becomes like a "midwife" (Belenky et al.'s term) who helps the participants "articulate and expand their latent knowledge; . . . [who] assists the student in giving birth to their own ideas." Midwife-teachers "encourage the students to speak in their own active voices" (Belenky et al., 1986, pp. 217-218). This process of articulating and expanding on one's own ideas and those of others sounds like exactly what the graduate students in urban planning were looking for.

A leader intent on process is more concerned with *listening* than with *telling*, more interested in *finding out where the participant has been* than in *telling a participant where to go*. In Belenky et al.'s view, midwife-teachers "assist in the emergence of consciousness" (p. 218) and try to create a nurturing environment, a "yogurt classroom" that "provides a culture for growth," as opposed to a "movie class" in which students are spectators (p. 221).

When students/participants use their "own active voices," true dialogue can occur. The value of dialogue is that it is less hierarchical and more egalitarian, as Freire (1971) explains:

> Both teacher and students engage in the process of thinking and they talk out what they are thinking in a public dialogue. As they think and talk together, their roles merge. Through dialogue, the teacher-of-the-students and the students-of-the-teacher cease to exist and a new term emerges; teacher-student with students-teachers. (p. 67; cited in Belenky et al., 1986, p. 219)

As a facilitator who enjoys evoking participants' responses, and who treasures their contributions, I nevertheless must admit to (and feel constrained to warn others about) an occasional sensation of loss while trying to lead with a midwife style. By *loss*, I mean that what I plan does not always happen, and then I wish it had, and I miss it because it did not. As much as I may deliberately profess that classes, workshops, or training sessions should be unstructured, and that leaders should use "more ambiguous and less predictable" methods (N. K. Miller, 1980, p. 5), I still value structure. I invest a great deal of diligence and imagination in outlining a session: I consider sequence, timing, logistics, and extra topics I am yearning to cover "if there is enough time." Then, as a particular group gets under way and takes on a life of its own, I watch in dismay as "my" structure begins to crumble a bit, sometimes feeling I am being "deprived" of what I had originally planned.

At these moments I feel the first twinges of loss: But what about my imaginative outline? My "brilliant" proposal? How will I ever have time to serve up all those delicious topics I so carefully prepared? How will the group survive without the pearls of wisdom that were supposed to have dropped from my lips? It is then that I force myself to switch gears and to visualize the session from the participants' perspective, a view that is probably quite similar to that expressed by the graduate student above: "We want more chance to be involved with what happens." I then remind myself that since one of my leadership goals is to accommodate ambiguity and allow for the unexpected, it is time for me to step back and encourage group members "to work together to maximize their own and each other's learning," as Johnson and Johnson (1988) phrase it.

Planned Unpredictability

How does a leader plan for and adapt to such ambiguity and unpredictability? How can one prepare a culture for growth so the yogurt—the participants' ideas—has time to ferment? One way to schedule this is to anticipate naturally occurring "holes" in the agenda or outline, gaps that might be called *deliberate unhappenings*. To facilitate these pauses, a leader can actually write some reminders into an outline:

- Allow leeway here.
- Take a break if it feels right.
- Have gestational gap at this point.
- Process new concept now!
- Give small groups more time here if needed.

These arranged hiatuses enable people to stray off course temporarily and gravitate toward what interests them, which produces
the anticipated messiness and planned disarray mentioned earlier, but which now is not so messy because it has been skillfully
arranged for.

Having thus *destructured* the time, the leader now feels free to
allow the session to rebuild and *restructure* itself. No longer pressing for a rigidly controlled agenda, the leader can relax and concentrate on building trust and rapport, lending support, encouraging teamwork, soliciting input, reaching for fresh or conflicting
viewpoints, and providing nurturing and constructive feedback,
a cycle Belenky et al. (1986) describe as "confirmation-evocation-
confirmation" (p. 219).

But what about the subject matter, you say; what about the topic
at hand? The secret here is that the loosely constructed outline is
always quite firmly in the leader's mind, and is also made available to the group before the session begins, so everyone becomes
familiar with it. Apprised of the major topics at the outset, participants are aware of, and reassured by, an agreed-upon underlying
structure. And should they stray too far from this basic format, the
leader gently reminds the group of its purpose, presenting the
next carefully wrought concept, which is always "up the leader's
sleeve," waiting to be utilized.

Confirmation-Evocation-Confirmation

How does a leader go about initiating this process of confirmation-evocation-confirmation? In a class or workshop, for example,
the leader waits until someone in the group shares an experience or
raises a particular question. As others begin to gravitate toward this
new concept (and the leader legitimates it as one of the established
subjects of the day), the leader can say, "I'm so pleased that you
brought up that issue; it just so happens that your question leads
directly to our next major topic." The leader then moves on to the
next point on the outline, as if it were all the other person's idea.

Imagine we are in a college class and the week's topic is "blatant
and subtle gender bias." The instructor, after delivering a brief
lecture on sexism, gender role stereotypes, and related topics, asks
the group, "What has been your personal experience as victim or
perpetrator of sexism? Have you ever experienced blatant or sub-

tle bias, or did you ever wonder if your treatment of others might be discriminatory?" The instructor then responds to, affirms, and builds on what students share.

Example 1

Female student: When I took a course from this one professor, and I would make a point during class, he would respond, "Uh-huh." But if one of the *guys* said something, the prof would go on and on—like this male student was *really profound*!

Leader: The sexism you describe is hard to detect because it's so subtle—you are very astute in your observation [confirmation]. Research in classrooms reveals that teachers often *do* pay more attention to males. It is also common for educators to give more lengthy responses to males' remarks, or to elaborate extensively on what boys and men say. Have any of the rest of you experienced similar bias? [Several students share similar episodes.] Let's now divide into small groups and discuss other instances when you noticed one gender being subtly favored over the other. Please be ready to share your experiences with the whole group [evocation].

Example 2

Male student: When I told my coworker she was a "cute chick" she walked away. I don't get it—I was just trying to give her a compliment.

Leader: Thank you for taking the risk to share that incident with the group [confirmation]. How do you think your coworker interpreted your words? [During this evocation the student admits that he might have "insulted" the woman.] Sometimes we use language—consciously or unconsciously—in a way that trivializes or demeans others. This is described as "linguistic sexism" by Henley and Thorne. Do you plan to follow through on this incident? If so, what might you say to your coworker?

[At this juncture, other students can be invited to offer suggestions; more evocation.]

Leader [to the group]: Class, your assignment this week is to make a list of slang phrases or demeaning words used to describe men as well as women. Compare the length of the lists, and be ready to discuss how you would feel if one of these terms were directed at you.

In the classes described in both the examples above, when students report back to the whole class (after having met in small discussion groups or completed the homework assignment), the leader supports and confirms their contributions, continuing the cycle of affirming, drawing out, and supporting. By responding in this manner, the leader evokes major concepts in the agreed-upon outline that participants, in their curiosity, have actually raised. The basic "hard" structure of the subject is maintained, but there is much "softness" and flexibility. Students have become teachers, and the leader, as teacher, has become student. What participants say has been acknowledged and supported, which draws out more of their responses, which are then reconfirmed.

I like to use the image of a spider's web to help envision this process of evocation, sharing, and confirmation (Figure 5.1). Webs illustrate a "delicate interrelatedness," suggest Belenky et al. (1986), in which no one position dominates over the rest. When we touch one part of the web, the rest of it quivers; when one person says or does something, it provokes or evokes a reaction in others. Learning in a weblike way means that each person in the group is "subject to the actions of others" (p. 178) and that "evolving thought can be tentative" (p. 221).

Images of weblike structures seem to be the wave of the future in corporations as well as in classrooms. Sally Helgesen (1990), who sees "women's ways of leadership" as an "advantage," describes women's management styles as being like webs or networks, rather than hierarchical. She reports that female managers perceive themselves not at the top of a management position reaching down, but as in the center, reaching out. "A hierarchy focuses on targeting a position, climbing the ladder and knocking out competition," Helgesen points out. "A web emphasizes interrelationships, building up strength and knitting loose ends into the fabric" (quoted in Laporte, 1990, p. 143; see also Peters, 1990).

Group process thus follows more of a spiral path than a linear sequence, suggests women's studies professor Patricia Samuel (personal communication, 1988). A group member, whether in a classroom or a corporation, might say something that does not have an "immediate point," in Samuel's words, but that leads, in a synergistic way, to the group's arrival at a new understanding. From the participant's point of view, this can be very refreshing:

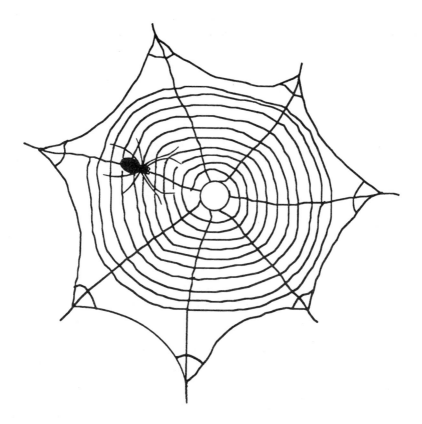

Figure 5.1. The "Delicate Interrelatedness" of the Learning Process

"We can all come to a conclusion which none of us started out with" stated one of the participants in Belenky et al.'s (1986) study (p. 220). (Or, in the words of the graduate student in urban planning: "The outcome would never be the same.")

Unfortunately, many organizations and institutions place a high value on predictability, and systems are designed to assure that both processes and outcomes *do* remain the same. The following example illustrates that the issue driving such systems is fear of loss of control.

A Question of Control

In an effort to provide more give-and-take in legal proceedings, an innovative technique was field tested in courtrooms (American Judicature Society, 1991). Specifically, this technique would allow members of a jury to take notes and submit written questions during a trial. Perhaps, it was thought, having this opportunity would help jurors clarify any issues raised during the trial that they did not understand. There was some concern, however, that the questioning would disrupt courtroom proceedings and the trial process; some attorneys actually feared jurors would "take over and run the show," according to law professor Steve Penrod, who served as consultant to the field study (personal communication, April 17, 1991).

A judge, in a radio interview about the innovation (July 19, 1989), seemed willing to try the method: "The jurors have to get the information eventually, so they may as well satisfy their curiosity during the trial, rather than wait until the deliberations," he said. When asked whether he might lose control of the courtroom, the judge responded:

> It's not a question of control, or of disrupting the lawyers' strategies. I can stop the questioning if it interferes with the process. The main thing is, it's an issue of getting at the truth.

It was to be hoped, stated Penrod in the same interview, that if jurors could submit written questions during the trial process, they would then "make more well-reasoned decisions and also pay attention better" during the trial. Although the results of the study ultimately showed that the technique was "neither harmful nor helpful," Penrod now reports that the jurors *did* "appreciate the opportunity to ask questions" (personal communication, April 17, 1991).

Any teacher, manager, or other leader already using such collaborative techniques as inviting team input and valuing the expertise of everyone in the room will probably feel these legal "innovations" to be elementary. It seems so obvious that a system that espouses government "of the people, by the people, and for the people" would place value on the people's being able to satisfy their curiosity by asking questions. Too often, however, we leaders, like the apprehensive attorneys who felt jurors might take over and run the show, may fear that this very questioning will lead to loss of control. It seems more convenient to maintain a predictable hierarchical structure than to allow the formation of a more "tentative" web, which might contain a few "loose ends." Not being in control may have been the very thing feared by the professor—described earlier—who, when challenged by his student, labeled her as "negative" and "disruptive."

Loss of control may also be the issue in the following critique, which contrasts one unilateral and highly restricted workshop presentation with another in which "teacher-student" merges with "students-teachers." The reader is invited to contrast the strategies used by these various leaders and to notice how the presenter who uses a collaborative pedagogy, which fosters learning as a communal enterprise, is the presenter who elicits the most empowering discourse.

Leadership Styles in Action

LEADER CRITIQUE 5.1

I had the opportunity to observe both peacock and midwife leadership styles at a conference on feminism and the family titled "Celebrating Women's Voices." Two workshop sessions I attended are compared and contrasted below.

Orating Peacocks

A session titled "Men's Responses: Feminism and the Family" was copresented by two men, who happened to be in the minority, as most other conference presenters, as well as participants, were women. The constituency of this particular workshop, however, was approximately 30% male, and both male and female participants seemed ready and willing to initiate discussion and enter into dialogue with the male presenters, both of whom were therapists.

However, a responsive, interactive mode did not seem to be what these leaders had in mind. They had a rigid, very constrained style: They read a lot of their material, and seemed compelled to cover every square inch of it. The men appeared very preoccupied with what they had to say and do, rather than with who was in the workshop and how they could interrelate with those participants. They tossed the lecture back and forth between themselves without missing a beat. The men seemed to be *competing,* not only with each other, but with their audience; they did not invite, or even seem to respect, questions and comments from participants. It seems ironic to reiterate that this conference was about "celebrating voices" when the voices of these presenters were the only ones to be heard.

I began to think that the rigid behavior of these two men was a function either of their minority status or their thesis: that men are victims, just as much as women are. Perhaps they had decided to keep talking as a defense against anyone's disagreeing with that stance, or perhaps they were afraid to give anyone a chance to question their statistics, which suggested that the same percentage of wives are violent to husbands as are husbands to wives, and that the majority of abuse occurs in families headed by women.

When a female member of the audience finally did ask, "Could you tell us where you got your statistics?" her question was glossed over and dismissed. This discouragement of doubt served to stifle the whole audience temporarily, which allowed the peacocks to continue their monologues.

Finally, an older man in the front row spoke up:

Attempted intervention: I wonder when you will stop for questions from the audience. I'd like to hear from myself and the others.

To which one presenter responded:

Intervention squelched: We will allow for questions later.

"Later" turned out to be seven minutes before the workshop was supposed to end; only then was audience input invited.

Evoking Midwife

The leadership style of the presenters above was quite different from that of Toni McNaron (1987), another presenter at the same conference who facilitated a workshop titled "Some Effects of Incest on Ideas of the Family." Like the men, McNaron—a professor of English and women's studies—also began with formal lecture, but she allowed and welcomed audience questions much earlier—approximately halfway through her

session. The comfortable rapport she established was evident in the
very personal nature of the questions raised by three different
participants, and in her responses to these queries:

> *First questioner:* Is it okay for a son to give his mother a back rub?
>
> *McNaron:* This is asking the son to fill an adult role; it is automatically
> *ishy.* . . .
>
> *Second questioner:* Why do female incest victims have such permeable
> boundaries?
>
> *McNaron:* Male members of the culture have been encouraged to
> take what they want when they want it; it has been the tradition of
> women to give it. . . .
>
> *Third questioner:* How do you break the silence if you're a victim?
>
> *McNaron:* When you break the silence, go where you'll be listened
> to. . . .

Through these interchanges between facilitator and participants a
warm climate was established—warm enough so that a male therapist
in the audience, although he was in the minority, felt comfortable
enough to admit, "In a therapy session with incest victims, it's
emotionally safer to blame the mother for what happened in the family
than to take on the father. At least if you're angry with the mom, she'll
stay *connected.*"

(The reader will recall that this therapist's assessment concurs with a
similar point made by Goldner, 1985, about "maternal centrality and
paternal marginality" noted in Chapter 1. That is, therapists often find
it easier to ask the wife/mother to be "switchboard" or "gatekeeper"
[p. 39] of the family dynamics—indeed, to hold her accountable for
these very dynamics—than to confront the husband/father, who may
be allowed to maintain a detached, and sometimes controlling,
distance.)

McNaron's midwife style enabled her to talk *with* us, not *at* us; she
was the personification of teacher-as-learner. She watched, she listened,
she interacted, she was connecting. Her commitment to a responsive
style of leadership was exemplified in her following statement:

> *The teacher must respond appropriately to the very first comment a student
> makes when a course is beginning. If you put them down or don't support*

them, they'll never speak again. It is not grandiosity or megalomania on my part to say this; it is the very nature of the instructor's role in the classroom to respond in this appropriate way.

McNaron's suggestion is an important guideline for any leader in any setting, no matter what the topic under discussion.

Analysis of Leadership Styles

Sociolinguist Deborah Tannen provides a clue as to why we may observe such strong contrasts in male and female leadership styles as evidenced in the two workshops above. Describing the confession of a colleague who was becoming more aware of his own defensiveness as a presenter, Tannen relates this insider's story:

> A male colleague of mine went to a conference and then told me he suddenly understood what women are doing when they give talks. A woman who was giving a paper at the conference kept saying, "Do you understand? Do you follow me?" And he said it blew his mind that her main concern really was that the audience understand her. When he gives a paper, he said, he's not concerned with that; *he's concerned that no one in the audience be able to stand up and put him down once he stops talking.* He's covering his ass (laughing). (quoted in Taylor, 1990, p. 33; emphasis added)

This man's description of his own presentation style sounds disturbingly similar to that of the two peacock presenters described above. In contrast, McNaron allowed herself to be interrupted, did not seem to worry about being contradicted, and also dialogued much more extensively with her audience. She structured her material so that there was a balance of *oration* and *evocation.* Subject matter was clear and concise, yet *she allowed time for her prepared remarks to be embellished and enriched by group members' experiences,* methods consistent with the tenets of learner-centered education, feminist pedagogy, connected knowing, and cooperative learning mentioned earlier. She also was authentic: She *said* teachers should be responsive, and she *was.* Her leadership exemplified Tannen's observation that it is most frequently the female who employs "rapport talk," using language to connect and "negotiate intimacy." The male leaders, on the other hand, appeared to view their presentation as a chance to negotiate status, which demonstrates, as

Tannen puts it, a concern for "who's one up, who's one down" (quoted in Taylor, 1990, p. 33).

(I wish to emphasize here that I have observed my share of female speakers who behave like peacocks, spending most of their allotted time displaying unreadable overhead transparencies, giving glowing accounts of their latest important client or book, expounding on obscurities irrelevant to their audience, or responding in a very cursory and unsympathetic way to audience input. I have also observed plenty of male midwife-style facilitators who wait patiently for participants to "give birth to their own ideas.")

The two workshops described above provide a clear-cut example of how a presenter who spends most of her or his energy "reporting," negotiating for status, or worrying about who's one up or one down may simply not devote enough time to establishing connection and understanding with group members. No matter what our leadership capacity—whether we be speakers, attorneys, clergypersons, or parents—if we are more concerned with making sure no one will criticize us once we stop talking than with being sure we understand and are understood, we are *not* creating hospitable climates for those we lead. As a result, very little learning may be going on.

One of the best ways we can create hospitable climates is to allow for pauses and moments of transition—periods of silence—during which participants can process information and prepare to verbalize their thoughts. Many leaders view silence as a very uncomfortable happening; some even perceive it as a "threatening experience" or the "ultimate nightmare." Yet, to those who have developed skills to deal with it, silence is an essential maxim of leadership.

Silence: A Symptom and a Tool

The Reasons for Silence

Silence during any process can make group members and their leader exceedingly self-conscious and uncomfortable. Microseconds seem like minutes; minutes feel like hours. Participants may be thinking: Why is it suddenly so quiet in here? Am I supposed to *say* something? Won't someone else *please* talk? For the leader, feeling stranded, the silence may provoke increasing anxiety: I'm up here in the limelight, so these folks must expect me to *do* something.

During these pregnant pauses, those of us supposedly in charge may make all sorts of discounting, disempowering assumptions about what is happening in other people's heads. For example, a teacher might assume a student is stupid, when actually the student is just thinking. A law enforcement official might assume a suspect is hiding information, when actually the individual feels intimidated. A doctor or nurse might assume an elderly person is senile or deaf, when actually she or he is merely trying to be discreet. A parent might assume a child is recalcitrant or disobediently rebellious, when in fact the child is depressed. A therapist or counselor might assume that a silent client is deliberately concealing important data, when actually the client feels unable to speak because the topic under discussion is too emotionally painful. And many of us, sad to say, may assume that when females are silent they are helpless, insecure, unable to cope, or maybe even incompetent. Let us examine some possible causes of silence.

Gender Role Extremes

My experience has taught me that episodes of silence may be driven by the extreme gender role behaviors discussed earlier (see Box 1.1). For instance, a dead calm might be triggered by a faction using *detachment/distancing* behavior as a form of *dominance* and control: We'll sit here in this corner or in the back row; if the leader wants participation, she or he will just have to *pry* it out of us. *No way* is this leader going to get *us* to talk. We're in control here!

This controlling, distancing maneuver has been attempted by male participants in several workshops I have facilitated over the years, but now I am wiser. Since I recognize how detached and privileged behavior interferes with process, I now have a regular practice of asking everyone—before a session even starts—to "shuffle" and "sit by someone you'd like to know better" or "sit by a coworker from another department." For example, I used this technique while facilitating a seminar for county employees after being forewarned by the meeting planner that the back row of the room would fill up with males "because certain men *always* sit there in these workshops." As predicted, the first males began to trickle in and assume their customary places, so I asked all participants to rearrange themselves, but I did not tell them why. This shuffling strategy allowed me to avoid confronting the gender issue directly, yet still prevented the sequestering of men or women into certain encapsulated areas. (Such a method might have been helpful for rearranging the sleepy male dental students discussed in the previous chapter who were acting "like they've got it made" in the back row of the lecture hall.)

Males sometimes withdraw out of discomfort, because they consider a topic "unmasculine" or a "women's subject." This stereotypical thinking may have been a factor in the males' quietude during the class on chemical dependency and family communication discussed in Case 1.3 (Chapter 1) when the leader felt she "gave away power" to the silent men. It may also help explain the behavior of the student, whom we will meet in Chapter 7, who sleeps through a human relations lecture on male violence against women.

Just as a group may fall silent because one of its factions tries to control through *detachment,* so also may a group fall silent because a different person or faction tries to control through *deference*: If we just smile sweetly and listen long enough, maybe somebody will ask us what *we* think; we can use the "silent treatment" to get people to pay attention to us. This deference may eventually intensify into angry frustration: How much longer do we have to sit here and accommodate to others before the leader will finally notice us! We saw this behavior in Theresa, the woman in the assertiveness workshop who threatened to drop out unless the leader could get Ted to "shut up," yet was not able to stop deferring to him and break her silence (Case 3.1, Chapter 3).

Other Possible Causes of Silence

Besides the gender role extremes of dominance or deference, there are many other human factors that can contribute to pauses in process, such as class, status, age, physical impairment, personality type, race, ethnicity, being a member of a linguistic minority, and even which section of the country a person comes from. Also to be considered are realities such as the room environment and temperature, the group's history, and the level of trust that has been established among members. (Appendix C of this volume provides a checklist on some of these items.)

Insensitive leadership. In addition to all these variables, it is also possible that painfully frustrating silences are driven by our own insensitive leadership. For example, the question the leader has asked may have been unclear; participants may be afraid to talk because the leader's body language is unsympathetic or even threatening; the leader may have shut off dialogue by making a discounting remark; or the leader may be exhibiting poor listening habits.

Time to process. Once we have assured ourselves that our techniques are effective, however, it is wise for us to take a rather benevolent view of silence, and to be gentle with ourselves as well as with our group. It is helpful to affirm ourselves inwardly: Yes, my skills as facilitator are sharpened; I don't need to be paranoid that I did something awful that caused this dead calm. It also helps to be very respectful and trusting of the group's process: Things are quiet here because something very important is going on. I'm going to be patient and find out what that is. There are people here whose voices need to be heard, and I need time to draw them out.

Gender-responsible leaders are able to trust these periods of silence, knowing that the unspoken may be as important as the spoken, and that what goes on "between the lines" of discussion may be even more significant than what is actually verbalized. Silence is a golden opportunity for a leader to become a midwife, to gain an insight into each participant's process—in short, for the *leader* to become the *learner*.

Females learn to be silent. An understanding of silence is especially significant if our goal is the empowerment of girls and women. In elementary school classrooms, Sadker and Sadker observed that girls sat for a long time with hands raised, waiting for the teacher to call on them—a silence enforced by the teacher's preoccupation with, and favoritism toward, male students. Silence may also be self-imposed, as Krupnick, in her study of college classrooms, observed: "Female students . . . tended to want time to think about a question before offering an answer" (in Fiske, 1990).

These studies and others indicate that—from toddlerhood through grade school, college, and beyond—females may be the more silent members of a group. In our commitment to encouraging greater involvement and participation of women, the technique of how to facilitate during a period of silence therefore becomes a particularly crucial leadership skill to master.

Nancy Goldberger (1989), during a workshop on "women's ways of knowing," explained that "silent women are the true victims of sex stereotypes." They are like the "received knowers" who are more likely to "accept the power differentials between women and men, turn to others for answers, be passive and not see themselves as agents of change." However, "silence is not just an issue for women," Goldberger clarifies, "but an issue for everyone" (personal communication, June 14, 1990).

One way for clinicians, educators, and policymakers to raise awareness about silence is to step out of their leadership role, walk momentarily in the moccasins of a group member, and honestly examine how they themselves would handle silence if placed in the position of participant instead of leader. Among other questions in a workshop handout for professionals, Goldberger (1989) provided these:

- Do I often silence my truest voice? Around whom or what kinds of people? In what kinds of situations?
- What do I imagine would happen if I spoke out—what would be the consequences?

Leader Discomfort With Silence

Mary Rose O'Reilley (1989), in her article "The Centered Classroom," describes silence as "the teacher's ultimate nightmare: what if I can't fill fifty minutes?" (p. 29). Other professionals—psychotherapists, for example—may also find silence frightening. Because of the ambiguity of silence—not knowing where others are "at," coupled with our own feeling of obligation to take up the time—we leaders may invade moments of quietude, trying to fill the vacuum. "We frequently do something counterproductive to break the silence and thus relieve our anxiety," explains psychologist Gerald Corey (1982), describing moments of silence during a therapeutic session. Corey, who thinks silence can be a "threatening experience," suggests we professionals may feel "compelled to rush in and give several interpretations" to what is being said, or to "intervene and talk [our] anxiety away" (p. 277).

For us to plunge in and interrupt a silence simply because we are apprehensive is a discredit to the group's collective intelligence, because it assumes that nothing valuable is going on. Not willing to live with our own discomfort, and assuming everyone else is just as "antsy," we seem unable to allow the group to be responsible for its own process. Instead, we mount a rescue operation, ostensibly to benefit the group, but mostly to benefit *ourselves*: I'll save all of you from your embarrassment about this pregnant pause so I will be less anxious.

It is particularly tempting, at such moments, for a leader to use sarcasm or inappropriate humor, as we saw in Case 1.3, when the presenter felt she was giving away her power. After a lengthy silence on the part of detached males was finally broken by one of them, she said sarcastically, "We finally heard from a male!" A similar example of such sarcasm is used by one of the facilitators in the following leader critique. Note the similarities and differences in the styles of the two educators as each tries to cope with a short period of silence. One leader seems like a peacock, focusing more on self than on the group, while the other resembles a midwife, trying to evoke the ideas of participants. (As is already evident to the reader, the criteria for being a midwife include being able to empower group members and "draw out" their responses.)

How Leaders Cope With Silence

LEADER CRITIQUE 5.2

Two experienced educators at a management training seminar in the upper Midwest are taking turns facilitating segments of a management training seminar for approximately 15 participants who are seated in a horseshoe arrangement.[4] The primary leadership skill on which we will focus is how each facilitator handles the "pregnant pause."

Presenter 1. This presenter delivers a minilecture on a management topic, and then, suggesting that it will soon be time for the group to become more involved and interactive, asks a question. The leader pauses after asking this question, as if to telegraph the thought, The ball is in your court now; it's your turn, but take your time responding—I'm comfortable waiting.

During this hiatus, which lasts as long as five or six seconds, the facilitator stands still, faces the group, maintains eye contact, smiles, and makes very few distracting gestures. In short, the facilitator models exemplary *listening* habits, letting the group know that silence is acceptable, usual, and comfortable. Participants, after some initial hesitancy, respond readily. A synergistic relationship has developed between leader and participants; dialogue and discussion ensue.

Presenter 2. In contrast, the second presenter seems to be talking *at* more than *with* the group. When this leader opens the discussion period with a question, the normal and customary period of silence begins. While the seconds tick away—two, three, four—the leader becomes visibly agitated, takes a step backward from the group, uses distracting hand gestures, and glances to the side, losing eye contact. Finally the leader interrupts the silence with these remarks: "Well, don't all talk at once!" and, after a short pause, "Wow! What a lively crowd we have here!"

This so-called facilitator is not only palpably apprehensive about the quietude, but finds it necessary to insult the group sarcastically rather than to live with this discomfort. The leader does not verbally check out where participants are in their process (Do you need more time to think?) or to empathize with this process (Take your time, we're in no rush). The leader also does not seem to be objective about personal pedagogical practices—Is my question unclear or could I explain the concept further? Rather, the leader's own anxiety is projected onto the group: Since I'm so uncomfortable, you must be too. As a matter of fact, you're probably to *blame* for my discomfort. So I'll jump in and insult you to get myself off the hook.

In the midst of these silent periods, during which participants are all acutely aware of each others' breathing, everything happening in the room seems blown out of proportion. One's concept of space is distorted: the imagination misinterprets and magnifies distances much the way the tongue exaggerates a tooth cavity—an area smaller than a pea feels like the Grand Canyon. The distance between ourselves and our constituents seems to widen into a vast chasm: Nothing's there, nothing's going on; when will something happen to close the gap?

The passage of time also becomes distorted, and "silent moments . . . may seem like silent hours," to use psychologist Corey's (1982) description (p. 277). Seconds tick by in such excruciatingly slow motion that we think our whole life will flash past until finally— finally—someone in the group will actually speak and rescue us from our agony. These periods of silence truly become a threatening experience, almost a nightmare, even for the most seasoned presenter.

Just what might be going on in the participants' heads during these silences? If we could monitor personal thought processes, these individual cogitations might follow the stages shown in Table 5.1. As is evident in the table, there is much activity going on "between the lines" during episodes of silence. Particular group members may feel especially vulnerable at this time. As leaders, if we discount, interrupt, insult, or make fun of a participant at any one of these stages, that person may become very discouraged, and it may be a long time before she or he again attempts to become actively involved in the group. As cautioned by Toni McNaron, the midwife leader above, we "must respond appropriately to the very first comment a student makes. . . . If you put them down or don't support them, they'll never speak again."

The leader who is committed to encouraging women's participation in the public forum will recognize that—since women sometimes have low self-esteem, a strong need for approval, a history of being discounted, and consequent hesitation about taking risks or speaking up—their reaction time may be slowed down, aggravating their possible existing tendency to remain silent. This leader will tune in to silent women in mixed-gender groups, aware that their silence is a reliable clue that something is definitely amiss. Silent women can be like a barometer indicating that the gender-driven power differentials, as described by Goldberger, need immediate attention. Like canaries sent into coal mines to test whether air is breathable, silent women are often the first symptom that a group's atmosphere is becoming unhealthy or even dysfunctional. To become responsible leaders committed to restabilizing gender-related power imbalances and to hearing the voices of women as well as men in our groups, each of us would benefit by learning to facilitate during periods of silence— to use silence as a tool.

Silence as a Tool

We have seen that silence can be an important *symptom*, an indication of nonproductive gender politics, dysfunctional power plays, group distrust and disarray, leader ineptitude, or multiple other factors. Silence can also be the facilitator's *sine qua non*—a treasured tool through which we demonstrate trust, both in the integrity of our participants and in our own ability to appreciate each stage of their inner process.

We leaders who are comfortable with, and know how to facilitate during, periods of silence have at our fingertips both a versatile key and a healing centering device. We can use silence as a key to "slow time," help find openings, and open doors for those who want to enter into the group's process more fully. We can also recognize silence as a personal time to become centered and to regroup—a welcome, peaceful pause in the rush of activity. As O'Reilley (1989) suggests, leaders could use this free time to be "quiet enough to pay attention" (p. 27), to appreciate everyone's specialness, to examine our leadership methods, and to watch ourselves watching ourselves—thus cultivating our own inner observer.

During this period of introspection we can ask: Have I helped to create a warm climate in this room? Do participants seem comfortable? Have I been clear in my language and expectations? Have I made any remarks that would cause a person to feel trivialized or marginalized? How is my pace? Too fast? Too slow? Am I treating participants fairly, and are the voices of *both* women and men being heard? Are there any extreme gender role behaviors that place either women or men at a disadvantage? Are there any power plays going on here that might interfere with process?

As we develop into midwife leaders we will become more comfortable with chasms in time, much as the conductor of a musical composition who "knows the score" can endure a grand pause in the piece. The grand pause serves an important function: Musical sounds that follow it have a more emphatic quality, seeming even more pronounced because of the preceding void. The same phenomenon occurs in a well-conceived painting, because the "negative space" in the work enhances the subject; what is *not* on the canvas highlights the importance of what *is*. In like manner, a midwife leader knows that *what is not being said* in the group lays fertile groundwork for *what will be said*.

Table 5.1   The Sound of Silence: Stages in a Participant's Internal Process

By being patient and trusting the process of silence, leaders can provide an opportunity for empowerment, because during this time sensitive group members are doing some fancy mental and emotional footwork. This rapid internal activity typically involves an evolution from a short period of self-consciousness, through an awareness of one's own emotional readiness, to an assessment of the group's process, and then to a decision to act or not act. Listed below are some typical stages in a participant's internal process during periods of silence.

(1) *Quick mental check:* How might I respond right now? Nonverbally? Verbally? What gesture, comment, question, or other contribution could I make? How might I react to the speaker or become involved in this discussion?

(2) *Self-consciousness:* I'd like to say something, but what if it sounds stupid? If I speak up, will my remarks be appropriate, or might I be criticized by other group members or the leader? If I smile or make a face, will they think I'm agreeing/disagreeing?

(3) *Check on emotional readiness:* Right now I feel anxious, unsure, distrustful (or relaxed, confident, accepted) as a group member.

(4) *Risk-taking check:* How much do I trust others in this group? How much of myself do I want to reveal to them?

(5) *Group process check* [looking around the room]: Is anyone else talking right now? Is anyone *preparing* to speak (clearing throats, raising hands, or the like)? Can I respond nonverbally or interject my comments without distracting others or changing the subject?

(6) *Decision to act/not act:* At this moment, nobody else is talking or seems ready to talk, and my response or remark seems correct/appropriate (or incorrect/inappropriate) so I will/will not share myself. [At this point, if the participant has decided to break the silence and to be verbally involved in the group discussion, the following steps ensue.]

(7) *Getting attention:* The would-be participant takes an audible in-breath, raises her or his hand, or otherwise attracts the attention of either the leader or the group member who currently has the floor.

(8) *Action:* Agreeing, disagreeing, affirming others, offering a new idea, stating an opinion, asking for clarification, and so on.

During periods of silence, the gender-aware leader will try to pace the group process slowly enough so there is time for women as well as men to sequence through these internal stages comfortably. At this slower pace, the leader will have more time to recognize and affirm a variety of participants—especially the quieter ones—and thus give many diverse voices a chance to be heard.

O'Reilley (1989) encourages leaders to "change our relationship to time":

> Many of us hate silence, especially in the classroom. It is the teacher's ultimate nightmare: what if I can't fill fifty minutes? . . . Silence is powerful. Sometimes when students seem indisposed to answer a question, it is useful to be quiet. What will happen then? Let me tell you, anything can happen then. Silence opens the void. . . . If you can learn to live peaceably with silence and slow time, all sorts of openings occur.
>
> Speech out of silence has an entirely different quality. It may, for example, be heard. (p. 29)

As we have seen in this chapter, leader behavior can literally make or break a group member's opportunity to develop credibility with others and to speak in her or his own voice. Clearly, it is time for leaders to relinquish some control, trust the cycle of confirmation-evocation-confirmation, and become learners. This requires much patience and personal discipline, but we can learn to trust ourselves and our group members enough to step away from the familiar "show-and-tell" peacock mode and assume a "watch-and-ask" midwife mode that draws others out. When leaders become learners and learners become leaders, a synergy evolves that accelerates the learning process—the hierarchical model of leader-follower gives way to a weblike network of collaboration and connectedness. Indeed, at this juncture in history, our world is in such an explosion of awareness, both of our inner microcosms and our macrocosm, that such a collaborative model of mutual empowerment seems eminently imperative: "There is no place for followers in this world anymore. If we don't all become leaders and join together and do [our] bit . . . , we haven't got a chance" (Menrath, 1988, p. 32).

Honoring silence and encouraging dialogue are two techniques that can empower *all* members of a group, allowing everyone the opportunity to transcend the role of participant and actually become a leader. If we are to ask people to share our leadership role with us, what steps do we take? Furthermore, if the leaders to whom we currently turn for guidance are setting a poor example, how can we tactfully suggest that they adopt a less sexist style? In short, what does a gender-fair leader look like, and what makes this person tick?

The two leader profiles presented in Chapter 4 depicted responsible leaders—one on a public commission, the other on a university accreditation team. As we continue our examination of effective strategies in the next chapter, we will learn additional appropriate ways for both leaders and participants to speak up when they detect imbalance, injustice, or insult. Chapter 6 provides clues for activating numerous interventions, illustrated with examples from a wide variety of settings, including community environments, professional meetings, dialogues between colleagues, and social occasions. We continue our search for persons who demonstrate versatility, credibility, and compassion in their leadership.

Notes

1. The issue of the father—searching for, demythologizing, reconnecting with one's male parent—has become a significant theme in men's movement literature and academic symposia. See, for example, the work of Minnesota poet Robert Bly. See also Schwenger (1987) and Thornbury (1987), as well as references to presentations that I have cofacilitated on such issues as becoming an involved male parent (Palm & Van Nostrand, 1987), females facilitating males in parenting groups (Van Nostrand & Breitenbucher, 1989), and the sexual politics of mothering and fathering (Palm, Van Nostrand, & Schmid, 1989).

2. The "Multicultural Gender-Fair Curriculum Rule" has been approved by the Minnesota State Department of Education. Local boards of education were required to adopt plans for curriculum changes by June 1, 1990. The purpose of the rule is to help school districts develop and deliver curriculum that addresses the issues of cultural diversity, gender equity, and disability sensitivity. For information, contact State of Minnesota, Department of Education, Capitol Square Building, 550 Cedar Street, St. Paul, MN 55101.

3. This quote is reprinted by permission of the Minneapolis *Star Tribune*.

4. I have purposely not mentioned the gender of the presenters in the text in order to avoid prejudicing the reader. Presenter 1 is male, and Presenter 2 is female.

Part II

ACTION

Implementing Interventions

◀ 6 ▶

INTERVENTION IS NEEDED, BUT WHERE ARE THE CREDIBLE LEADERS?

The practice and structures by which a class of white males maintains privilege endanger not only women, but also people of color, the third world, children, and even life on earth. For survival and a just world we must listen to and heed the voices of the oppressed. . . . [As men], will our new concern with our inner lives . . . become one more tool for extending male privilege, dominance, self-involvement and woman-blaming? Or will we make it the means to know and engage with those who are not us?

(National Organization for Changing Men, *Ending Men's Violence*, 1990)[1]

A woman's scream pierces the sunlit morning as I walk to my downtown office. It is a high-pitched, tight, fearful scream: "NO! LEAVE ME ALONE! NO!" Across the street, in the parking lot next to a pizza joint, I see a red and white pickup, a man in the driver's seat, and beside the truck another man and a young woman. This second man—tall, dark, slender, perhaps in his 20s—is roughing up this small and very frightened woman, trying to shove her into the truck. Although I am defenseless—my arms laden with briefcases and workshop materials—something urges me to cross the street.

Seeing my approach, the assailant forcefully maneuvers the young woman away from the truck toward the restaurant's brick wall, between two parked cars.

Through the truck's open window I address the driver: "What's going on?"

"Oh," replies the driver nonchalantly, "he's just trying to get her to go with him, and she doesn't want to."

My worst suspicions confirmed, I find myself moving toward the young woman and man, compelled by some hidden force. I am a witness, amazed at my own fearlessness, and aware that I may also appear somewhat foolish. I plant my feet, stand my ground, and simply *witness*. Everything I ever taught, and learned, while facilitating assertiveness training workshops tells me to stay centered, stay grounded, use eye contact. Even though he is wearing glasses, I am very aware of the assailant's eyes—as dark as he is threatening.

The young woman's eyes are large and frightened; her face is blanched. Like a rabbit feeding at night by the driveway, captured momentarily by approaching headlights, she is frozen and encapsulated in time. I feel a bond with her; she is another woman, a sister, yet young enough to be one of my daughters. And she is in trouble.

The man, only inches from her, his mere proximity enough to inhibit and restrain her movements, begins a monologue of obscenities largely directed at me: "Keep the fuck your nose out of this. This is none of your goddamn business."

Just then I see, approaching from the county courthouse to the north, a prominent local attorney. Another witness? Possible support? I inch a few sidesteps toward the lawyer and, gesturing toward the pair, I whisper urgently, "I think there's an assault going on over here!" He walks over to the assailant, and—with his back toward me—asks a brief question that the assailant answers just as briefly and inaudibly. The attorney then exits the parking lot toward the pizza joint. So much for support.

Again I approach the attacker and his victim—I am simply unable to leave the scene. The bond I feel with the woman, my own rage, and the outrageousness of the situation have me firmly planted.

"Who the fuck do you think you are, sticking your nose in our business?" continues the assailant's diatribe.

"I'm concerned," I reply, amazed at my own calmness.

"What the fuck gives you the right to stand there and watch this?"

"I'm concerned," I repeat, continuing to look him in the eye, hoping I'm not boring him with my persistence.

The attacker continues his verbal abusiveness, becoming preoccupied with lambasting me, uttering every insult he can muster. His frustration is mounting; his voice grows louder, his dark eyes more fiery. I am aware that he could strike me, the young woman, or both of us at any moment. Still carrying my professional trappings, I realize I am ill equipped to protect myself.

I glance to my left to see if there is any trace of the attorney. Sure enough, peeking around the restaurant's facade, I see his pink-cheeked, inquisitive face.

"Keep your fucking nose out of this," the attacker continues, his body turned completely toward me now, totally preoccupied with his own ranting. I see the young woman glance around furtively, realizing her opportunity. Suddenly she turns and bolts for her life, dashing between parked cars, darting across the busy street toward the courthouse. Her assailant is scarcely aware she has departed as he nails me with his final question, one so ambiguous I am still haunted by its possible meaning: "*Where were you before, when all of this was going on?*"

I am momentarily taken aback. What does he mean? That he has beaten her many times before and wishes someone had stopped him then? That he *himself* was victimized and no one was there to protect him?

Too concerned with the whereabouts of the young woman to ask him to clarify his astounding question, I turn and see her fragile form disappear behind the courthouse.

I direct myself toward my office. The perpetrator walks over to the truck, climbs in next to his male companion, and the vehicle turns in the direction of the victim's escape route.

When I relate this episode, some listeners are full of free advice about What Should Have Been Done:

"Did you get the license plate number?"

"Why didn't the lawyer *do* something or at least call the police?"

"What about the truck driver—how could he just *sit* there?"

And the most cynical comment of all: "What good did you do? Domestic abuse situations are impossible, and she'll just go right back to him anyway."

Although there were many alternative measures that could have been taken, I realize that my being a witness and implementing an on-the-spot intercession was quite effective. Somehow the cycle of violence was interrupted long enough for the victim to leave the scene.

What seems even more significant is that the young man began to be more aware of, and to introspect about, the possible origins of his oppressive behavior. This out-of-control controller paused long enough to ask a question that caused a shift in his consciousness—and in mine—and a departure from his exploitive behavior. Even though he began by coercing, intimidating, and depersonalizing others, he then moved (in terms of the Male/Female Continuum, Figure 2.1) through a stage in which his anger surfaced, to a different plateau of listening, asking questions, and becoming increasingly introspective.[2]

There is no doubt that the attacker was blatantly out of line; he was committing an atrocity. He used threats of violence as "one more tool for extending male privilege, dominance, self-involvement and woman-blaming," an issue of concern to many in the men's movement. But what about the subtle sexism embedded in the lawyer's behavior, his tacit collusion in the attacker's overall strategy? What about his silent retreat to the sidelines, where he hung around covertly satisfying his curiosity as if the goings-on were a titillating sideshow? When one man witnesses a brother extending male privilege, shows no disapproval of this oppressive behavior, and actually lingers nearby to watch the behavior spin itself out, is this not a covert sanctioning of this very privilege?

Sexism by Default

It is obvious that the perpetrator's behavior belongs at the far end of the Male/Female Continuum under "violence and sexual exploitation." But the lawyer's behavior can also be found on the Continuum; he fits under the category of "discrimination" because, by his inaction, he also devalued the female victim. In his decision to "courteously" leave the scene, he demonstrated covert bias. He did not coerce the woman, but he condoned coercion. He did not beat the victim; rather, he beat a hasty retreat. The attorney exhibited sexism by default.

Many of us are like the attorney. We are not guilty of *bias by commission*—we do not verbally attack others or blatantly shove people around. But we may fall into the trap of *bias by omission*—we fail to intervene; we turn our backs and walk away.

The attorney's indifference is especially troublesome because he—like the assailant—is male, and men's willingness to challenge each other's misogyny is an essential component of gender-responsible leadership. As a community leader, he is supposedly a "decent" man. What is behind this "complicity of the decent man in acts of atrocity against women" (Dworkin, 1991)? Does the attorney believe that one man's violence is not another man's business?

All Men Benefit When One Woman Is Violated

There are "past and ongoing inequities and distortions" between the sexes, states William Doherty (1989), that "many men prefer to ignore. Men have many entitlements under the present gender arrangement," he continues, "and women overall have been on the short end of it." In Doherty's view, women will not find men credible until men begin to admit the enormous benefits they reap at women's expense:

> Men must willingly acknowledge our privileges and entitlements, and not just concede these matters defensively or pretend that we have not personally benefitted from them. (Entitlement can be as familiar as the air we breathe, and as difficult to see.) Failure to acknowledge these historical realities means that no meaningful dialogue between men and women is likely to occur. We will not be credible with women. (p. 3)

In some ways, the young assailant was more credible to me than was the lawyer—at least a rudimentary dialogue began between us. The attacker was willing to pause, look at, and verbalize a possible distortion in his present gender arrangement. It is not clear to me whether the lawyer detected any inequities or distortions, but his retreat would suggest that he found the attacker's exploitiveness within fairly acceptable bounds.

"The problem is, after all, men and male culture," Niessen-Derry reminds us, speaking from his vantage point as a leader who regularly confronts male batterers. We also remember his poignant admission, "Part of my process in becoming a 'feminist male' was learning how much I had to give up" (personal communication, 1989). For the lawyer or any other male to have empathized sufficiently with the female victim to have intervened on her behalf, he would have had to admit how much he and other men benefit every time a woman is roughed up and shoved around, and how this kind of violation serves to solidify further their own status and privilege.

Decent, gender-responsible men will not ignore male entitlement, but will name inequality. Such honesty may be exceedingly difficult, because to name inequity is to admit complicity, and admitting complicity means sacrificing status. Nevertheless, honest male-to-male confrontation is an absolutely crucial step toward credibility and colleagueship. "Why didn't the lawyer *do* something?" people asked. Why, indeed?

When I later described to a friend this entire parking-lot drama, including an account of the lawyer's hasty retreat, my friend gave quite a succinct assessment of the attorney's behavior: "That fink" was all he said, or needed to say. The attorney's behavior stands as a symbol of the ignorance and numbness to violence within each of us. In him we see every reluctant leader who witnesses discrimination and refuses to deal with it, who colludes in a system of dominance and subordinance without intervening, who blames victims or leaves them to fend for themselves, and whose bias by default ultimately reinforces male entitlement.

Our task as leaders—whether we are in parking lots or workshops, city streets or boardrooms—is to sharpen our sensitivities in order to detect bias, tighten our courage to name it, and hone our skills to implement interventions. We need to become "accomplices in awareness" and let perpetrators know: *Any* woman's oppression is definitely our business; coercive behavior is not acceptable in this group or in our community; we are watchers and witnesses—we are authentic and we act. When we take such action, no one will need to ask, Where are the responsible leaders?

Full Spectrum of Oppression:
It's Only a Matter of Degree

Although being a Samaritan against sexism is the purview of us all, we rarely witness such overtly oppressive behavior as that exhibited by the parking-lot assailant. If we keep our eyes and ears open, however, we *will* notice many less obvious, and thus much more insidious, behaviors that discount others. Like the lawyer's indifference, these actions are insidious because of their very subtlety: Why do those people have their backs turned toward me and what are they discussing? Why is information being withheld from me and others in this department? Why were no females appointed to this committee? Is there a threat behind what that person just said or did? As noted earlier, these covert maneuvers can be the most damaging because the persons involved are not always fully aware of the depth of the bias.

Subtle Bias: So Insidious, So Dangerous

A recent study at the University of Minnesota revealed that 56% of the female and 36% of the male undergraduates said they had been sexually harassed and that "the largest category of harassment was of the *mildest* form" ("U of M Sexual Harassment Study," 1990; emphasis added). This included "unwanted teasing, jokes, remarks or suggestive looks [that contributed] to a discriminatory environment." (Roughly 30% of the men reported being harassed by other males.) Women's Center Director Anne Truax, who wrote part of the report, stated:

> [This study] tells me that "baby" hasn't come as long a way as we'd hoped. . . . There is still a great deal of sexual discrimination, and it's the kind that's so ingrained, so unconscious that it's extremely difficult, not only to get rid of, but to identify in the first place. (p. 88)

The kind of disparagement Truax describes as ingrained and unconscious is what both victims and perpetrators may fear most, be the most ambivalent about, and have the most trouble identifying. Those who bear the brunt of such degradation may feel the way people do when they are just coming down with a virus. Things don't seem quite normal, but they can't diagnose exactly what is causing their discomfort and malaise.

Thus when a group member appears helpless, frozen, and intimidated, indications are that there is a malady afoot, and it is time to take a specimen of the situation—to "culture" the group's "culture." It is important for a leader to examine carefully all possible causal factors, including the leader's own sexism, because in many settings much of the discounting and devaluing that goes on is the result of very subtle, nearly invisible, but virulently pervasive forms of bias. Consider the following three examples of highly contagious subliminal sexism.

Example 1: No Woman Need Apply

A very capable woman, who has loyally served an organization for years, informs her CEO that she would like to run for the Board of Directors of the local Chamber of Commerce. Her boss cautions her that this is ill advised because, in their corporation, the privilege of applying to community boards of directors is reserved for only the "higher echelons" of management. This woman reports feeling very discouraged and frustrated; her initiative has been shot down.

Example 2:
"He tore up her honeymoon plans right in front of everyone!"

The mother of a young woman related this story to me:

You want to hear about sexism? I can give you an example of the kind of bias women experience in the workplace.

My daughter, who is only 24, started working for a large corporation. For a vacation-scheduling meeting in October, all employees were asked to submit to the boss—in writing—their vacation plans. Since she was to be married the following May, she submitted on a sheet of paper a plan that outlined the dates of her wedding and proposed honeymoon trip.

At that meeting, in front of other employees, the boss took this piece of paper and just tore it up! He just tore up her honeymoon plans right in front of everyone! Although she felt close to tears, my daughter held her own during the rest of the meeting. Then, afterward, she went to her boss's office, asked to speak with him, and told him to close the door. She went nose-to-nose with him, shook her finger in his face and [gave him a piece of her mind]: "Don't you ever do that again! Don't you ever treat me that way again!"

After this incident, she started keeping a personnel file on him, ready to record any more incidents.[3]

Is the boss's behavior a form of harassment? Many will say that his actions are a blatant, offensive, and illegal abuse of power. Others will blame the young woman, saying she was overreacting, the boss was just kidding, and boys will be boys. Some may even suggest, as did a few senators in the Clarence Thomas/Anita Hill hearings, that the victim is emotionally unstable. The diagnosis depends on which standard is used as a yardstick.

If our unit of measure is the progression of sexual harassment, this scale extends all the way from forcible rape, to unwelcome sexual advances, to blocking a person's passage through a doorway, to displaying offensive visual materials, to creating an environment that is "hostile, intimidating, or demeaning" (University of Wisconsin, 1990-1991, p. 7). But many observers start measuring halfway along the scale, ignoring such intangible guidelines as hostile environment. Insisting that psychological intimidation is insignificant, they choose to take action only when overwhelmed with evidence proving a person has been physically harmed. They perceive ripping up someone's work to be a boyish prank executed all in fun, and that the victim who complains has "lost her sense of humor."

"The notion that women's role in life is to be available for men's sexual amusement is pervasive in our society," explains attorney Lynn Schafran (1989b) in an article titled "Sexual Harassment Isn't Unusual; It's Routine." Because of this distortion, women may not be taken seriously when they report harassment; instead, they may be blamed for being "oversensitive."

The boss's action in this case is *definitely* harassment because it was threatening; it interfered with his employee's work performance, and it created a hostile, demeaning, and isolating working environment. Our responsibility, as authentic and credible leaders, is to take psychic violence seriously: to start measuring discrimination at the very beginning of the yardstick, and to put a stop to paper-shredding, woman-denigrating episodes before the virus spreads.

The sad reality in this case, as in the case of law professor Anita Hill, is that the burden of proof to diagnose and try to remedy the harassment rested with the victim. Although other males witnessed the honeymoon-plan shredding, they—like the attorney in the parking lot—took no action to confront the inequity. It is this sexism by default that gender-sensitive males are beginning to address.

Example 3:
"Why does she choose to get herself mistreated like this?"

A final alarming example of subtle bias emerged as I engaged in dialogue with a colleague, related here in Case 6.1.

CASE 6.1

Is Sauce for the Goose Also Sauce for the Gander?
Androcentric Bias and the Double Standard

I am engaged in conversation with another professional speaker, Herb, who lives in a neighboring state. Since we are both former public school teachers, Herb and I have much in common—we both present motivational workshops for educators and are also interested in promoting good self-concept in young people.

Herb believes humans are in charge of their own thoughts—we can change personal patterns if we just change our attitudes. Each of us is responsible for our own behaviors, he says. Herb describes his upcoming presentation for school administrators on this very subject to fire them up for the coming school year.

Herb: Let's talk about self-concept in young people. Take some 16-year-old girl, for example. She's been going out with this guy for three years, but he mistreats her and even beats her. But for three years, she keeps going out with him. And then later, at age 19, she even *marries* the guy! We've got to do something about changing the self-concept and behavior of kids like her so they won't get themselves into these situations!

Catharine: What about the guy? What about his behavior?

Herb [speaking more loudly and continuing on the same tack]: But why does she keep going out with him? He calls her up for a second date—she probably already knows he's not treating her right—and she says *yes!* Why does she say yes? And then she spends three years with this guy and eventually even *marries* him. She's responsible for her own behavior; she could make different choices. *So why does she choose to get herself mistreated like this?*

Catharine: It sounds to me as if you're blaming the victim. This boyfriend is responsible for his choices and his behaviors too: He is choosing to mistreat this woman.

Herb [raising his voice even more]: But why doesn't she speak up? Why doesn't she stop him? She should say NO to him when he calls. Why does she keep going out . . . ?

Catharine [interrupting in frustration]: That's not the point. The point is, he's beating her. He's choosing to mistreat her and he is responsible for his own behavior just as much as she is responsible for hers. If you and I are going into communities, giving speeches to educators about self-esteem, we'd better be fair and present both sides of the coin—ask them to look at the whole system. *This man gets by with his behavior because our system lets him get away with it.* [pause] If he were a school administrator, and she were a teacher being harassed, what should be done?

Herb [melting just a bit]: The teacher should speak up.

Catharine [feeling indignant]: What if she *is* being harassed, and what if she *has* spoken up, and what if *nothing* is being done? What if this teacher is afraid to be alone in her own classroom because of this administrator's harassment? What if she has filed a formal complaint, but he is still on the payroll? [I then describe such a situation in a nearby, but anonymous, school district.] What if the whole system protects violent males like this administrator and this student? What should be done then?

And what about consultants like you and me, who are hired to go in and "educate these educators"; how can we make a difference? How can we expect students to shape up, get confident, and defend themselves against battering boyfriends when, perhaps even in the same building in which they are supposedly being educated, their own principal may be a perpetrator of violence? Furthermore, how can you and I then give presentations to these same administrators suggesting that women are to blame for their own victimization?

The restrictive stereotyping, subtle maneuverings, public humiliation, and victim blaming in the examples above are not as harsh as physical assault, but these subtle put-downs form a daily pattern of harassment. They are miniassaults on a woman's self-esteem, somewhat like Chinese water torture, and they contribute

to the constant challenging of women's egos. In each example of
subtle bias a woman is categorized, criticized, trivialized, and
marginalized: She is not capable enough for the board of directors,
not worthy enough to have her plans respected, not uppity enough
to just say no to the batterer. The female is blamed while the oppressive system continues.

The above sexist scenarios—women being shunted aside, publicly
humiliated, and vehemently blamed—are all part of the "collusion
of dominance and subordinance" illustrated on the Male/Female
Continuum (Figure 2.1). As discussed earlier, the Continuum extends all the way from murder, battering, and other violence at
one end to mutual respect and shared power (colleagueship) at
the other. We could refer to movement along the Continuum as a
"gender role journey."

Gender Role Journeys

Both females and males are very defensive early on in their
journeys: The male who will *intimidate, touch,* or *tease* has a counterpart in the female who will *endure* or has *anger frozen inside.* The
male in a stage of *discrimination* corresponds to the female in a
stage of *manipulation;* the male who will *exclude* women or try to
avoid them is matched by the *seductress.* As each person becomes
less defensive, and willing to journey toward colleagueship, she
or he makes the *decision to learn.* This person then moves into the
"transition" phase, and it is in this phase that the real psychological work is done. In transition, men begin *listening and asking
questions* and become *increasingly introspective,* while women begin
to *acknowledge their own power* and to *stop introspection from freezing
[their] actions.*

Women Move First

Ideally, women and men would arrive at the transition phase
together, but according to Carol Pierce, "dominants never move
until subordinates start. A woman must be way ahead on her
journey before a man starts to move on his" (personal communication, 1990). We might even say we have a new kind of gender
gap here, a gap that is a cause of considerable tension between the

genders.[4] "It is this tension of some women moving along [the] Continuum far beyond specific men that forces these men to look at themselves," explain Pierce and Page (1990), and "the tension makes it difficult to stay connected" (p. 10). We live in a "very resistant time," according to Pierce:

> Women who journey far ahead of men are *punished constantly*. To be understood, and to avoid such punishment as avoidance, silence, unresponsiveness, or verbal abuse, women must continually "cycle back" on the Continuum to "catch" the male where he is. (personal communication, 1990)

As difficult as this gap may be for all those who make the journey, Pierce urges diligence, because "colleagueship is never assumed until the work is done in this transition phase" (personal communication, 1990).

The examples in this chapter vividly illustrate Pierce's contention that when subordinates move, the collusion abates somewhat: When the victim ran from the parking lot, her assailant had no one to abuse. When I challenged my sexist colleague Herb with the words, "What about the guy's behavior. . . . It sounds to me as if you're blaming the victim," I was refusing to collude with his misogynist attitudes. And when the young employee went nose to nose with her paper-shredding boss, she was refusing to acquiesce to a dysfunctional system of coercion and intimidation.

Men Resist Because of Their Entitled Position

While many females are moving beyond subordinate responding, many males who find themselves left behind on the other side of the gender gap seem determined to retain a dominant position. Because "people try to maintain the status quo when they benefit from it" (Ridgeway, 1983, p. 199), and because it is not in the interest of *any* privileged group to change, these males seek to serve their own self-interest by ignoring their own entitlement, downplaying the privilege of other males, and doing nothing that would dilute either.

Other men may recognize women's second-class status only to exploit its more sensational aspects and to continue to blame the victim: Tsk, tsk, did you hear about the poor gal who got herself beat up in the parking lot? About that meeting when the boss tore up that new employee's honeymoon plans? About that lady law-yer who followed her boss to another government agency even though he was allegedly harassing her? Why do women choose to get themselves mistreated like that?

Social Work Denial

Still other men may take their concern a step further and actively protest violence, by marching in a "Take Back the Night" demonstra-tion, for example.[5] They may be very vocal about women's plight without ever dealing with the antecedents of, their own perpetuation of, and even their own victimization by, the patriarchal system that causes that very oppression. These demonstrators, states Jim Lovestar, may be really hurting underneath, but on the surface they are "going through the motions in their public life, while in their private life, they're in denial." Lovestar, former chairman of the Twin Cities Men's Center (Minneapolis/St. Paul), calls this stance "social work denial" (personal communication, April 1992). That is, a man who has been victimized or abused may cover up his own hurt by working for "politically correct" organizations: He may be a do-gooder for a righteous cause without ever exam-ining what pain motivated his interest in the first place. For example, a consultant might give presentations on the low self-esteem of high school females without ever examining the origins of his *own* poor self-concept; or a group of men would sit on the board of directors of a rape crisis center, never admitting to themselves—or to each other—that every one of them had been a victim of childhood sexual abuse.[6] None of these men would have reached the level of honesty temporarily attained by the parking-lot assailant, who at least began fleetingly to examine "all" that was "going on" in his own past.

Men who fight for good causes, suggests Tom Witt (1990), are not believable unless these men demonstrate an ability to criticize and a "commitment to resist the patriarchal value system" (p. 5). Defining patriarchy as "social organization marked by supremacy of males," Witt makes it clear that male unwillingness to compro-mise for fear of appearing "soft" conspires with the equating of violence with virility to create a system governed by insecure males who refuse to dialogue or negotiate, insisting that "macho" is best. When people like this are in power, we can have a real problem on our hands:

> Thus we have a group of people who are profoundly insecure, with poorly developed nonviolent conflict resolution skills and a deep-rooted sense of entitlement, who feel a need to prove themselves through aggression, achievement and competition. These people, who are the least equipped to deal with absolute power, are then put in position of absolute power, from the heads of families to the heads of nations. (Leghorn, quoted in T. Witt, 1990, p. 4)[7]

How can men learn ways to resist and reform their own patriarchal systems? Perhaps the place to start is with behavior change—perhaps a man's willingness to analyze his own (and other men's) privilege comes later. When the parking-lot assailant, insensitive boss, and the consultant Herb encountered resistance, each man showed just the slightest shift in behavior: Each began to *listen*. We do not know whether any one of these males was actually willing to acknowledge his assumptions about male entitlement. All we know is that each modified his actions to a very subtle degree.

At this point, we again resurrect the nagging question: Why does the burden of intervention fall on victims? There were males who witnessed these female-shoving, paper-shredding incidents. Why did they not intervene? Imagine the impact a few words from a concerned brother could have had in the parking lot or the vacation-scheduling meeting. What if the lawyer had said, "You're mistreating her!" or even, "Can I help you?" What if a male employee had addressed the paper shredder with the low-impact intervention, "I'm uncomfortable with what's happening here"; or, "The way I read our policy manual, this organization's values do *not* include the degradation of women." These missed opportunities lead many to assume that men do not intervene—in fact, appear not even to notice—because to do so would require them to fight against their own ultimate, systematic self-interest: the collective subordination of women.

Many men continue to be unwilling to examine, much less to acknowledge, how they benefit by women's oppression. There is still strong pressure on men to "stand up to her"; "Don't let her push you around"; "Don't listen to all that 'feminist' stuff about women's rights—what about men's rights?" Defensiveness of this sort precludes meaningful dialogue that could enrich the lives of both women and men, a dialogue that will not be possible, in the view of some, unless men stop ignoring the distortions (Doherty, 1989) and show commitment to resist the patriarchal value system (T. Witt, 1990).

We have seen how crucial it is for each of us to heal our own hurt before we try to help others. Any person stuck in the social work denial stage must move beyond that stage. Such healing may be an important first step toward less distorted relationships. But what about the next step? After the introspective stage, are men then willing to stop acting like victims, acknowledge their privilege, and take proactive steps to treat women as respected equals?

There is a disturbing "men's rights" element that urges men not to succumb to women's agenda, but to defend themselves against any criticism of their actions. After all, these men ask, are men not oppressed too? The thesis that males are suffering victims in the war between the sexes, suffering under women's criticism of their behavior, is an absurdity in the view of Charles Niessen-Derry (1991a):

> The absurdity of a man talking about men's rights is lost in the environment where those rights are the norm, often exercised at women's expense. . . . Twenty-two women were murdered [in 1990] in Minnesota. . . . One in four women are beaten regularly and half to two-thirds are assaulted at least once. . . . One in three women will be raped and all women live under a state of siege due to these assaults. The "enemy" . . . is men. . . .
>
> This attempt to silence women's reality of men's oppression of them is the most consistent tactic used by male culture and individual men to maintain their privileged position.
>
> . . . Men are not in control of every major cultural institution by accident. We maintain that power through distinct and accepted forms of violence and coercion. It's time for men to *stand with* feminist women and end our sexist oppression and violence against them, rather than "*standing up to* them." Women have experienced men "standing up to them" for too long. Maybe it's time we sat down and listened instead. (emphasis added)

Listening was the positive first step taken by the assailant, the boss, and Herb; it is the absolutely crucial step each man can take to begin journeying beyond defensiveness and move into the transition stage. When a man is denying and defensive, it is an especially "resistant time," as Pierce (1990) explains. A woman in a stage of extreme anger and a man in a stage of extreme defensiveness create a difficult and most frustrating gap. Upon learning I was designing interventions for confronting such gender-driven power imbalances, Pierce said:

> Men need to see their behavior and recognize what they're doing. We need books which make available skills to call men on their behavior, interventions to guide them toward more desirable behaviors and *show them what they need to do.* (personal communication, 1990)

Action: Notice and Intervene

That leaders need to "call men on their behavior" is a suggestion echoed by psychologist and author Nancy Goldberger (1989). Addressing an audience of psychologists and educators, Goldberger explained how important it is to intervene in both personal and professional settings when one detects an environment detrimental to women, or processes during which women's voices are not being heard:

> Men don't notice whether women *do* or *don't* speak. . . . It is important to make this discrepancy overt and not to just fall silent. For example, at a dinner party the men might be doing all the talking and the women all the listening. A woman might think, How long is this going to go on? She might speak up later saying, "Did anyone notice or *care* that we women weren't saying a damn thing?" A male might reply, "Why didn't you speak up? We're not stopping you!"

Goldberger then challenged the audience to fulfill their responsibilities as professionals and as leaders:

> We must notice and comment on the group process. Say, for instance, that you serve on a committee discussing the dissemination of a project initiated and researched by women. The females have done *all* the work and they are the experts. During the meeting, the males turn to each other for "expert" advice, ignoring the females in

spite of the fact that it is the women's project. *We must notice and intervene; we must comment.*

We professionals must foster an environment for women in which men don't take power or interrupt. *Don't worry about protecting the discussion. Stop it and help those people dominating the conversation to see that they can learn by being silent.*

Following Goldberger's suggestions, how can we notice and comment or notice and intervene to help dominators see that they can learn something? What are some simple guidelines one can follow so that when bias is confronted, the strategy is initiated appropriately?

Basic Guidelines for Intervention

An intervenor can follow two simple guidelines when confronting others about sexism and trying to motivate them to modify oppressive behavior:

(1) The intervenor is nonjudgmental and respects the integrity of the process.
(2) The intervenor uses few words and begins the intercession at a minimal level.

Using earlier case studies as examples, let us examine each of these recommendations in turn.

Guideline 1: The intervenor is nonjudgmental and respects the integrity of the process. For example, during the public meeting of the government commission, when the member threw his pencil, the female member followed this guideline. She first spoke with her peers, and then requested time on the next meeting's agenda to discuss group process. Her initial interventions were nonjudgmental because she used *naming* rather than *blaming*. She described the disruptive and depersonalizing event and indicated that she prefers a less confrontational style. The value of naming is that we give an opinion "to which we are entitled" rather than making a "personal judgement on the receiver," which would be *labeling* (Pierce & Page, 1990, pp. 36-37). Labeling is usually unproductive for three reasons: It is disrespectful, it imposes our values or perspectives on others, and—most significant—it increases defensiveness.

Notice also that this commission member initially used a short, self-disclosing statement: "I did not appreciate the way you spoke to me at the public meeting." Such verbal simplicity conforms to the next guideline.

Guideline 2: The intervenor uses few words and begins the intervention at a minimal level. In the parking lot, when I addressed the attacker, I used only two words: I'm concerned. This sort of simple "I statement" is called, in assertiveness training parlance, a *minimal assertion*: I disagree, I prefer, I care. My personal term for this method is *low-impact intervention*; that is, in order to transcend interpersonal barriers, the intervenor communicates in as non-confrontive a manner as possible. So, in spite of the attacker's mounting frustration, I repeated my low-impact assertion, trying not to alienate or escalate. By simply reiterating, "I'm concerned," I used the repetitive method known as the "broken record technique" (Smith, 1975).[8]

I tried to respect both the assailant and myself, both his process and my process. However, to heed Goldberger's admonition, I did not worry about "protecting the discussion" between the perpetrator and victim; nor did I try to protect the discussion between him and me. I did not try to minimize, cover up, or ignore the oppressive dynamics of either interaction. Rather, I tried to enter the encounter at a low-impact level, use minimal verbalization, and name my own concern rather than blaming the perpetrator for his violence. Although I was indignant, the perpetrator saw mostly compassion. In terms of the Male/Female Continuum, some "new dynamics" were happening between us: He began listening and asking questions and became increasingly introspective, which moved him (temporarily, at least) into the transition phase. He was asking for feedback and we were both becoming more aware of process—characteristics of the state of colleagueship.

Sensitive Leadership and Compassionate Precision

The interventions used in the parking lot, by the official in the committee meeting, and in my dialogue with Herb all demonstrate the quality of "compassionate precision," a quality taught in a training program in professional leadership at the Oasis Center in Chicago. Those who lead with compassionate precision, according to the program brochure, will learn to "combine the precision of clear knowledge, the guidance of intuitive insight and the strength of compassion," skills that can help professionals lead "groups of diverse people, in diverse settings, toward any ethical goal" (Oasis Center, 1989, p. 37). An ethical goal is defined as one that fosters *integrity*:

> All worthwhile leading rests upon insightful perception of, and informed response to, the ever-changing dynamics of the live situation. . . . *The best techniques are those developed during a unique situation and used but once.* (emphasis added)

The program description continues: "[This technique of] elegant *precision* focused and informed by loving *compassion* . . . is difficult to practice, but simple to define:

> *Precision:* knowing exactly where to go next;
> *Compassion:* seeing through the barriers which cause alienation."

When we use this elegant precision in our leadership, there will be an authentic melding between the happening, our sensitivity to the oppressiveness of the situation, our insightful ability to see through the alienating barriers, and our action to remedy the inequity. Some sort of remediation may even occur; someone may even wonder, Where were you before, when all of this was going on?

Such a stance is a form of dissent, and it is a potent antidote to an established dysfunctional system, whether the system involves assault and victimization in a personal relationship, intimidation and degradation in a corporation, or even oppression and disenfranchisement of a people by their own government.

Some of the dissidents active in China at the time of the June 1989 Tiananmen Square massacre showed this synchronicity of awareness, authenticity, and action. Among the most prominent of dissidents was Fang Lizhi, who was given—in absentia—a First Amendment Award for his embodiment of the principles of free speech. Fang Lizhi "could not but speak the obvious"; he dared to "say the unsayable," according to those who described his courage.[9] In his behavior was no moment of "fear, reflection, and censorship" but a "direct line from thoughts to action."

Praxis

This clear channel from theory to practice, from thoughts to action, is termed *praxis*. Used in the context of feminist pedagogy, praxis means that we seek "to foster an active sense of agency and to connect ideas to liberating action" (Shrewsbury, 1984; cited in Bell, 1987, p. 79). If we value gender equity, we will find *immediate* ways to actualize our values and encourage such immediacy in others. One of my students describes her action plan:

> When I suspect sexism or feel put down, I'm going to say something right at that moment like, "This conversation doesn't feel right to me." I'm not going to deny my feeling or let the chance slip away— *I'm going to speak up right then.*

As we engage in this spontaneous process, such phrases as "I'm concerned," "The point is, he's beating her," "I did not appreciate the way you spoke to me at that meeting," and "Don't you ever treat me that way again!" will become second nature. Precise, well-timed interventions in parking lots, committee meetings, and workplace settings will become everyday, effortless occurrences.

When to Intervene?

How will we recognize whether a situation requires an outside intervenor or whether people should be left alone to work out the imbalance themselves? The Male/Female Continuum provides a clue: When we observe that the behaviors of women or men are directly opposite one another on the Continuum, an outside intervention will probably be necessary. For example, in the parking lot, the young woman was frozen because she was stuck exactly opposite, and was in direct collusion with, the attacker's intimidation and harassment. Because each person was entrapped in collusion, neither could envision colleagueship, and the help of a third party was therefore necessary.

On the other hand, when women and men are at different stages on the Continuum, they can probably rectify the imbalance themselves, because one of them can cycle back to challenge the other. For example, in the pencil-throwing incident, the female commission member is further along in her journey. She envisions women and men having more flexible role options and she is able to initiate change. Because her awareness demands a more collegial position, she is able to return to the male member's level and speak in a manner to be understood.

Although all of the above examples depict females as being further along on their journeys and having to cycle back to catch the males where they are, this role can be played by males as well. Men who support equality and mutual empowerment can cycle back and challenge women's collusion: "Could you be more direct about your wishes—you can be more assertive with me!" or, "I know you're angry about something; please give me some honest feedback!" But most of all, men can challenge other males: "You have no right to beat her!" or, "I find your behavior in this meeting very offensive."

As men accept the concept of mutual empowerment, colleagueship will become reality. Men will be more credible not only to women, but also to other enlightened men. Then more meaningful inter- and intragender dialogues can begin. Each person will individually make a decision to learn, and the gender gap will begin to narrow.

The course of action recommended here is an ambitious one. For women as well as for men, gender-responsible leadership requires not only that we be willing to deal with our own historical hurts, but that we also be sufficiently indignant about injustice perpetrated upon others to avoid colluding in it. Such indignation suggests that we go beyond the question, Why does this individual allow herself or himself to be mistreated? We need to move to a new level of inquiry:

- Why does that perpetrator feel entitled to exploit that victim?
- What system allows that perpetrator to continue such oppressive behavior?
- What part do I play in that system?
- How can I stop my collusion?
- Is intervention appropriate? If so, what could I say?

If minimal assertions such as "I'm concerned" or "We must deal with our conflict" can be so effective in such extreme cases of female disempowerment, it would seem that all one would have to do when encountering a sexist professor, harassing boss, or demeaning committee member would be to plant one's feet and face the offender in confident, patient silence. However, we all know that more forceful interventions are often necessary.

In Chapter 7 we will examine nine categories of intervention, including limit setting, abrupt interventions, and other more confrontive strategies. Each strategy is demonstrated in the context of a practical situation needing remediation, and is shown in combination with other techniques that enhance the effectiveness. The difference between *direct* and *indirect* strategies will be addressed, and I will demonstrate why procrastination—delaying an intervention until a more opportune time—is sometimes beneficial. Then, as we examine the final case study, we will see that it provides a comprehensive capstone to the major concepts found throughout this volume.

Notes

1. This quote is from a brochure distributed at the 15th National Conference on Men and Masculinity, Oglethorpe University, Atlanta, Georgia, May 31-June 3, 1990. The conference was sponsored by the National Organization for Changing Men (NOCM), now known as the National Organization for Men Against Sexism (NOMAS). "Men Stopping Violence is an organization dedicated to ending violence against women by confronting the social norms that support it" (NOCM, 1990). For more information, contact NOMAS, 798 Penn Avenue, Box 5, Pittsburgh, PA 15221. For more about male violence and NOMAS, see Diane Mason (1990).

2. I am grateful to Carol Pierce, coauthor of *The Male/Female Continuum* (Pierce & Page, 1990), for clarifying concepts and language from her book that are used throughout this chapter.

3. The boss in question was subsequently terminated from his position after numerous complaints about harassment were filed by other employees. Because the targets of his taunts were men as well as women—fat and thin, gay and straight—his behavior now appears to have been not solely gender biased, but that of an "equal-opportunity bigot."

4. The term *gender gap* traditionally refers to the differences in female and male values as represented in voting patterns, for instance, in the 1984 U.S. national elections. Here, *gender gap* is used to describe the disparity between women's and men's awareness of inequality or readiness to change. The term could also describe

the wide discrepancy between numbers of female and male students enrolled in traditionally male subjects such as mathematics; see the discussion in Chapter 4.

5. "Take Back the Night" marches/demonstrations are held in communities across the United States and internationally to protest violence against women on the streets and in their homes. These events are a "symbolic way for women to reclaim our power," according to Jane M. Olsen, M.A., Women's Center director, St. Cloud State University (personal communication, May 18, 1992).

6. This example of social work denial—male victims serving on boards of directors of women's organizations—is a true-life case: I attended a male-facilitated conference presentation during which every person on the panel, to a man, admitted that he had been a victim of sexual abuse and had been trying to resolve his rage by volunteering to work on behalf of female victims.

7. The purpose of Witt's article, titled "Sexism and Militarism," is to show the "connections between war, masculinity, and the oppression of women." In this passage, Witt quotes author and lecturer Liz Leghorn (the original source of her words is not given).

8. The broken record technique, described by Smith (1975), is based on the premise that "calm repetition—saying what you want over and over again—teaches persistence." According to Smith's "Glossary of Systematic Assertive Skills" (in his book), practicing this technique "allows you to feel comfortable in ignoring manipulative verbal side traps, argumentative baiting, irrelevant logic, while sticking to your desired point" (pp. 301-302). ("Argumentative baiting" seems an accurate description of tactics tried by the parking-lot assailant with whom I used this method.)

9. Fang Lizhi was given the First Amendment Award because he exemplified the principles of free speech. This presentation, accompanied by a panel discussion, was broadcast on *The New American Gazette*, National Public Radio, June 9, 1990.

◖ 7 ◗

APPROPRIATE INTERVENTIONS

How to Choose, Implement, and Evaluate Intervention Techniques

I had to intervene. I couldn't go on lecturing about how men oppress women and have oppression happening before my very eyes. I had to say something.

(Charles Niessen-Derry, facilitator of groups for male batterers)

You have to help me—tell me when I step over the line. I just jump into these roles without thinking. I feel silly, and I'm really sorry. I'm glad you got upset because it made me wake up.

(male graduate student to female graduate student)

In a previous chapter we found ourselves in two very different situations in which women were disempowered. Our first encounter was with a parking-lot attacker who treated a woman as something to shove around. We then observed a pencil-throwing commission member who treated his peer as though she were stupid and incompetent. In spite of the varying degrees of real or implied violence in these two situations, and the fact that the dominance represents very different stages on the Male/Female Continuum, the intervenors who confronted the offenders used amazingly similar tactics. Each intervenor (a) respected the process and the person(s) involved in the incident and (b) interceded at a minimal level, using just a few words.

Sometimes, however, such minimal, entry-level techniques are not strong enough to be effective. Sometimes our "few words" are not heard, not taken seriously, or —worse—are met with even greater aggression. When we encounter such resistance, we may find that we need to escalate to a more confrontive level of intervention. *Escalation* is a process by which we assert ourselves as simply as possible at first, and—if unsuccessful—then initiate a graduated series of stronger and stronger messages.

In Table 7.1, nine suggested intervention strategies are sequenced from least to most confrontive. Phrases enclosed in quotation marks are the exact words used during one of the real-life episodes described in this book. Readers are requested to submit, using the Reader Response Form (Appendix A), additional ideas for interventions that have been field tested in various settings.

The versatile leader who is able to implement a wide variety of interventions is well equipped to cope with bias, bigotry, and sexism in all their guises. A variety of techniques are provided in the three main sections of this chapter. The first of these sections details the nine techniques shown in Table 7.1, explaining each strategy's purpose, offering one or more examples, and showing the benefit/outcome of intervening. The second section illustrates ways to *combine* some of these interventions, synergistically increasing their effectiveness. These concepts are then synthesized in the final section in the timely testimony of a graduate student.

Nine Intervention Tactics

Descriptive Intervention

Purpose

We use *descriptive intervention* when we wish to be "reporters": merely to observe an interaction and give an account of what we perceive. By commenting on what is happening without criticism—*naming*, not *blaming*—we demonstrate our respect for the participants and the integrity of their process. The guest lecturer in Chapter 1 who confessed, "I gave away my power" used, among other less effective tactics, a descriptive intervention; her experience is summarized below.

Example

In a presentation for a college class, a female guest lecturer interacts almost exclusively with the female students (who are in the majority), while the males—one of them black—isolate themselves in the corner, sitting in hostile silence. During most of the discussion the males do not participate, but when the African-American man is finally the first to speak, the lecturer, after a bit of indirectness and sarcasm ("At last we heard from a male"), says, *"Up to now the males have not shared themselves, and I'm very aware of that."*

Benefit/Outcome

The benefit of a descriptive intervention is that it raises awareness. When we describe what we perceive, participants know that we are "tracking" the group dynamics. Since we are trying to describe without judgment, no particular individual feels blamed, and more members of the group may take responsibility for what is happening.

Nurturing/Empathic Intervention

Purpose

When a leader nurtures and shows empathy for someone, it helps that individual to feel more accepted, supported, and psychologically safe. This technique is a tremendously effective way to reinforce any person who is making an effort to be more gender fair, taking risks to be more self-disclosing, or becoming aware of—and admitting to—being biased.

I had an opportunity to use a nurturing intervention at a social gathering. Even though my new friend displayed a possibly prejudiced point of view, I chose to praise his *awareness* of this bias, rather than to be critical of the opinion itself.

Example

I am conversing at a social gathering with a man named Bill, whom I have just met.[1] We are discussing a recent news item describing how female students at an all-women's college protested the institution's efforts to become coeducational.

Table 7.1   Gender-Responsible Interventions

When a leader detects bias and decides to intervene, the choice of which intervention to use depends on the situation. Sometimes discrimination is so blatant or sexism is so out-of-bounds that an *abrupt* or *limit-setting* strategy is necessary. At other times, the bias seems to arise out of the unwitting offender's ignorance or lack of awareness; in these cases it helps to show some measure of understanding, using an *empathic* intervention. Patience is important here, because the offender is just beginning to be sensitive about (or willing to admit ignorance of) issues of gender equity.

The strategies listed below are arranged from *least* to *most* confrontive; the language of most of these interventions is excerpted directly from case studies presented in this book.

(1) *Descriptive intervention:* Name, don't blame; report on what is observed or perceived; try to raise awareness without judging.

I notice . . . . I perceive . . . . I am aware that . . . . It appears to me that this is happening . . . . "There is a very strange dynamic going on here."

(2) *Nurturing/empathic intervention:* Show support, understanding, and acceptance for the other person's position (this helps build both individual and group trust).

You must be uncomfortable when . . . . You seem to understand women's reality. I appreciate the way you . . . . You have my support. "Thank you for sharing." "It's refreshing to see your level of awareness." "I like what you just said."

(3) *Humorous intervention:* Use humor, lighthearted teasing; temporarily *deflect* the sexism so it will *reflect* back on the perpetrator.

You can't be serious . . . . Give me a break . . . . You may call me "Lizzie" if I can call you "Bobby." "Affirmative action won't come in your lifetime? Are you really *that* old?"

(4) *Self-disclosing intervention:* Reveal your feelings, opinions, and personal point of view.

I feel . . . . I disagree . . . . I care . . . . "I really resent that." "I'm concerned." "I feel uncomfortable—I feel patronized."

(5) *Inquiring/fact-finding intervention:* Gather facts; seek and contribute hard data; try to understand other person's perspective, based on

all available facts. (This clarification process may involve informing and educating the other person.)

Tell me more . . . . Are you aware of these data? What brought you to that conclusion? "Could you tell us where you got your statistics?" "What about recent research?" "Will you please clarify what you mean?"

(6) *Transformational intervention:* Envision positive change; make creative, practical request or suggestion for improvement in group process. (May require group consensus to be implemented successfully.)

I have a suggestion. Perhaps this way would work better. What about this method? "Could we please change this seating arrangement?" "Let's put the outline on the chalkboard and all work through it together."

(7) *Limit-setting/disciplinary intervention:* Lay out definite ground rules; delineate parameters and set clear boundaries; let the offender know exactly why her or his behavior is inappropriate or discourages mutually respectful relationships.

This is what I expect . . . . There are certain conditions/ behaviors/remarks that I do not tolerate. We don't do that in this institution. "We all need to be sensitive to one another as well as [to] ourselves." "I don't teach in such a climate." "Your confrontational style does not move us forward—it's not task-oriented behavior." "Don't categorize my answers!"

(8) *Consensus intervention:* Activate group energy; encourage group members to "sense [bias] together" and to be mutually responsible for confronting it.

The group feels . . . . We have all noticed that . . . . What can we do about this? As we have discussed . . . . "We must deal with our conflict." "Are we getting anywhere?" "Why don't you all turn around and look at him."

(9) *Abrupt intervention:* Be spontaneous, immediate (usually reserved for the most blatant sexism).

Please stop that! That is enough—no more! "Don't you ever treat me that way again!" "Bite your tongue!" "Did anyone notice or care that the women weren't saying a damn thing?" "Listen to your people, your employees—listen to what they're saying!"

continued

Table 7.1 Continued

Important Points to Remember About Interventions

(1) *Begin the intervention at a minimal level.* When first approaching an offender, it is best to follow the preliminary steps recommended in Chapter 6:

Respect the person and the process
Use few words, beginning at a "low-impact" level.

Only after observing these entry-level procedures should one then escalate to more forceful strategies.

(2) *Use direct, honest intervention language.* Interventions should be carried out in as direct and unambiguous a manner as possible. Indirect interventions (using sarcasm, manipulation, hurtful humor, backbiting, and other "double messages") are ambiguous and may cause the receiver to misinterpret and distort your purpose. For example, saying "Your behavior really bothers me" (direct) is more clear than "Do you act this way in *every* committee meeting?" (indirect).

The effective leader respects persons and their process, initiates interventions at a minimal level, and uses straightforward communication. In addition, the leader can employ each of the nine strategies above in one or both of these ways:

(3) *Combine interventions.* For greater impact, blend two or more intervention techniques. For example, try an empathic comment before escalating to more confrontive remarks: "You may disagree with our course content, but I notice you keep showing up for class every week."

(4) *Delay an intervention.* Although most tactics are best initiated spontaneously at the very moment bias is suspected, a strategy can be activated after the fact: "Dr. Jones, I didn't feel comfortable raising the issue of your harassing behavior when it occurred last month, but I'd like to discuss it now."

Whether a leader uses an intervention singly or in combination with others, if the strategy is direct and honest, and initiated at a low-impact level, it has a better chance of being heard and well received by the listener.

Bill: I feel like the female students were "male bashing." I mean, the way I interpret the press coverage, the women overreacted. They were wearing T-shirts and carrying signs that said things like "Better Dead Than Coed" and "Don't Let the Rape of Women's Education Happen Here" [Kelly, 1990].[2]

Catharine: Do you see any merit to the college's remaining an all-female school? I mean, there are even colleges in our own neighborhood that have remained single-sex institutions.[3]

Bill: Women are going to have to live and work with men in the real world eventually. They may as well study side by side with men in college.

Catharine: Some of the articles I read cited research demonstrating that women develop self-confidence and leadership skills more readily if they don't have to compete with men in the classroom. What about that?[4]

Bill [modifying his position a bit]: You have to understand, because I am a male, I react to situations first as a *male* and then later as a *whole person.* I react first from my *gut* and then later, sometimes after reflection, from my *head.* My male, gut reaction is, These women are really out to get men; this is really male-bashing. Then I become more rational and say to myself, "Maybe the female students are not *really* against men—they just want a good education."

Catharine: I like what you just said. I think you show a lot of awareness of your own process, and I appreciate the way you can stand back and look at your own biases that way. Where did you learn that?

Bill: Well, I didn't start out that way. I began to be more aware of my own biases about five years ago when I met my wife-to-be, who had served as president of the local chapter of NOW, the National Organization for Women.

Catharine: It's really refreshing to see that level of awareness.

Bill: Thanks.

Benefit/Outcome

It is very important to give credit where credit is due. Just as Bill gives credit to his wife for educating him about bias, he needs to be given credit for acknowledging it. Leaders can be especially helpful when they reinforce persons who share their evolutionary struggle toward gender fairness. A nurturing intervention that utilizes a compliment or other reinforcer is an effective way to demonstrate appreciation and empathy for this struggle.

Humorous Intervention

Purpose

Humor is a very effective way to *deflect* sexism, suggests management psychologist Barbara Mackoff, discussing humor in the workplace. Through the use of comicality, we hold up a mirror to sexism, turn it around, and *reflect* it back in a lighthearted way. One of Mackoff's examples is cited by business columnist Dick Youngblood (1990b), in an article titled "The Key to Women Moving Up Is Know [*sic*] Laughing Matter":

> Elizabeth, a businesswoman, . . . was having lunch with a client who persisted in calling her Lizzie. Rather than making an emotional issue out of the patronizing behavior, she simply quit calling the man Robert and started calling him Bobby.
> "Several Bobbys later," Mackoff reported, "he said, 'Oh, you prefer to be called Elizabeth, don't you?' " (p. 8D)

This kind of "deflecting/reflecting" intervention may involve not only humor, such as that used by the businesswoman above, but even teasing or other roundabout strategies. Humor is valuable because it helps lighten up the process, providing a breather or a moment of comic relief. However, since it is indirect, humor can be dangerous, because we often use it when we are adamant, ambivalent, or embarrassed about something; perhaps that is why sex, race, religion, and politics are frequently the subjects (and objects) of jokes. When we are oblique, our messages are open to misinterpretation, and so we need to use humorous interventions judiciously.

Example

I am attending a meeting at a university. In this particular institution, there are very few females who hold the position of department chair or dean. After our meeting, some of us informally discuss how concepts in this volume might be used to address such inequities. "Well," says a male faculty member to me, "we could certainly use some of the ideas from your book on this campus. We have problems here, and there's a need for some changes—for example, in the area of affirmative action. But the change won't come in my lifetime."

Upon hearing his remark, I experienced that old sinking feeling, but I did not respond. Once again I was hearing discouraging words to the effect that, This is just the way things are and there isn't much anybody, certainly not *I*, can do about it. This man's bias is of the genre described earlier by an administrator at another large university:

> [Some leaders] are examples of the perpetuation of subtle bias: [They know] the issues but think "that's just the way it is." . . . Males must be affirming of change, but by refusing to tackle issues, they thereby perpetuate them.

Later, while leaving this meeting, I brainstormed with another consultant about possible ways one might respond to remarks such as the professor's. My colleague suggested this humorous intervention: "*Affirmative action won't come in your lifetime? Are you really that old?*"

Benefit/Outcome

The professor seems to indicate that affirmative action is not his responsibility—none of his business. However, the consultant's technique, were it to be implemented, would refuse to let him off the hook. Again, the value of using humor and other gently teasing methods is that we raise awareness in a roundabout manner. We let others know that we are cognizant of their prejudice, but we express ourselves using more oblique methods. Such indirectness is often more effective than the abrupt expression of anger and hostility, which can sometimes raise the defenses of your typical "knee-jerk sexist," to use columnist Youngblood's term. As an alternative, psychologist Mackoff suggests, "If you invite him to look in the mirror and see the silliness of his comments . . . you may render the office dinosaur extinct" (in Youngblood, 1990b, p. 8D).

Although my friend's hypothetical intervention was never actually activated, its benefits are obvious: The person initiating such a strategy is able to assert her or his values in a manner that promotes and preserves a playful, collegial atmosphere.

Self-Disclosing Intervention

Purpose

This intervention is almost the exact opposite of the previous method. Whereas the humorous intervention is roundabout, uncovering feelings and opinions in an oblique, lighthearted manner, the self-disclosing method is very direct, to the point, and reveals much more about the speaker. When we self-disclose, we try to be as open, honest, and transparent as possible in order that the listener may have direct access to our "insides"—our values, opinions, and passions. Of course, we try to be authentic persons during *all* our interventions, but we are especially true to ourselves here; we really show our colors.

We may express emotions all the way from simple frustration to actual outrage; we state opinions using techniques as simple as minimal disagreement or as complicated as formal debate. Because this form of intervention is so heartfelt, and uncovers so much about the speaker, an individual may actually become more vulnerable as a result of taking such a forthright position.

Because the self-disclosing intervention is very effective, and because I believe its use is a crucial skill to be mastered, I will demonstrate its appropriateness in two situations. The first is a conversation with a dear friend who confronted me regarding my own stereotyped assumptions about gender roles. Our dialogue is significant because it depicts intragender (in this case, woman-to-woman) confrontation.

Example 1

I am with one of my best friends and we are discussing our respective careers. She is an experienced and empathic teacher, and her husband is also a very competent and caring professional.

> *Catharine:* It's so great that you are providing a second income for the family.

> *Female friend:* Catharine, I really resent that. I work very hard at what I do, and I take it very seriously. I consider myself just as much a professional as my husband. We have an equal relationship, and we each carry equal responsibility for supporting the family.

Catharine: I'm so sorry—that was insensitive of me. My assumption that the male is the primary breadwinner is so deeply ingrained that I don't realize my bias until someone brings me up short. Thank you! What you just did is sisterhood at its best; women being able to love each other enough to be confrontive.

Benefit/Outcome

The transparency and honesty of the self-disclosing intervention clears the air. Like my friend, when we use it, we "lay our cards on the table." However, we take a risk in baring ourselves: We may be criticized for being too "open," "angry," "opinionated," or "touchy." Nevertheless, the outcome of such action is often beneficial: Because our values are expressed so clearly, others may feel free to be candid about their own. This promotes a deeper knowing of each other.

An adult education class provides another opportunity when self-disclosure would be appropriate.

Example 2

A group of parents meets regularly to discuss problems of child rearing, sharing household responsibilities, and other issues crucial to two-income families. The topic for the evening is "time management." This group is facilitated by a female leader in training who is being observed by a professor of child and family studies. Participants are all female, except for the professor and one token father, Wayne, seated next to his wife.

Facilitator/leader in training [turning to the only male participant]: Well, Wayne, how do you manage your time?

Wayne [giving his wife a patronizing pat on the shoulder]: Well, I really don't *have* to manage my time. My wife takes care of all those details at home, and at work my secretary does it.

A possible self-disclosing intervention in response to this statement, suggested later, but never actually implemented by either professor or facilitator, is: *"I'm feeling uncomfortable right now, because I detect some condescension in your remark. If I were a woman [or, As a woman] in this group, I would feel patronized. Could you*

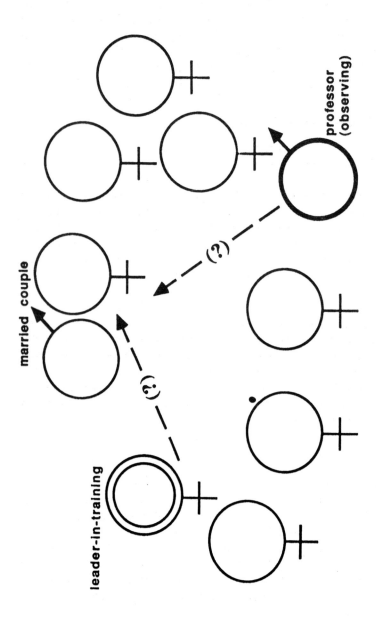

Figure 7.1. Who Should Intervene, and How?: "*I feel uncomfortable . . . I feel patronized*" (Self-Disclosing Intervention Suggested)

clarify what you mean?" Were this tactic to be used, it would actually be a *combined intervention*; the intercession begins when the intervenor self-discloses ("I'm feeling uncomfortable") and then moves to an *inquiring/fact-finding intervention,* as described below: ("Could you clarify . . . ?"), during which an effort is made to solicit information about the other person's point of view.

Analysis: Leadership Dilemma

As the frustrated professor described the parenting group above, he explained that neither he nor his leader in training actually confronted this man's sexism at the time, but he wishes one of them had. For those of us who supervise or evaluate others, this episode provides serious food for thought: Should we override the leadership of our trainees or not? If the professor *had* intervened, would his interruption have sabotaged his student's influence and undermined her confidence? Which issue do you deal with: the misogyny of a group member or the ego of the fledgling trainer?

A word about ethics and approximate propriety. These questions bring us to an important issue: What about the ethical issues associated with intervention? When we intervene, we always take a risk. We risk exposing private information, unearthing buried history, causing embarrassment, aggravating an already touchy situation, eliciting underlying hostilities, possibly provoking a member's departure from the group. Interventions are definitely a "jolt"—a disruption in process.

Therefore, before taking action, each of us needs to ask: What is appropriate? How might the offender respond to my intercession—would it be hurtful or helpful to the person involved and to group process? Is my tactic moving the group forward toward its goal, or will it cause more friction? Will I lose members of the group? Then we need to ask the toughest question of all: Is my action itself motivated by bias—am I so unconsciously prejudiced against females or males that my intervention is actually punitive, rather than just a consciousness-raiser? It is absolutely essential that the leader not foist her or his own unresolved conflicts or hang-ups about gender issues onto others, using intervention as a vehicle or weapon.

In Wayne's group, for example, if the leader has experienced (or been hurt by) men who refuse to share household responsibilities and who cannot be trusted to fathom the family's schedule, then the leader might dismiss Wayne's remark in exasperation: He's hopeless; I'm not even going to talk to him! Or a leader who is smarting from past injustices might take out personal anger on Wayne, using blaming humor or harshness: "Wayne, you're really a slippery character; do you try to wriggle out of *every* tight situation this way?" Or, "Wayne, how did your wife manage to marry such a dolt?"

On the other hand, if a leader firmly believes that males have every right to excuse themselves from being equal partners in a relationship, and that there are certain jobs that men *just don't do,* then the leader might say: "Right on, Wayne—hold your own!" or even, "I don't blame you, Wayne, I don't handle the scheduling in my life any more than you do." In either case, the leader is responding from the depths of her or his own prejudiced needs and assumptions, rather than examining how this biased leadership undermines group rapport, exacerbates stereotypes, and discourages women and men from developing collegial relationships in which they explore more flexible role options.

Another leader might give Wayne inordinately special consideration, reasoning that because we need more fathers in parenting groups, we must not do anything to challenge those who do come. This type of overprotective treatment would be a parallel form of the classroom chivalry described earlier that is sometimes used in the presence of females, and would be equally damaging to group process.

As is evident from the discussion about Wayne, we have many factors to keep in mind as we try to be ethical leaders. While monitoring both our own biases and group interactions, we must constantly try to be *proactive,* not *punitive.* We need to "pick our battles," making a judicious choice of technique only after first acknowledging our own blind spots and assessing the group's dynamics. Sometimes it is helpful to revert to a more entry-level method—the nurturing/empathic approach: "It must really be unsettling to be the only male in this group, Wayne; do you feel uncomfortable?" Or perhaps an inquiring/fact-finding intervention would be better: "Wayne, please clarify—did you mean your

remark as a compliment to your wife?" By refraining from prema-
ture judgment, we place the responsibility for clarification on the
participant and hold our own assumptions in check, rather than
impose them on the group.

Inquiring/Fact-Finding Intervention

Purpose

An easy way to remember this strategy is with the phrase, "Give
me the facts—just the facts." When we activate this intervention,
we attempt to gather as much information as possible about the
other person's point of view, and also to seek and contribute as
much hard data as we can muster. We try to get clarification and
let the other person know we want to understand, and are willing
to listen to, her or his side of the story.

An inquiring intervention usually involves an open-ended
question: How did you gather your information? What brought
you to that conclusion? Could you please clarify? What is behind
that for you? We use who/what/when/where/why questions.
One might activate this intervention to deal with someone like
Wayne (from the parenting group above) by asking, "Wayne, how
do you mean your comment 'My wife or secretary handles all of
the scheduling'; will you explain further?"

The fact-finding intervention can also be of the more rhetorical
variety, as were those questions I asked Bill when he declared that
the female students were "male-bashing." In my inquiry ("What
about recent research? . . . Do you see any benefit to a college's
remaining coeducational?"), I was trying to lead Bill toward my
own position: I was trying to educate, inform, and instruct as well
as to find out more about his position.

The inquiring intervention "Could you tell us where you got
your statistics?" was used by a participant in the conference
workshop led by the two "peacock" presenters discussed in Chapter 5. Unfortunately, her question was never answered, and the
pressures in the controlling climate militated against escalation to
a stronger intervention.

Transformational Intervention

Purpose

The transformational intervention is useful when we envision a constructive step that could be taken toward more gender-fair process—perhaps a practical improvement in group procedure. Our request is predicated on the condition that we have the suggested change firmly in mind—that we know what we want before we ask for it.

Because this strategy involves some creative imagining, it commands a greater level of sophistication than the previously described techniques, in which we simply describe what we see, nurture others, disclose feelings and opinions, or gather data. Constructively altering the dynamics of an imbalanced situation requires not only that we perceive the inequity, and have the courage to mention it, but that we have a concise plan for remediating the problem and believe enough in our plan to propose it. Practical remediation was used in the discussion of "territorial sexism" in Chapter 2. That vignette, from my own experience, is encapsulated below.

Example

At a regional conference, a woman has just attended my interactive workshop, during which we discussed how some group members may control process while others remain disenfranchised. As this woman enters her next workshop session, she sees female participants all seated in one semicircle, with males in an opposite arc encircling the male facilitator. Addressing the workshop leader, she makes her request: *"I just came from a session in which we discussed how stereotyped gender roles can disrupt group process. With the layout in this room, we could automatically be off to a bad start. Could we please change this seating arrangement?"* The leader readily complies with her suggestion and asks participants to rearrange themselves in a more gender-integrated fashion.

Benefit/Outcome

When group members' innovations are listened to, they feel more ownership of the group process, which can then be more tailored to meet their individual needs. If only a few members—

leader included—can envision a creative change toward a more equitable arrangement, and take initiative to verbalize it, then the group can more readily get on with its business. (Transformational suggestions also provide a good vehicle for taking care of routine "housekeeping" details that promote smoother process, but have nothing to do with gender. For example, a participant could request that the leader speak more audibly, or that the room be darkened to permit easier viewing of overhead projector transparencies.)

When leaders reinforce this kind of imaginative petitioning, it encourages members to take initiative, hear their own voices, challenge nonproductive dynamics, test themselves in the public forum, and gain self-respect in the group. And as the leader begins to implement their suggestions, participants know they are being taken seriously, which helps to raise their trust level and warm up the group climate.

Using a simple, well-timed request, the woman who suggested the change in seating was spontaneously sharing her vision for a more gender-fair arrangement. Such spontaneity is vastly preferable to using a delayed tactic—sitting in hostile silence through the entire workshop, fuming about the males' privileged position in the "power place," and then blowing up later.

Although the intervenor here happened to be a female critiquing males' "territorial sexism," she and other women should be aware that a similar power imbalance might develop sometime when *they* are leading a group. That is, a female facilitator might surround herself with female participants, not realizing how this arrangement could be perceived by males as a "shutout." This leader could then expect justified criticism from males, who might complain: Look at the room layout here; this doesn't feel right to us. You as a female leader seem to be showing favoritism to other women, placing us men at a disadvantage. Could we please change the arrangement?

Limit-Setting/Disciplinary Intervention

Purpose

We use limit setting to clarify our own boundaries—to set definite parameters on what is, and is not, acceptable to us. Limits can be delineated during group discussions as well as in one-on-

one conversations. For example, Geraldine Ferraro, in her debate with George Bush (see Chapter 2), made her boundaries clear by cautioning her opponent: "Don't categorize my answers!"

As we lead groups, we can use disciplinary intervention to let members know exactly what we expect of them. A clear definition of ground rules is best accomplished in the first session, when the group is just forming: The leader sets out guidelines on such matters as parliamentary procedure, confidentiality, syllabus requirements, attendance, or customary format that are specific to the group's particular purpose. For example, if the topic is something about "How does one intervene when one detects gender bias?" the ground rules could be similar to those suggested earlier in this chapter. The leader says, "I want all of you to understand that if you *do* decide to confront me or another participant about possible sexism, the following guidelines are recommended: (a) The intervenor respects the other person and her or his process, and (b) interventions take place at a minimal level."

Sometimes, however, we neglect to clarify our expectations. If we, in the beginning, do not define what we expect of participants (and let them know what to expect of us), we may have to do it in the middle of a session. Of course, it is always best to discipline in private; if possible, the leader may need to ask to see the offending party later. However, if certain participants are drifting into inappropriate, disrespectful, or disruptive behaviors, the leader may need to repeat, revive, or invent a ground rule on the spot—right in front of the rest of the group.

The following two examples are from classrooms. The suggested technique, which could be activated in either situation, was contributed by an experienced educator.

When a Limit-Setting Intervention May Be Necessary

Example 1. In a noncredit community education class, one adult male student insists on wearing his notebook on his head, like a hat. He does this repeatedly throughout the session. Not only is the facilitator annoyed, but this man's behavior is very distracting to the rest of the class.

Example 2. In a dental school lecture hall, a group of male students—purposely choosing the back row for this express activity—proceed to sleep through the professor's lecture. (The reader will recognize this as a reprise of Case 4.1.)

A limit-setting/disciplinary intervention that might be appropriate to both of these settings would be something like the following: *"I'd like to remind the group that wearing one's notebook on one's head [or sleeping through lectures] creates an environment that interferes with learning because others are distracted by the exercise of privilege. I don't teach in such a climate. Therefore, if these behaviors continue, I will have to ask certain individuals to leave."*

Outcome/Benefit

When one or more group members are disruptive, not listening, calling attention to themselves, making distracting gestures, or trying to assert status, the climate is not conducive to learning. Other participants are focusing on the individuals who are allowed this entitlement (How come they can get away with that?) rather than on the topic at hand. When we set limits on this kind of out-of-bounds behavior, we model positive leadership standards and redirect the group's attention to its purpose. By using a limit-setting intervention, we set clear boundaries: This is what I expect; I do not teach in such an environment; there are some behaviors that are inimical to productive group process.

Consensus Intervention

Purpose

Consensus has tremendous potency because it involves group energy—energy that can be activated by leader, participants, or both. The consensus intervention is the strategy used in the public meeting episode (described throughout this text) when the female member, tired of being criticized, trivialized, and marginalized by a pencil-throwing male, garners peer support and confronts the offender. By first soliciting support and then clearly defining what is and is not acceptable behavior for that group (limit setting), she stimulates the energy of the whole commission, who agree that her action helped "turn the tide" regarding the pencil thrower's behavior.

The following example of a consensus intervention, activated in a university class, is probably the most futuristic, forward-looking technique in this manual because it depicts a rarity: a male confronting another male about his sexism. The presenter is Charles Niessen-Derry, a facilitator of groups for male batterers. He describes this incident in his own words.

Example

I am a guest lecturer for a human relations class. The topic is male violence against women. I see this guy asleep in the back row. It's at the end of my lecture, and I am discussing how men typically react to feminist analysis and confrontation.

As one of my examples, I say, "Take the guy in the back row who's been sleeping through this entire presentation. Maybe he was up all night, but how many of you were also up all night?" (There is a show of hands.) "*Why don't you all turn around and look at him.*" (The whole class turns and looks at the sleeping student.)

Then I say to the class: "*This is a good example of a man indicating that male violence against women is unimportant; it's an example of how men ignore women's reality.*" (This is being said as the student is coming out of his sleep and sees about 150 faces looking at him.)

I continue: "*Now his friends can explain to him what's going on.*" (His friends, seated nearby, are not having anything to do with him at this point; they're leaning way to the other sides of their chairs.)

After this episode, I close with comments on how men need to take responsibility not only *for their own oppression* of women, but also for *other men's oppression* of women. Through this intervention I named an oppressive tactic—a male sleeping through a lecture about how males are violent to women—as it occurred. I wanted the class to turn and look at the oppressor so they recognized and remembered him. In this way he can be held accountable for his behavior on some level. Men must do this with one another and also facilitate it institutionally; that is, in a formal lecture setting.

Outcome/Benefit

As Niessen-Derry demonstrates, the consensus intervention has great potential for making change, because (a) the group shares responsibility for the confrontation, thereby relieving the leader of a solo role; and (b) the sheer weight of peer pressure and public opinion helps the offender recognize the inappropriateness of his "oppressive tactic."

The consensus strategy can best be used when a leader has sufficiently developed a trusting rapport so that participants know, and
feel partially responsible for, each other and the group's success.
Members then have become "important 'shareholders' in the group's
enterprise" (Quick, 1986, p. 57). As leaders, if we respect our group's
process, properly define sexism, clearly set boundaries, demonstrate
the appropriate use of minimal interventions, and empower group
members to do the same, we will not have to say or do much other
than identify inequity; the group takes over from there.

Abrupt Intervention

Purpose

This tactic is useful when bias is so blatant that we feel compelled to confront it summarily, on the spot, or immediately
thereafter. We are so offended that we spontaneously and inci-
sively utter our reaction, trying to deal with the situation. The
abrupt intervention is best activated at the *very moment* we detect
injustice; we do not pause to propose changes, suggest limits, or
reach consensus, much less to nurture the person, say something
amusing, or gather more data, as with earlier strategies.

The abrupt intervention was implemented on the spot in one of
the vignettes used to illustrate dysfunctional female-male dynamics at the beginning of Chapter 2 (Example 4). A committee member announces, "Let's get this meeting wrapped up; I have to
hurry home and beat my wife—otherwise she'll miss it." Another
member decides this is no time for sweetness and light, and when
she retorts, "BITE YOUR TONGUE!" she is being entirely appropriate. Note that she receives immediate support and affirmation
from a male peer, who agrees, "Yes, that was a *very* sexist remark."

An abrupt intervention can also be used very appropriately and
effectively after the fact, as demonstrated by an example in the
previous chapter: The boss publicly tears up his young employee's
written honeymoon plans; she restrains herself through the rest of
the meeting, and then goes directly to his office and warns, "Don't
you ever treat me that way again!" This is a *delayed intervention.*

Another delayed abrupt intervention was described during a
workshop by Nancy Goldberger: At a dinner party, males are
dominating the conversation, doing all the talking while women

do all the listening. Goldberger (1989) suggests this after-dinner, delayed intervention: *"Did anyone notice or care that the women weren't saying a damn thing?"* That this intervention is activated after the fact does not dilute its abruptness; the precipitous nature of the utterance is probably aggravated by the long period of patient but frustrated silence that precedes it. (See Chapter 6 for comments made during Goldberger's lecture and the discussion that followed.)

Yet another abrupt intervention, although never actualized, was suggested by a physician assistant when I queried him about the internal workings of an organization with which he was familiar (Barry Radin, personal communication, summer 1989).

Example

Van Nostrand: Can you tell me anything about the structure and culture of this particular organization?

Physician assistant: Well, it's very hierarchical. A few males at the top make the decisions without much input from the support people at the bottom. Morale is poor; there's a lot of turnover, and many of the other professionals have already left.

Van Nostrand: What is the gender of the support people?

Physician assistant: Mostly female.

Van Nostrand: Is it fair to say this organization is sexist?

Physician assistant [laughing at the understatement]: *Definitely,* yes. If you could just *see* how other similar organizations work, how employees are kept informed, told how the business is going, asked for their input. . . .

Van Nostrand: If someone asked your advice about how to make positive change in this organization, what would you say?

Physician assistant: I would go to the powers that be, the "uppity ups," and I would grab them by the shoulders and shake them and say, *"LISTEN TO YOUR PEOPLE, YOUR EMPLOYEES: LISTEN TO WHAT THEY'RE SAYING!"* Then I would go to the support staff, the "underlings," and I would say, *"QUICK! THEY'RE READY TO LISTEN TO YOU NOW. GO IN THERE AND TALK TO THEM!"*

Outcome/Benefit

A spontaneous outburst of indignation, frustration, or anger is often the most appropriate way to deal with an entrenched situation. When insensitive behavior and unfair treatment have been part of an organization's culture for a long time, without relief, a rude awakening may be necessary.

The nine strategies suggested above are useful for confronting behaviors that are sexist, exploitive, discounting, patronizing, or condescending, or that otherwise reinforce and perpetuate privilege of one gender (or one person) over others. We have depicted women confronting men, women confronting each other, and—crucially important—men confronting other men. In addition to more abrupt tactics, we have explored less confrontive techniques, such as nurturing interventions for reinforcing and encouraging gender-fair attitudes and humorous interventions for raising awareness in a more lighthearted fashion.

Like the tactic suggested by the physician assistant, a few of the above interventions are hypothetical, but the majority of the suggested methods were field tested both inside and outside of professional settings, either by me or by other seasoned group leaders.

I have found that when concepts about gender-responsible leadership are presented to groups for discussion, participants are often eager to concoct new intervention strategies and to suggest innovative ways they may be combined. The five-step method presented in Box 7.1 can be used to guide aspiring leaders in creating and field testing original techniques.

Remembering our caveat about leadership ethics and propriety, it should be reemphasized that the appropriateness of any given intervention depends on our awareness about personal prejudices, plus our sensitivity to the particular situation: How well do we know ourselves? How well do we know our group members? What is the group's history and gender makeup? If the group has developed a comfortable cohesiveness, how will our intercession affect this rapport? Is our intervention *proactive,* moving members toward greater mutual understanding and deeper personal growth, or is it *punitive*—merely a projection of our own hang-ups? And, finally, if we *do* decide to intervene, are we able to initiate the strategy at a minimal level, respecting the person and her or his

BOX 7.1

Creating New Interventions

This training sequence will guide aspiring leaders to devise, critique, experiment with, and reevaluate various intervention techniques.

Step 1: Share experiences. Leader or group member shares an experience of sexism or gender bias, describes the setting, and diagrams the incident's power dynamics on a blackboard or flip chart with figures similar to those in this book.

Step 2: Brainstorm solutions. Participants disband into small groups to devise potential strategies for confronting the sexism in the described (or a similar) setting.

Step 3: Discuss suggested interventions. After about 20 minutes, all reconvene and share strategies. Special attention is given to whether the proposed intervention language would be appropriate and respectful, and to creative ways to combine this technique with others.

Step 4: Field test designated interventions. The group chooses a few strategies that seem most applicable to the case in question, and everyone writes them down. "Homework" is then to field test these original techniques when confronting bias in similar upcoming personal and professional interactions.

Step 5: Report outcomes. Participants report homework results. Were these interventions responsible and effective in remediating discrimination? Did they help to create a more collegial climate? If not, the group brainstorms alternatives.

Each group is invited to submit its most effective "creations" to the author, using the Reader Response Form (Appendix A).

process? (Appendix C provides a checklist on some of these leadership considerations.)

After a leader has mastered most of the techniques outlined above, she or he can then begin to *combine* interventions when necessary. Several useful combinations are suggested in the following section.

Intervention Synergy

There are times when one intervention strategy alone is not sufficient. It is at precisely these moments when combined interventions prove valuable. When strategies are joined, one technique is reinforced with another to potentiate the impact of each. For example, we might find that a certain situation calls for a nonjudgmental description of what is happening, plus a bit of humor thrown in for good measure (joining descriptive and humorous interventions). Or we might begin with a fact-finding intervention, trying to gather hard data and appreciate the other person's point of view, only to discover that this person has no understanding of, or interest in, *our* point of view. At that point, we need to be much more definitive and incisive in naming the bias (limit-setting or abrupt intervention).

The combinations of interventions discussed below are but a few of the many ways to increase synergistically the effectiveness of the nine strategies introduced earlier.

Descriptive Plus Humorous Interventions

A workshop series, led by a female facilitator, meets weekly. One male member of the group repeatedly questions this leader's competence and credibility; she feels his behavior is not only sexist, but detracts from the workshop's purpose and undermines her leadership. So she intervenes, beginning with a simple observation and moving into slightly "flip" banter to challenge him in a lighthearted way: "*I notice you seem to be challenging some of what is discussed here* [observes/describes], *but that doesn't seem to keep you from showing up week after week"* [uses humor to deflect the bias and reflect it back to the perpetrator].

Another way this facilitator might convey her message would be to mix an empathic/nurturing intervention with a playfully descriptive strategy: *"You may disagree with what is said here* [shows understanding], *but I notice you keep coming back every week"* [describes with humor]. (The language of the above interventions was suggested by experienced family educators who lead parenting groups.)

Descriptive Plus Inquiring Interventions

The following combined intervention was field tested by Glen Palm, associate professor in the Department of Child and Family Studies, St. Cloud State University. Palm is especially concerned that men learn to be more nurturing and involved in parenting and family life, and—as is evident in his testimony—he tries to emphasize these values in his classes:

> I read parts of a preliminary manuscript of your book and it made me start looking at the settings I'm in, and to start thinking about gender issues in my classes. For example, I teach a parent/child class of 45 students: 38 women and only 7 men [see Figure 7.2]. The men sit in the back of the room and make joking comments during class—they're not taking things seriously.
>
> So I decided to try some ideas about gender-responsible leadership and see how they fit. I divided the class into small groups and put one male in each. I then asked them to discuss the topic "how men function in groups." I wanted to be honest with the men—I think it's important for the instructor to be honest. So I said to the class: *"Men don't usually do as well as the women in this class. They don't take the subject as seriously. Child and family studies and parent/child classes are considered a 'women's subject' "* [descriptive intervention, with slightly abrupt overtones].
>
> Then I asked the men: *"Do you want to learn about the nurturing parts of yourself? Do you want to be an androgynous man or an androgynous father?"* [inquiring intervention]. And the male students said things like "Not now"; or, "If I act androgynous, people will think I'm gay."

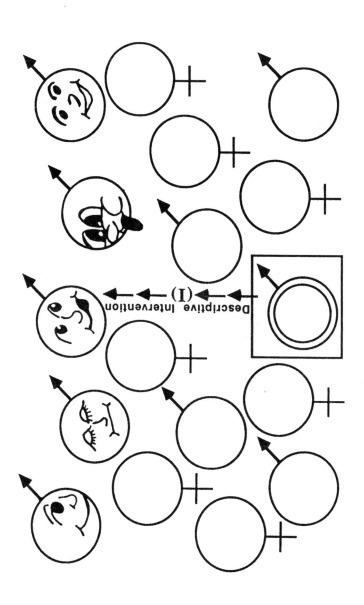

Figure 7.2. Professor Challenges Disruptive Males: *"Men don't take the subject as seriously."*(Descriptive Plus Inquiring Interventions Used)

227

Here I sit, an instructor in the middle of this campus, surrounded by young males. It is a critical time in a young man's development for him to explore his nurturing side, but there is *nothing* in college that promotes nurturing in males. The emphasis, the promotion, is on sports or the sciences. What are we instructors doing in our classes to promote nurturing in young men? How can we get them to take such issues as parenting seriously?

What this professor is saying is that our own leadership behaviors, or the behaviors we let students get away with, may exemplify the *exact opposite* of what we are trying to teach about. If the course is about nurturing, family responsibilities, or child care, and some students act disinterested or indifferent—not viewing the subject seriously—then they are behaving in a nonsupportive, irresponsible, and uncaring manner (for more on the subject of men and parenting, see Palm & Van Nostrand, 1987; Palm, Van Nostrand, & Schmid, 1989; Van Nostrand & Palm, 1986).

The goal of education in general (and this topic in particular) is to create a cooperative environment in which people feel involved, connected, and respected. Yet if the instructor allows group members of one gender to joke from the back row, discount the subject matter, or call attention to themselves, then he condones an atmosphere inimical to his goal—a climate of detachment, not involvement; separation, not connection; disparagement, not respect.

Through his combined intervention, this educator demonstrated the essential leadership components of *awareness, authenticity,* and *action.* He stimulated the students' awareness, even as he revealed his sensitivity; he tried to create congruent links among subject matter, gender-role stereotyping, student behaviors, and his own leadership methods. His action showed authenticity because he refused to conduct a class during which *process* contradicted *content.* By describing the dynamics he saw, and pointedly asking the males to introspect about their attitudes and behaviors, he also modeled admirable intragender (male-to-male) honesty.

Nurturing Plus Limit-Setting Interventions

We saw how both nurturing and limit-setting techniques could have been activated in the assertiveness workshop described in Case 3.1. As the reader will remember, eight women and one man were participants in the workshop, for which I acted as facilitator.

The man, Ted, was going through a divorce and emotionally unloading on the group—calling attention to himself, using his neediness to control the process.

The following intervention, suggested by a woman who had experienced similar attention seeking in other settings, seems helpful, timely, appropriate, and incisive:

> I've been in a situation like this one, where there's one male, the rest women, we're discussing issues we all share, and he's talking— we're all listening. I intervened by letting him know that I was supportive of his talking out (*"Thank you very much for sharing"*) and then I said, *"We all need to be sensitive to one another as well as to ourselves."* I left it there and let people take it where they wanted to. He finished up what he had to say, on his own, and the women were able to open up more.

Note that this intervention nurtures and supports the male's taking a risk to reveal himself and be vulnerable ("Thank you . . . for sharing"). However, the leader also sets a limit on his behavior by suggesting he might be less preoccupied with himself in order to connect more effectively with others. This clear definition of boundaries opens the door for the group process to work its own magic— another preliminary step toward a consensus intervention.

Inquiring/Fact-Finding Plus Abrupt Interventions

I combined interventions during my dialogue with my colleague Herb (the one who was going to speak to school administrators about self-esteem), whom we met in the previous chapter. As Herb continued to insist that the 16-year-old student was "choosing to get herself mistreated" by her battering boyfriend, I first used an inquiring intervention, questioning him about the young man's responsibility in the relationship (*"What about his behavior?"*). Then, because Herb did not seem to acknowledge my position or even to hear me, I escalated to an abrupt technique: *"It sounds to me like you're blaming the victim. . . . The point is, he's beating her."*

In addition to learning how to combine interventions, there are two other important concepts for the prospective intervenor to

consider: (a) the difference between direct and indirect intervention, and (b) when to try a delayed intervention.

The difference between direct and indirect intervention. An intervenor's
language should be as direct and honest as possible. Forthright
expressions are much clearer and less confusing to the listener.
However, sometimes an indirect or devious intervention is effective. A benign form of indirectness is the humorous strategy
mentioned earlier: The businesswoman Elizabeth, having lunch
with her client Robert, starts calling him Bobby so he will stop
calling her Lizzie. She does not come right out and ask him to
change his language; she simply drops a devious hint by changing
her own wording.

A more problematic example of indirect intervention would be
to malign an offender deliberately within earshot so that the person—whom you fear confronting directly—cannot help overhearing
your criticism (as in Case 7.1, presented in the next section).

Physical demeanor can also send indirect messages; we verbalize one idea, but our body language betrays us and we transmit
an entirely different signal. This is called a double message or
"mixed message." For example, one might say something polite,
but the scowl on one's face would betray underlying hostility; or
a person might insist that she or he was not hurt or embarrassed,
yet all the while that person would be blushing and feeling very
offended. The mixed message confuses the listener, who may
interpret the incongruity as dishonesty or even manipulation.

Although an indirect intervention may temporarily put a stop
to offensive behavior, it is not as effective in the long run as being
direct and forthright—that is, if one feels safe enough to have
intervened in the first place.

The *direct intervention,* on the other hand, is clear and has no
hidden meaning: "I disagree"; "I don't teach in such a climate";
"Your behavior is inappropriate." The language of most interventions suggested so far has been very direct.

Of course, either direct or indirect strategies may backfire because other persons, as we shall see in Case 7.1, are simply not
ready to receive *any* kind of message. They may be so unwilling

to face their own privileged or oppressive behavior that they become defensive no matter what sort of intervention is activated.

When to try a delayed intervention. We sometimes find ourselves in situations in which we detect bias, but at that instant, we simply do not have the words or the energy to implement an intervention. Or perhaps it does not feel appropriate to raise the issue then, and we decide to say something later. (We have already established, for example, that the employee whose boss publicly shredded her honeymoon plans made a wise choice *not* to confront him during that meeting; her intervention was much more strategic because she waited until she could speak to him in private.) When others seem especially defensive, when we feel emotionally fragile, or when our intervention seems ill timed, it is wise to wait awhile and then subsequently try the same or a different technique.

When we implement an intervention after the fact, and ask others to consider the incident of discrimination after it is all over, this is a delayed intervention. After-the-fact strategies are also a useful form of escalation: When a first attempt makes no dent in the problem—or is inappropriate, misunderstood, or ignored—we resurrect the issue later to let others know we are still concerned.

In the following case study we meet Natalie, a graduate student who feels trivialized, criticized, patronized, and marginalized by her male classmates. Natalie describes how she combines a variety of interventions to alleviate oppressive sexism, each combination apparently less effective than the last. One reason her interventions may not achieve optimal effectiveness is that she alternates between direct and indirect strategies. That is, at one moment she is clear and concise in expressing her opinions, and at the next— when she sees that clarity and directness do not work and her suggestions are being discounted—she reverts to indirect strategies that are met with even more resistance. This roller coaster of responses motivates her to try a direct strategy again. Ultimately, Natalie resorts to a *delayed* intervention during which she reiterates and rephrases her concern, urging more group cohesion and consensus.

Changing Behavior, Changing Consciousness: Gendered Behaviors, Self-Esteem, Participation Levels, and Group Morale

CASE 7.1

"I'm glad you got upset, because it really made me wake up"

Natalie is a graduate student in urban planning at a large university who is enrolled in a class on urban planning theory and methods. Students in the class have been divided into teams to work in various committees to research one aspect of a particular neighborhood, after which each team was to meet again to compose a final report for presentation to the entire class. Natalie describes what happened:

The research team [as described by Natalie]: On our team there were three women and two men—I'll call the men Male A and Male B. Although we had worked together on research committees, this was the first time we had met to discuss the actual presentation itself. Our meeting started well, though we felt pressured: The presentation was in one week and we had no group product. We had all done hard work but we had no consensus as to who would do what in the final presentation.

Because of the time pressures we felt, I suggested that at our next meeting we use the chalkboard to facilitate our discussion; we needed to work together to brainstorm ideas for a presentation we could all agree on. My suggestion was readily accepted and we adjourned.

At that next meeting, Male A chose a piece of chalk, went to the board, and began writing out his outline, assigning a major section of the presentation to himself. He had taken *my* idea to post the outline where all could see, and had just gone ahead with it! He was so caught up in what he wanted to say that he was oblivious to how he excluded others—he just didn't "get it." Then Male B entered the room, picked up another piece of chalk, and stood next to Male A at the board. There they were, both standing at the front, discussing things and making decisions between themselves. The women sat in a circle in the middle of the room, waiting to be involved in discussion.

Direct strategies [Natalie combines self-disclosing and nurturing/supportive interventions]: The men continued writing the outline on the board. When they arrived at a certain section of the topic that one woman found particularly interesting, she suggested they include a specific important reference. The men dismissed the reference as irrelevant, and carried on. Since I thought the reference was *very* pertinent, I said, "I disagree. I think we should consider her idea [direct; self-disclosing]; I think her idea is quite relevant" [giving support]. But the men kept on writing.

The women were providing important feedback, but the men were deciding what the whole group would do. The men became the teachers, the women became the students. I was disturbed about the barriers in the setting—the men standing at the board, the women sitting in a circle—let alone the rules being established.

Combined indirect and direct strategies: After several more incidents during which the women made good suggestions that the men disregarded or vetoed altogether, I began to lose my patience. I leaned over to the other two women and whispered, "Did you notice there's just guys up there at the board?" [descriptive technique used *indirectly*]. One woman said she *did* notice; the other shrugged as if she did not. The men heard me, and said that they noticed. The situation continued, nevertheless.

At that point the men slowed their discussion. I wanted to participate more, so I stood up, took a piece of chalk, and asked the men, "Do you mind if I rework one of the sections that seems to be confusing the discussion?" [*direct* transformational or fact-finding intervention]. I went to the board and started waving my piece of chalk around and writing, as they had been doing [*indirect*]. One of the men moved to another part of the outline and just kept on writing.

Finally, the men said we were running out of time (all of which, up to this point, had been taken up by them), and they would work on the two central portions alone. These portions were the only sections to which all of our group had contributed fieldwork and slides. The men were making no effort to distribute these major sections equitably among members, but, in all fairness, neither were the women.

Male A continued to the end of the outline on his own terms and arrived at a point that required recording on paper. So, as a planner comfortable with words, I volunteered. But Male A (a more visual/architectural person) evidently had expected me to record the pictures found in his brain, because as he was speaking I was writing his words, but he demanded that instead I draw his images. Male B said sarcastically, "Boy, you really *are* a planner, aren't you?" I said,

"Please," and walked out of the room. It was obvious that this was becoming an interdisciplinary as well as a gender conflict.

I went into the women's rest room and began to cry—there is only so much of this shit I can take. One of the women joined me there and just listened. She said she understood, but did not say one way or the other how she felt. Then I went out into the hallway and by the water fountain Male B, the one who had uttered the last insult, came up to me and apologized. He said, "I'm glad you got upset because it really made me wake up. I knew I was doing something wrong." Male A never approached me nor apologized.

Direct strategies tried again [combining self-disclosing and transformational interventions]: I lost sleep over this episode, feeling as if I wasn't being "cooperative." At the next meeting I read a few ideas that I had prepared and felt strongly about including in the presentation. The other women were again silent. The men said that everything was pretty well set and our presentation was already "overloaded"; overloaded, of course, with their disproportionately large sections. They said not to worry about the grade: "Not all of us have to be in the presentation; after all, the group is graded as one." This made me even more upset, because I am an A student, had taken some of the slides that were to have been shown, and knew I could contribute detail that the presentation needed. After all, were we there only for the grade? I thought our process—for example, whose ideas were taken into consideration and how we made decisions—was just as important as the grade itself.

One of the women took the only remaining section, leaving the bulk of the material taken. I asked the third woman if she had a particular interest. She said that at that point she didn't care, and would rather not talk at all! The men suggested, "One of you could take the intro, the other the conclusion." How could this be anything but a clearly oppressive situation to these people?

I said I would take the conclusion, which, given the newness of the assignment, I had to prepare overnight. I molded it into a comprehensive conclusion that included the topics raised during our team's research, one of which was the issue of group dynamics: that the process is as important as the product. (After all, if we are going to be *planners*, we have to be able to *plan* with each other!)

In our presentation, everyone performed well. Of course, the guys had the long parts. The men were very entertaining and they presented with a lot of flair and joking. We women had the short parts. Later that day, Male B (the one who had said "You woke me up") thanked me again, and asked me to correct him in the future. He said, "You have to help me—tell me when I step over the line. I just jump into these roles without thinking. I feel silly and I'm really sorry. You really made me wake up." I told him I still wanted to talk to both the men to sort out how we did. I said, "We need to talk about our process" [preliminary suggestion of consensus building]. (I didn't specifically ask the women to come, but I wish I had.)

Natalie finally tries a delayed, consensus-seeking intervention: When I met with the men again, I asked how we could have done things differently [seeking consensus]. Male A, the one who had not yet spoken to me, said, "A reality check would have worked; you could have stopped the group and asked, 'Are we getting anywhere?' " I agreed and said we could have begun there, and that I had no answers to these problems, which was why I needed their input. I also said I knew we got into problems with our presentation, and I didn't know if it was a gender issue or not, but I *do* know we all fell into roles that weren't fair: the women's ideas were discounted and the men were making decisions for others.

Analysis of Case 7.1

Natalie experimented with both direct and indirect strategies in an attempt to find some method that was effective. Her initial effort was direct, assertive, and nurturing: When the males rejected the female student's suggestion to include an important reference, Natalie disagreed with the men and showed support for the woman's idea. When the men continued to downplay and denigrate input, and it appeared that her direct strategies would not work, Natalie next tried two indirect methods: whispering audibly to the other women and going to the board, waving a piece of chalk around. In the midst of this she also tried an intervention that could be seen as either fact-finding or transformational: She attempted to enrich the presentation by reworking a section of the outline, an effort the men tried to terminate by complaining that the team was "running out of time."

At their next meeting, Natalie, undeterred that her initial attempts had seemed ineffective, again tried direct methods. She brought up specific new material she felt strongly about and believed should be included in the outline. This suggestion was also rebuffed by the men. Ultimately, after the presentation was all over, Natalie implemented two delayed consensus-seeking interventions: "We need to talk about our process" and "How could we have done things differently?"

Natalie is the very embodiment of many of the women we have met here who have been categorized, trivialized, criticized, marginalized, and even ostracized within a male-dominated system. Her story provides fitting closure to this volume because it illustrates most of the major themes:

(1) Women and men may display extreme gender role behaviors, occupying space and using language in ways that skew participation levels.

(2) These differences lead to a system of dominance and subordinance that inhibits colleagueship and in which females are acutely disadvantaged.

(3) "Women's ways of knowing" (and learning) must be revalued.

Let us consider each of these points in turn.

Extreme Gender Role Behaviors

The Four D's of gender role extremes—male *dominance* and *detachment*; female *deference* and *diagnosis* (Box 1.1)—are clearly delineated in Natalie's experience. Although in the minority, the two men manage to dominate the team meeting by unilaterally choosing for themselves the most prominent and favorable sections of the presentation, by writing on the board, and by doing most of the talking. "Physically and verbally" they allow themselves space, to use Adrienne Rich's (1979) description; they make the "assumption that people will listen even when the majority of the group is female" (p. 243).

The male students, by standing and by positioning themselves in the front of the classroom, try to take control of the territory. As a matter of fact, they exemplify almost perfectly the five characteristics of "male talk" (Box 2.1): *dominance* (of both discussion and space), *problem solving, self-listening, finding fault* (with other peoples' ideas), and *topic selection* (deciding the outline's format). The men also threaten to *detach* when things don't seem to go their way.

Female students, meanwhile, defer (mostly to the men, and sometimes to each other). The terms Natalie uses to describe her own behavior and that of the other women include "silent," "shrugged," "said she didn't care," "again silent," and "did not say how she felt." This language denotes passivity, disenfranchisement, and lack of agency. The internal and external pressure on women to conform to this passive role is so great that when Natalie departs from passivity and steps into a more instrumental role, she even blames herself, at one point, for not being cooperative.

Seated in a circle in the center of the room, the women find themselves reduced to the role of "students" while the males play "teacher." Although Natalie remains in this enclosure and defers for a while, she also tries to remove herself from the circle long enough to play the "scouting" role of *diagnosing detective,* trying to sniff out the men's strategy: "Did you notice there's just guys up there?" This diagnostic role is frequently assumed by token persons in groups, or those who, because they feel less powerful, try to influence decisions in a relatively oblique manner (Powell, 1988). Natalie later tries to involve her male team members in this diagnostic process: "How could we have done things differently?"

The Male/Female Continuum

Concepts from the Male/Female Continuum (Figure 2.1) are also played out among these graduate students: The males *intimidate* by making unilateral decisions and by refusing to dialogue with the women or even to sit down and join them in the circle, a gesture that could reassure everyone that "we're all in this together." Choosing not to enter into joint decision making, the males instead devalue the females by discounting or ignoring their suggestions. Also, they show *paternalism* by "letting" the women have the less prominent parts of the presentation, the introduction and conclusion. When Natalie tries to assert her leadership, the men become even more defensive and offensive. Throughout most of their planning meetings, Natalie (and perhaps also the other women) sits with *anger frozen inside.* Although Natalie does seem to try to *control through helping* (volunteering to record ideas on paper), she and the other women mostly *yield.* Their role of deference is symbolized by Natalie's asking the men if they would "mind" if she goes to the chalkboard.

A hopeful note is sounded when Male B comes out into the hallway and admits, "I knew I did something wrong." He has *made a decision to learn* and seems genuinely open to feedback. His openness is evidenced in his subsequent plea to Natalie: "You have to help me—tell me when I step over the line." It appears Natalie *also* learns from the episode: She decides it is in her best interest to again be assertive and direct. Even though she is very emotionally upset and losing sleep, she continues to contribute her ideas. Perhaps she envisions the possibility of colleagueship; in any case, she clearly advocates more *flexible role options*, suggesting that all five students could share decision-making and leadership functions, rather than having these roles appropriated only by the males. She, as a woman, is seeking *autonomy*; perhaps one source of conflict in this mixed group is that the men not only seem threatened by Natalie's expression of autonomy, but apparently feel very little need to develop connection and to seek *intimacy*.

Women's Ways of Knowing

In addition to illustrating basic concepts about the Four D's, male talk, and the Male/Female Continuum, Natalie's experience also provides a clear justification for the thesis that women do not learn well in an adversarial climate, preferring instead a more cooperative setting (Belenky et al., 1986; Keith, 1987; Rich, 1979; Spender 1980). In this highly competitive atmosphere, Natalie and her female classmates have the choice to "wait forever to be asked or [to] get a word in where they can," a phenomenon documented by others (Latour, 1987, p. 31).

The women on this team seem to make conscious efforts to do the "linking" (Eisler, 1987) and "maintenance" work in the group: to cooperate and keep the channels of communication open, even if it involves only listening. Natalie says the other women "made good suggestions" and "provided important feedback." Natalie herself suggests the outline be shared and written on the chalkboard so all team members can work on it together. At least two of the women demonstrate nurturing: When another woman suggests a certain reference, Natalie supports her idea; and, of course, one of the women very much nurtures Natalie by being present and listening as Natalie weeps. These are clear examples of linking, rapport-building, cooperative behavior.

The males, meanwhile, seem to prefer functioning in a competitive "ranking" mode, appropriating the prominent parts of the presentation for themselves and making decisions for others. They want to be the "reporters," staying in the limelight and keeping the focus of attention on themselves to maintain status. The women's efforts to create a climate of connection seem overshadowed by the adversarial atmosphere established by the males.

At this juncture it must be acknowledged that no group can make decisions if there are too many leaders and not enough followers: some individuals *must* agree to follow in order that others can lead. Some might argue that, to expedite matters, it was very helpful when the males seized the initiative and made most of the decisions. Helpful, that is, if this behavior fits with your value system. The males' values seemed to be: Let's get the job done; somebody has to do it; we are the best qualified, so we should take charge. Natalie's values, however (and perhaps those of one or both of the other women), may have lain in a much different direction, something like: We have a job to do that will require input from all of us; since we are all equally qualified, what will be our process so we may all be involved?

This case clearly demonstrates that when a climate is overly competitive, and a hierarchy is established prematurely, some participants become so discouraged that they abdicate their chance to be an equal participant. They may say, as did one female student, "I don't care; I'd rather not talk at all!"

What could have motivated this group to interact as a more cohesive team with balanced participation and empowerment of all members? A gender-responsible leader could have sensitized students to the peculiarities of mixed-group process *before* the team ever met. For example, the subject could have been introduced as a separate lecture on how to research projects and plan presentations in a mixed-sex group. Thus forewarned, classmates would not have had to spend valuable time and emotional energy dealing with power plays and doing reality checks. Rather, they could have *enjoyed* sessions working together as colleagues focused on a common goal.

Undoubtedly, each of us will, through trial and error and based on personal experience, conjure up many more combined or delayed strategies for confronting bias. Like Natalie, we may experiment with indirect strategies and find that the direct ones are more effective. We may try to be spontaneous in our intervention, and, finding that our efforts meet with resistance, try again later. As stated previously, the choice of which intervention to use (or whether to intervene at all) depends on one's rapport with the group, the depth of the sexism, one's ethical sense of propriety, and sometimes even one's feeling of safety.

The key to intervening effectively is to try to appreciate each person's gender role journey, know what is appropriate, weigh the possible consequences of our actions, choose a remedy appropriate to the severity of the bias, and—above all—to intervene with compassionate precision.

Notes

1. Bill Vossler is a free-lance writer and a North Dakota Arts Council writer-in-residence. His wife, Nikki Rajala, acknowledged as the person who raised his consciousness about women's issues, had recently been president of the St. Cloud, Minnesota, chapter of the National Organization for Women (personal communication, May/June 1990).

2. Several sources provide reports about, and views for and against, women and men being educated together. For example, for newspaper coverage of protests against coeducation, see Kelly (1990, p. 1D). For editorial comment on similar protests, see Zettersten (1990), who describes what he considers to be feminists' "twisted philosophies" and tries to discredit some student demonstrators, who, according to the editorial, belonged to lesbian groups. For a discussion on "what it means for a college . . . to be coeducational today in light of feminism and the women's movement," see Warch (1990). Finally, see Adrienne Rich's 1978 essay, "Taking Women Students Seriously," which proposes that the concept of coeducation is "misleading" because even though "women and men are sitting in the same lectures, reading the same books . . . they are not [receiving an equal education] because the content of education itself validates men even as it invalidates women" (Rich, 1979, p. 241).

3. Two Benedictine schools, the College of Saint Benedict (women) and Saint John's University (men), are single-sex institutions in Central Minnesota; however, students from each college attend classes at the other.

4. One researcher who has documented how female students are disadvantaged in coeducational classrooms is Catherine Krupnick (Harvard Graduate School of Education), who videotaped classroom interactions—see discussions in earlier chapters. Krupnick's work is cited in articles by Kelly (1990) and Fiske (1990). Other researchers who have observed similar disadvantage among female students include Hall and Sandler (1982, 1984); Sandler, (1986), Latour (1987), and Sadker and Sadker (see Griffin, 1990; Schmidt, 1982), to name a few.

APPENDIX A

Reader Response Form

Instructions for Submitting
Your Personal Case Studies
and Field-Tested Interventions

Think about your experience of sexism in mixed groups: What happened, and why was the incident discriminatory? What inappropriate language and behaviors indicated that you or another group member was at a disadvantage, a victim of bias, or otherwise thrust into an unwelcome role? If an intervention was used, who activated it and how? Was the intervention effective?

This is your chance to share successful or unsuccessful intervention techniques you have devised or have watched another person implement. Please submit details on the form that follows. Describe the group's purpose, setting, and gender mix; the incident of bias; and the type of intervention used and what was said. Give the exact wording of the intervention and then assign it a category from Table 7.1 (for example, humorous intervention) or devise a new category of your own.

Your contribution must be original and not previously copyrighted. If you adapt from the work of others, please acknowledge the original source.

Please provide your name, address, and phone number; also attach a brief biographical sketch (up to 40 words) that includes your title, position, affiliation, background, and experience with mixed-sex groups. I would like the option to include your example in possible future editions of *Gender-Responsible Leadership* or to use your case study in workshops on gender equity. Please indicate whether—should your submission be chosen—you will permit me to mention your name and affiliation publicly.

Follow the format of one of the two examples below. Example A describes an incident from the point of view of the intervenor; Example B is told from the perspective of an observer watching someone *else* intervene.

Example A

Setting and incident [described by male intervenor]: I am a trial lawyer and I frequently try cases with another attorney in my firm—I'll call her Louise. Last week, just an hour before our case was going to trial, the judge called Louise and me into his chambers. Because I was delayed gathering some papers, Louise entered his chambers first; I could hear him joking with her and propositioning her for a date. Louise responded very crisply to the judge—I knew by her voice that she was flustered and angry. He was making very unwelcome and inappropriate advances, was undermining her professional stature,[1] and was definitely throwing her off track, which was perhaps his intent.

Intervention: I had heard enough, so I quickly grabbed the rest of my papers and stepped into the room. Louise's face was pale, her fists were clenched, she looked very upset. I walked over to the judge and said, "Your honor, I couldn't help overhearing your remarks. I feel your comments are quite inappropriate and out of place here" (combined *self-disclosing* and *limit-setting* interventions).

Outcome: Considering this judge's insensitivity, and the fact that in the past I have seen him treat other women in a similarly unprofessional manner, I was amazed at his response. After some initial nervous laughter, he actually (but halfheartedly) apologized to me: He said, "Sorry, I might have been a little out of line." However, I never heard him apologize directly to Louise.

Example B

Setting and incident [described by female observer]: I was facilitating a workshop on gender issues for volunteer coordinators in human services agencies. In this group there was only one man—we'll call him Jerry—and 19 women.

These coordinators explained that in their workplaces they were frequently expected to do stereotyped jobs just because of their gender; for example, it was assumed that women would always make coffee. So I asked everyone to divide into small groups, choose a spokesperson, and discuss how they handle these expectations. (Of course, since Jerry was a "token," I realized he would be the only male in his cluster.) Then I walked around the room, watching to see how they would handle this assignment.

Sure enough, the same on-the-job stereotyping they had been complaining about was happening right there in the workshop: Because he was male, everyone in Jerry's group turned to him, expecting him to be the spokesperson!

Intervention: Many men would have taken on this leadership role without questioning the biased assumptions behind it. But Jerry confronted the women quite honestly on his own behalf. He said, "Do you expect me to lead just because I'm a guy? I'd prefer someone else do it—there are many others in this group capable of being spokesperson!" (combined inquiring, self-disclosing, and limit-setting interventions).

Discussion: As workshop facilitator, I then asked Jerry to share his intervention with the entire group. This prompted a lively discussion about how men do not like to be pigeonholed into certain prescribed roles any more than women do. Women dislike having to make extra phone calls or provide refreshments for meetings just because they are female, and men do not want jobs "dumped" on them either, just because they are male. We talked about how an organization is strengthened when diversity is valued, because then people can develop competence in a variety of tasks rather than forever being expected to fit into some rigid role slot.

Outcome: The outcome was very gratifying. Participants said they could *definitely* use these ideas back in their agencies. The women said Jerry's honesty had inspired them to return to their offices and protest if asked to make coffee! Especially interesting was Jerry's confession that this workshop experience had enabled him, for the first time in public, to verbalize his anger about the limitations of masculinity and the confines of having to play the "expected" male role. He also admitted that our discussion helped him develop empathy for the many "invisible" jobs women traditionally perform in organizations that he heretofore had not fully appreciated.

Note

1. The legal scenario in Example A is adapted from a letter to the editor in *New Directions for Women* written by a tenant's attorney in New York City, who, with her female adversary, was greeted in open court by a male judge who asked, "Hi, girls. Can I call you girls? . . . Can I call you up for dinner?" No explanation should be needed, writes the attorney, of "how demeaning his so-called levity was to my professional stature and character" (McGuire, 1990). This quote is reprinted by permission of *New Directions for Women*, 108 W. Palisade Avenue, Englewood, NJ 07631.

READER RESPONSE FORM

Describe mixed-group *setting* and demographics, *incident* of bias, category and language of *intervention*, and *outcome*.

Setting and incident: _____

_____

_____

_____

Intervention (category and exact words used): _____

_____

_____

_____

Outcome: _____

_____

_____

_____

Your Name and Position/Affiliation: _____

_____

Address: _____ZIP: _____

Phone: Work: (   )_____Home: (   )_____

Attach biographical sketch (up to 40 words)

If your case study is chosen for publication, or as workshop example, may I mention your name and position? yes___ no___

Please submit to:

Catharine Herr Van Nostrand
36854 Winnebago Road, St. Cloud, MN 56303-9657

APPENDIX B

Gender-Specific Interventions: Leadership Language Targeted Especially to Women or Men

Leaders may find it necessary to confront a certain female or male about sexist attitudes or stereotyped behaviors. However, before asking others to change, authentic leaders will first demonstrate personal sensitivity to—and willingness to remedy—their own assumptions, prejudices, and methods. The following interventions segue through these stages from *awareness* to *authenticity* to *action*.

Awareness: Leader Stimulates Group's Awareness

To generate more sensitivity, and to set clear parameters about acceptable behaviors, the leader first defines sex role stereotypes and explains how these extreme roles disrupt process. Then the leader asks the group to watch for the following:

Imbalanced participation:

Some educational research reveals that boys are eight times more likely than girls to call out answers in class. This behavior tends to marginalize females. If any of you notice a similar pattern in our group, will you please mention it?

Gender-typical linguistic patterns:

Linguists report that males frequently use language to assert status and center conversations on themselves, while females use language to establish connection and intimacy. If similar patterns existed in our group, how might they affect our discussions?

Biased or sexist comments that go unchallenged by group participants:

We've established a group guideline that we will not stereotype individuals on the basis of gender, or make assumptions about their capabilities. For practice, let's analyze the bias in the following examples: (a) "Women will never make good managers, because they're not willing to pay the price for success"; (b) "Men are such insensitive clods, they'll never really understand how the glass ceiling impedes women's advancement."

Males asserting privilege:

When the teams presented their research projects today, I noticed that in each team, males presented the more prominent sections of the topic, while females were left with minor parts like the introduction and conclusion. This happened in every case, in spite of the fact that our class has a 50/50 ratio of females to males. I'd like you to return to your research groups and discuss this phenomenon: "By what process did our team decide who would appropriate the major and minor portions of the presentation?" Be prepared to share your decision-making process with the whole group. (See Case 7.1.)

Authenticity: Leader Admits Personal Bias

After defining sexism and raising the group's awareness about behaviors that perpetuate sexism or disrupt group process, the leader then establishes credibility by admitting personal tendency to collude, and demonstrating willingness to change.

Leader shows awareness of own biased body language:

I just realized that my eye contact has been almost exclusively with the men [or women] in this group. I'm going to turn so I can face all of you.

Leader comments on use of noninclusive language:

I'm aware that in my lecture I used the pronoun "he" when referring to certain occupations. Let me correct that: "The doctor will decide how SHE or he will treat the patient."

Leader reveals how personal favoritism toward one gender discourages participation by the other:

Mary and John raised their hands at the same time, but I noticed that, partly because of my own need to be chivalrous or to gain female approval, I called on Mary first. However, Mary has already had two chances to speak. John, what did you want to say?

Leader acknowledges own discomfort or risk taking:

As a guest lecturer/newly appointed chairperson here, I realize I don't yet know all of you, and I feel somewhat uncomfortable speaking up, but I must say that I find that last remark very sexist.

Leader admits possible collusion and asks for feedback:

This discussion feels out of balance to me. Perhaps I have encouraged some of you to the exclusion of others. Is there anything about my leadership that is collusive or is aggravating this unbalanced participation level?[1]

Action: Leader Confronts/Supports Females or Males

This section provides specific strategies for responding to members of each sex. First we see a leader confront either males or females about how their extreme behaviors of dominance, detachment, or deference (Box 1.1) interfere with effective group process, inhibit gender role flexibility, or both. Also included are a few nurturing/supportive interventions for reinforcing actions that contribute positively to the group's interest.

Interventions for Confronting/Supporting Males

To male who interrupts another speaker:

(1) John, I noticed that you've interrupted Mary twice now while she was speaking. Were you aware of that?

(2) John, I'd like Mary to have a chance to finish her comments before you interject yours.

To male whose comments up to now have been gender sensitive, but who inexplicably reverts to female-degrading remarks:

John, up to this moment you have been quite supportive of women in the group. I'm surprised you just made that derogatory remark about Mary. Could you please rephrase your comment?

To male who shows ability to relate in the abstract to emotions of others, but does not appear comfortable sharing his own experiences and feelings:

John, I notice when you read that passage about the scientist's spiritual experience, your voice shook and you seemed very moved. Have you had a similar experience that affected you deeply?[2]

To males who freely give advice to a woman (as she shares a highly charged issue), but who seem intent on advice giving and problem solving rather than in quietly empathizing with and attending to her:

"I would like the men to stop giving advice. Men have been giving women advice for centuries" (Houston, 1988).[3]

To male who either is not listening or is trying to control the discussion by switching to a subject with which he is more familiar:

John, during our discussion just now, you changed the subject. Is it possible you haven't been listening or following the conversation, or that you're unfamiliar with (or uncomfortable with) the topic? Men sometimes do this in groups—is this pattern common for you?

To male who becomes more sensitive, stops using "male talk" behaviors of self-listening and faultfinding (Box 2.1) and begins to affirm others:

John, I like the way you attended to and complimented Pete/Helen just now. When we support each other this way, it gives our group more cohesiveness.

Interventions for Confronting/Supporting Females

To female who allows herself to be interrupted:

Mary, I notice you stopped talking when John interrupted you. Are you aware of that? How did it feel? Can you explain where you learned to do that? Would you like to continue?

To females who seem to appease men:

Mary, Sue, and Jane, I observed you all laughing just now when John told that sexist joke. But in the past, all three of you have complained to the group about jokes that degrade women. Can you tell us what's behind that for you?

To female who employs self-deprecating, status-weakening linguistic patterns:

Mary, your part of the debate was presented in a generally confident manner, but I notice your final statement ended on a note of uncertainty—like a question mark. This is called a "tag question," and some researchers feel these "overly polite," "hesitant," and "submissive" behaviors are associated with lower status in women.[4] Such a linguistic pattern may serve to weaken your argument. Please state your closing remark again, firmly, without letting your voice rise at the end.

To very bright female student (after class) who had appeared quite withdrawn during the session:

Mary, in reading your journal for this course, I'm impressed with how much you share your knowledge, thoughts, and experiences on paper. Yet during class discussions we don't hear nearly as much from you as we'd like. Could you tell me more about this?[5]

To female who repeatedly disparages men:

(1) Tracy, are you aware that your comments seem to reveal a strong antimale bias?
(2) Tracy, do you recognize that some of your remarks about men could be perceived as very hurtful?

To previously indecisive female who begins to play a more instrumental role in the group:

Natalie, you were confident and decisive in helping your research team to get organized, arrive at decisions jointly, and decide how to present your group project. I'm pleased with your strong leadership. (See Case 7.1.)

Please use the Reader Response Form provided in Appendix A to share any original gender-specific interventions you have experienced that may be similar to those here.

Notes

1. Admitting one's flaws and opening oneself to feedback is the skill of *negative inquiry.* An assertiveness training technique that reduces defensiveness between people, negative inquiry "allows you more comfortably to seek out criticism about yourself . . . while prompting the other person to express honest negative feelings and improve communication" (Smith, 1975, p. 302).

2. I used this language successfully in an informal, leaderless adult study group when I urged a usually reticent male friend to self-disclose, which he did, describing how profoundly in touch with nature he felt while observing a wild owl.

3. Jean Houston—author, philosopher, consultant, and seminar leader—used this intervention in one session of a week-long workshop (October 1988) during which a female participant "came out" about having been sexually abused. Dr. Houston asked male participants to gather around this woman and give her support. Instead, most of the men began giving her advice: "You must be strong"; "You can go back home and cope"—examples of the impersonal problem solving and topic selection typical of "male talk" (Box 2.1). Dr. Houston then spontaneously implemented her abrupt, limit-setting technique. She requests that it be made clear that her "words were used

in a very specific context. They were not meant to be a catchall statement concerning men's relationships to women" (personal communication, September 16, 1991).

4. For discussion of female linguistic patterns that may weaken a woman's argument, and thus contribute to her powerlessness and possible lower status, see Hall and Sandler (1984, p. 5, and the accompanying note 21); see also the discussion of "linguistic sexism" in Chapter 2.

5. Sudie Hofmann, instructor in human relations at St. Cloud State University, actually implemented this intervention with a female student who freely shared her thoughts in her course journal, but participated at only a minimal level in class (personal communication, 1988).

APPENDIX C

Are You a Fair Facilitator?
Checklist/Discussion Guide
for Group Leaders

When females and males are grouped together, a leader may grant privileges to one sex that are not assumed by the other. This collusion upsets the balance of power and disrupts participation levels, which may already have been thrown off balance by room setup, group's history, and other factors. Taking many of these factors into consideration, this checklist provides a guide to stimulate greater equity in mixed-sex interactions.

How to Implement This Checklist

Use this assessment to examine a group's physical environment and its demographics, as well as to critique any actions of its leader that seem (a) to favor one sex more than the other, (b) to allow certain factions to control the group, or (c) to discourage full participation by either females or males. Leaders can implement this assessment either as a self-audit or as a way to evaluate other leaders. Group participants can also use it to analyze the power dynamics among themselves.

Before critiquing another leader, do a preliminary self-audit and ask yourself: Am I a fair facilitator? Do I notice how women and men arrange themselves in a room? Am I sensitive about status differentials already existing in the group and how these differences may disrupt process? Do I monitor my own verbal and nonverbal behavior for signs of sexism? For example:

- Do I ever respond more energetically to, or show more tacit approval of, one gender than the other?
- Do I ever recognize and reward participants who dominate and try to assert status, ignoring those who collaborate and nurture others?
- Do I ever appease controlling factions in the group?

The leader you are about to evaluate may believe that she or he is an "equal-opportunity facilitator" who is perfectly gender fair; however, you will probably detect subtle behaviors that indicate bias. This will be, by necessity, a subjective evaluation, because as you critique this other leader (or yourself), your responses will be clouded by your unique attitudes and perceptions.

There are many factors besides gender that may affect group functioning, such as the age, race, and professional status of each participant and the leader. Although these other factors are also important, we will focus primarily on the issue of the leader's possible sexism.

Note that the word *facilitator*, as used here, applies to any person who guides others in an educational, therapeutic, business, or other setting. Also note that at the end of each section you have an opportunity to add your own comments and observations.

The Room: Physical Distribution of Group Members

Chair arrangement: How are chairs arranged: Semicircle? Circle? Participants seated around tables? Theater seating? Other? _____
Is there anything about this setup that gives one gender an advantage over the other? If so, does the facilitator take action to rearrange people? Describe: _____.

Segregation by sex: Are women and men separated from each other? Are a few (or all) members of one sex isolated from the rest of the group? If so, does this segregated arrangement seem to have any effect on group dynamics? If an adverse effect, what does the facilitator do to correct the problem? _____
_____.

Space and status: Does any person (besides the leader) occupy a dominant or "power position," such as at the head of a conference table, center of a semicircle, behind the podium, or writing on the chalkboard? Does anyone try to control group process by (a) standing when she or he could instead be sitting, or (b) taking up extra space, such as placing an arm over the back of another person's chair, or putting feet up on another's desk?[1] If so, what is the sex of this "controller"?_____.

Issues of proximity: Do any persons try to "cozy up" to the leader by crowding around her or him, by choosing the front row, addressing the leader frequently, or sitting directly opposite the leader at a table? Conversely, do any persons try to exercise control from a distance, such as a back row or corner of a room? What is the sex of these individuals who want to either endear themselves to or detach themselves from the leader and the rest of the group? How does their attachment/detachment affect the group's power dynamics?_____
_____.

Add your own observations: Is there anything else that concerns you about the physical layout of the room or the way participants take up space? _____
_____.

The Group Itself: Gender Balance, Rapport, and Other Considerations

Group's purpose and history: What is this group's purpose—why are people together? Is this a one-time-only session, a regular meeting, or part of a series? If an ongoing group, how long has it been functioning? _____.

Group composition and gender balance: (a) List numbers of (or percentages of): females __ males__ . (Give exact figures, if possible.) (b) If group composition is "skewed" and one sex is vastly outnumbered (thereby becoming "token females" or "token males"), how do these tokens act, and how are they treated? Do they tend to isolate themselves? Are they singled out because of their minority status and either *overchallenged* or *underchallenged*? Do others make assumptions about them? (For example, "She's the only woman on our committee—let her be secretary and take notes.")_____
_____.

Cliques: Are there any couples, partners, or people who joined as close friends or coworkers? To avoid the formation of cliques, and to enhance more balanced process, should these pairs be separated? If the leader *does* separate pairs, how is this accomplished? (For example, people could be asked to sit next to someone they do not know.) If reshuffling takes place, is this request made at the beginning of the session or later? Do partners react positively or negatively to the request?_____

_____.

Rapport: What sort of rapport or "group spirit" appears to have developed? Assess the trust level: Do members seem wary of each other or comfortable together? Do you have a feeling of teamwork?_____.

Status and power differentials: Are you aware of any preexisting status or power differentials that could cause some participants to feel less confident and even intimidated? (For example, a group might contain experienced professionals and a few college-aged students, or high-status male administrators and lower-status female support staff.) If marked differences exist, what effect do they have on who chooses to (or refuses to) participate?____

_____.

Other demographics: Besides issues of history, gender, and status, what other factors should be considered, such as age, race, ethnicity, physical disability? For instance, are any participants differently abled? Are any of them members of a linguistic minority—less fluent in the language of the majority? How might these additional factors influence process?_____

_____.

Your additional observations:_____

_____

_____.

The Leader

Consider the leader's race, age, and professional standing—what effect do these factors have on ability to lead? Consider especially sex: Is the leader the same sex as or the opposite sex from the majority of members? Does the leader's sex make her or him any more or less credible with the group, or have any effect on who becomes involved in discussions? (For example, if the group is predominantly male and the facilitator is female—or vice versa—note whether this difference seem to enhance or inhibit participation by all members.)

In addition to the above factors, consider the question of whether the leader—verbally or nonverbally—either colludes with certain persons or discriminates against individuals on the basis of gender. (If you answer yes to any of the following questions about sexism, provide details.)

Nonverbal bias:

(1) Does the leader pay more attention to members of one gender than the other (stand closer to, turn toward, have more eye contact with, nod or smile at, slap supportively on the shoulder, and so on)?

(2) Does the leader seem to seek more approval from, or show favoritism toward, members of one gender? (In other words, does the leader "play to" one segment of the crowd?)

(3) Does the leader show veiled annoyance, embarrassment, or amusement at inappropriate sexist remarks without honestly confronting the sexism?

(4) *Additional observations:* In what other ways does the leader nonverbally collude with men or women?_____
_____.

Verbal discrimination:

(1) Does the leader use exclusive language or stereotype people into rigid categories by gender (saying *fireman* instead of *fire fighter,* for example)? If a group member uses noninclusive language, does the leader correct the linguistic sexism or ignore it?

(2) Does the leader utter put-downs or jokes at the expense of any person because of gender, race, age, disability, sexual orientation, or other immutable characteristics?

(3) Does the leader trivialize or condescend to anyone? (For example, "Do the ladies have anything to add?"[2] or, "I'm sure you guys wouldn't know about things like that.")

(4) Does the leader give lengthier answers, more elaborate instructions, or more precise and dynamic responses to members of one sex?

(5) Does the leader call on, and seek input from, one sex more than the other, or (once the discussion is rolling) continue to question participants of the same sex?

(6) Does the leader cut off questions asked by members of one sex, or disregard, belittle, or deprecate these questions?

(7) Does the leader criticize individuals who exhibit behaviors atypical for that gender role stereotype? (For example, a teacher could imply that a female who answers more questions than other students is an "overachiever.")

Additional observations: What else do you notice about this group and its leader? Share and be ready to discuss additional observations about the room arrangement, leader's verbal and non-verbal behaviors, and the gender-driven power dynamics within the group.

Notes

1.This example of "territorial sexism" ("spatial bias") was provided by Roberta M. Hall, coauthor of *The Classroom Climate: A Chilly One for Women?* (Hall & Sandler, 1982), who also suggested several other items on the checklist.

2. The patronizing question, "Now, do any women have something to add [to the discussion]?" is a "common pitfall" that perpetuates male oppression in groups, say Moyer and Tuttle (1983, p. 26). Such paternalistic remarks deprecate females because they give the impression that everything worthwhile has already been said, and a woman's contribution would therefore be merely a postscript.

REFERENCES

Adler, Alfred (1980). *Cooperation between the sexes: Writings on women love and marriage, sexuality and its disorders* (H. L. Ansbacher & R. R. Ansbacher, Eds. & Trans.). New York: Jason Aronson. (Original work published 1910-1945.)

American Judicature Society. (1991). *Toward more active juries: Taking notes and asking questions* (Larry Heuer, Principal Investigator; Steven Penrod, Consultant). Chicago: Author.

American Medical Association, Department of Women in Medicine. (1990). *Women in medicine: Data source, 1990* [Brochure]. Chicago: Author.

Aries, Elizabeth (1976). Interaction patterns and themes of male, female, and mixed groups. *Small Group Behavior, 7*, 7-18.

Association of American Colleges, Project on the Status and Education of Women. (1988). Report on *Looking for more than a few good women in traditionally male fields. On Campus With Women, 17*(4), 12.

Association of American Colleges, Project on the Status and Education of Women. (n.d.). *Looking for more than a few good women in traditionally male fields.* Washington, DC: Author.

Belenky, Mary F., Clinchy, Blythe M., Goldberger, Nancy R., & Tarule, Jill M. (1986). *Women's ways of knowing: The development of self, voice and mind.* New York: Basic Books.

Bell, Lee (1987). Hearing all our voices: Applications of feminist pedagogy to conferences, speeches, and panel presentations. *Women's Studies Quarterly, 15*(3/4), 74-80.

Bergquist, Kris (1990, September 2). Women make strides in world of medicine. *St. Cloud* (Minnesota) *Times*, pp. 1C, 9C.

Bernardez, T., & Stein, T. S. (1979). Separating the sexes in group therapy: An experiment with men's and women's groups. *International Journal of Group Psychotherapy, 29*, 493-502.

Borisoff, Deborah, & Merrill, Lisa (1985). *The power to communicate: Gender differences as barriers.* Prospect Heights, IL: Waveland.

Bormann, Ernest G. (1990). *Small group communication: Theory and practice* (3rd ed.). New York: Harper & Row.

Bunker, Barbara B., & Seashore, Edith W. (1977). Power, collusion, intimacy-sexuality, support: Breaking the sex-role stereotypes in social and organizational settings. In Alice G. Sargent (Ed.), *Beyond sex roles.* St. Paul, MN: West.

259

Chandler, Rich (1992). *22 surefire ways to slash your business insurance costs: A practical, easy-to-use risk management manual.* St. Cloud, MN: Risk Publishing.

Corey, Gerald (1982). *Theory and practice of counseling and psychotherapy* (2nd ed.). Belmont, CA: Brooks/Cole.

Desjardins, Carolyn (1989a). The meaning of Gilligan's concept of "different voice" for the learning environment. In Carol Pearson, Donna Shavlik, & Judith Touchton (Eds.), *Educating the majority: Women challenging tradition in higher education* (pp. 134-146). New York: Macmillan.

Desjardins, Carolyn. (1989b, April). *Morality of rights/morality of response.* Handout distributed during the conference, Strategies for Success: New Definitions, sponsored by Forum of Executive Women, St. Cloud, MN.

Doherty, William J. (1989, October). Step one in a gender dialogue. *Newsletter of the Feminism and Family Studies Section* (National Council on Family Relations), No. 2, p. 3.

Driggs, John H. (1990, December). Overcoming male privilege. *The Phoenix* (Roseville, MN), p. 9.

Dworkin, Andrea (1991, July/August). [Review of *The women of Whitechapel and Jack the Ripper,* by Paul West]. *Ms.,* p. 82.

Eisler, Rianne (1987). *The chalice and the blade: Our history, our future.* San Francisco: Harper & Row.

Findhorn Foundation. (1989, March-November). *Guest programme of the Findhorn Foundation* [Brochure]. Findhorn, Scotland: Author.

Fiske, Edward B. (1990, April 25). Survey finds pro-male bias at colleges. *Star Tribune* (Minneapolis), pp. 1E, 5E.

Folkins, Carlyle, Pepitone-Areola-Rockwell, Fran, Vando, Rosemary F., Vando, Alan, Spensley, James, & Rockwell, Don (1982). A leaderless couples group postmortem. *International Journal of Group Psychotherapy, 32*(3), 367-373.

Freed, Alice (1985, May 29). What we teach kids about language, about themselves. *Star Tribune* (Minneapolis), op. pp.

Freire, Paolo (1971). *Pedagogy of the oppressed.* New York: Seaview.

Geis, Florence L., Carter, Mae R., & Butler, Doré (1982). *Seeing and evaluating people* [pamphlet summarizing scientific research]. Newark: University of Delaware.

Getting more women into science [Editorial]. (1990, January 8). *Star Tribune* (Minneapolis), p. 8A.

Gilligan, Carol (1982). *In a different voice: Psychological theory and women's development.* Cambridge, MA: Harvard University Press.

Goldberg, P. A. (1968, April). Are women prejudiced against women? *Transaction, 5,* 28-30.

Goldberger, Nancy (1989, June 2). *Women's ways of knowing: The next questions.* Workshop presented for Minnesota Women Psychologists, College of St. Thomas, St. Paul, MN.

Goldner, Virginia (1985). Feminism and family therapy. *Family Process, 24*(1), 31-47.

Goleman, Daniel (1990, April 16). "Mr. Moms" affected by new sexism. *Star Tribune* (Minneapolis), pp. 1E, 2E.

Goodman, Ellen (1990, September 28). "Ladies" still have long road to equality. *St. Cloud* (Minnesota) *Times,* p. 6A.

Goodman, Hal (1983, August). Up in arms. *Psychology Today,* p. 78.

Grady, Kathleen E., Brannon, Robert, & Pleck, Joseph H. (1979). *The male sex role: A selected and annotated bibliography* (DHEW Publication No. ADM 79-790). Washington, DC: Government Printing Office.

Griffin, K. R. (1990, February/March). Attending to equity. *AAUW Outlook, 84*, 10-15.

Hall, Roberta M. (1986, March). *He said, she said: Gender and classroom climate.* Address delivered as part of the Gender and the Curriculum Project, College of Saint Benedict/Saint John's University, St. Joseph, MN.

Hall, Roberta M., & Sandler, Bernice (1982). *The classroom climate: A chilly one for women?* Washington, DC: Association of American Colleges, Project on the Status and Education of Women.

Hall, Roberta, & Sandler, Bernice (1984). *Out of the classroom: A chilly campus climate for women.* Washington, DC: Association of American Colleges, Project on the Status and Education of Women.

Halvorsen, Donna (1990, June 19). Gender-diversity training urged for all lawyers. *Star Tribune* (Minneapolis), p. 6.

Hayden, Elizabeth (1990, March 14). *The court system from the inside looking out.* Paper presented at a meeting of the American Association of University Women, St. Cloud, MN.

Helgesen, Sally (1990). *The female advantage: Women's ways of leadership.* Garden City, NY: Doubleday.

Henley, Nancy, & Thorne, Barrie (1977). Womanspeak and manspeak: Sex differences and sexism in communication, verbal and nonverbal. In Alice G. Sargent (Ed.), *Beyond sex roles.* St. Paul, MN: West.

Hill, Fred (1988). Formal presentations and demonstrations. In William H. Kemp & Anthony E. Schwaller (Eds.), *Instructional strategies for technology education: 37th yearbook, Council on Technology Teacher Education* (pp. 125-142). Mission Hills, CA: Glencoe.

Holland, Norman (1975). *Five readers reading.* New Haven, CT: Yale University Press.

Houston, Jean (1988, October). *Pangaia: Whole system transition and the earth's new story: A mythic event.* Workshop sponsored by the Oasis Center, Chicago.

Johnson, David W., & Johnson, Roger T. (1988, January). *Cooperative classrooms, cooperative schools.* Minneapolis: University of Minnesota, Cooperative Learning Center.

Johnson, Rita J. (1991, October). *Woman to woman: Celebrating our differences.* Keynote address delivered at the annual fall conference sponsored by the Forum of Executive Women, St. Cloud, MN.

Kanter, Rosabeth M. (1977a). *Men and women of the corporation.* New York: Basic Books.

Kanter, Rosabeth M. (1977b). Some effects of proportions on group life: Skewed sex ratios and responses to token women. *American Journal of Sociology, 82*, 965-990.

Kanter, Rosabeth M. (1977c). Women in organizations: Sex roles, group dynamics, and change strategies. In Alice G. Sargent (Ed.), *Beyond sex roles.* St. Paul, MN: West.

Kanter, Rosabeth M. (1989a, May). How the kinder, more cooperative corporation wins. *Working Woman*, pp. 118-120.

Kanter, Rosabeth M. (1989b, July 27). [Speech to the City Club Forum of Cleveland, OH, based on concepts from *When giants learn to dance: Mastering the challenges of strategy, management and careers in the 1990's*]. National Public Radio.

Keith, Sandra (1987). A strategy for the female math student in the battle. In Hilde L. Nelson & Marian Rengel (Eds.), *Gender and the curriculum: Theory and practice, selected papers* (pp. 87-95). St. Joseph/Collegeville, MN: College of Saint Benedict/Saint John's University.

Kelly, Dennis (1990, April 30). Will finances foreclose tradition? *USA Today*, pp. 1D, 2D.

Laporte, Suzanne B. (1990, September). Advantage: Women [Review of *The female advantage: Women's ways of leadership*, by Sally Helgesen]. *Working Woman*, p. 143.

Latour, Trudi (1987). Language and power: Issues in classroom interaction. *Women and Language, 10*(2), 29-32.

Levin, Jack (1991, January/February). Hate crimes against women: Being as nasty as they want to be. *Bostonia* (Boston University), p. 60.

MacVeigh, Virginia (1988, September). Speaking up [Letter to the editor]. *Ms.*, p. 16.

Martin, Leslie (1988, March 16). Sexism is still alive and sick in the workplace [Editorial]. *Star Tribune* (Minneapolis), p. 13A.

Mason, Diane (1990, November 2). The men who abuse women: Their credo spawns violence. *Star Tribune* (Minneapolis), p. 19A.

Mattessich, Paul W., assisted by Heilman, Cheryl, & Wagner, Todd (1989). *Career paths of Minnesota law school graduates* [Study commissioned by Minnesota Women Lawyers]. St. Paul: Wilder Research Center.

Matyas, Marsha (1990). Cultivating a new generation of women in science and engineering. In Sandra Keith & Phillip Keith (Eds.), *Proceedings of the National Conference on Women in Mathematics and the Sciences* (pp. 5-13). St. Cloud, MN: St. Cloud State University.

McClelland, Averil E. (1988). Connected knowing, teaching, and learning: The connected classroom. *Gender and Education, 1*(3/4), 4, 6.

McGuire, Colleen F. (1990, November/December). Sexism again [Letter to the editor]. *New Directions for Women, 19*(6), 2.

McNaron, Toni A. H. (1987, September 18). *Some effects of incest on ideas of the family.* Workshop presented at the conference, Celebrating Women's Voices: A Conference on Feminism and the Family, Minneapolis.

Megargee, E. I. (1969). Influence of sex roles on the manifestation of leadership. *Journal of Applied Psychology, 53*, 377-382.

Meier, Peg (1989, February 12). Study notes gender "tags" in toddler talk. *Star Tribune* (Minneapolis), p. 1E.

Menrath, Nina (1988, Summer). My shadow, my friend. *One Earth: The Findhorn Foundation Magazine, 8*, 30-33.

Miedzian, Myriam (1991). *Boys will be boys: Breaking the link between masculinity and violence.* New York: Bantam.

Miller, Jean B. (1976). *Toward a new psychology of women.* Boston: Beacon.

Miller, Nancy K. (1980). *Mastery, identity, and the politics of work: A feminist teacher in the graduate classroom.* Unpublished manuscript.

Minnesota State Bar Association. (1990). *Report of the Committee on Women in the Legal Profession* [Executive summary]. St. Paul: Author.

Minnesota Supreme Court Task Force for Gender Fairness in the Courts. (1989). Final report. *William Mitchell Law Review, 15*(4), pp. 827-948, 1A-76A.

Minnesota Women's Fund. (1990). *Reflections of risk: Growing up female in Minnesota.* Minneapolis: Author.

Minnesota Women's Fund. (n.d.). *Back-to-school report card for Minnesota's women and girls* [Brochure]. Minneapolis: Author.

Moczygemba, Carol (1990, Spring). Gender studies: "Just plain intrinsically interesting." *Lawrence Today* (Lawrence University, Appleton, WI), 70, 19.

Moen, Jesseli (1990, May). *Women and chemical dependency.* Speech presented at a meeting of the Forum of Executive Women, St. Cloud, MN.

Mosak, H. H., & Schneider, S. (1977). Masculine protest, penis envy, women's liberation and sexual equality. *Journal of Individual Psychology, 33,* 193-202.

Moyer, Bill, & Tuttle, Alan (1983). Overcoming masculine oppression in mixed groups. In *Off their backs . . . and on our own two feet.* Philadelphia: New Society.

National Organization for Changing Men. (1990). *Ending men's violence: Pathways to a gender-just world* [Conference brochure]. Pittsburgh, PA: Author.

Niessen-Derry, Charles (1991a, April 26). Men must speak out to prevent violent acts against women [Letter to the editor]. *University Chronicle* (St. Cloud State University), p. 5.

Niessen-Derry, Charles (1991b, April 28). Homosexuals, women oppressed for same reason [Letter to the editor]. *St. Cloud* (Minnesota) *Times,* op. pp.

Noddings, Nel (1984). *Caring.* Berkeley: University of California Press.

Oasis Center. (1989, January-March). [Brochure]. *Training program in professional leadership: The mark of the exceptional leader is compassionate precision* [program selection], pp. 36-38. Chicago: Author.

Obsatz, Michael (1975, July). *Boy talk: How men avoid sharing themselves.* Unpublished manuscript.

Obsatz, Michael (1989, July 1). To stop the "boys will be boys" syndrome, men and boys need to be taught empathy [Commentary]. *Star Tribune* (Minneapolis), p. 11A.

Ognibene, Elaine R. (1987, February). *Mentoring males: Feminist men are made not born.* Paper presented on the panel, Men and Feminism: Theoretical Aspects (Harry Brod, Moderator), at the conference, The New Gender Scholarship: Men's and Women's Studies, University of Southern California, Los Angeles.

Olson, Lynn C., & Heilman, Cheryl W. (1989, October). Two roads diverged: Reflections on a study of career paths. *Bench & Bar of Minnesota,* pp. 31-34.

O'Reilley, Mary Rose (1989, September/October). The centered classroom: Meditations on teaching and learning. *Weavings: A Journal of the Christian Spiritual Life, 4,* 20-31.

Palm, Glen, & Van Nostrand, Catharine (1987, October). *Becoming involved male parents: Strengths and obstacles.* Workshop presented at the Midwest Regional Men's Conference, Hamline University, St. Paul.

Palm, Glen, Van Nostrand, Catharine, & Schmid, Karen (1989, November). *The sexual politics of mothering and fathering: Implications for family educators.* Panel presentation during the conference of the National Council on Family Relations, New Orleans.

Peters, Tom (1990, September). The best new managers will listen, motivate, support: Isn't that just like a woman? *Working Woman*, pp. 142-143, 216-217.

Pheterson, G. I., Kiesler, S. B., & Goldberg, P. A. (1971). Evaluation of the performance of women as a function of their sex, achievement and personal history. *Journal of Personality and Social Psychology, 19*, 114-118.

Pierce, Carol, & Page, Bill (1990). *A male/female continuum: Paths to colleagueship.* Laconia, NH: New Dynamics.

Porter, N., & Geis, F. L. (1981). Women and nonverbal leadership cues: When seeing is not believing. In C. Mayo & N. Henley (Eds.), *Gender and nonverbal behavior.* New York: Springer-Verlag.

Powell, Gary (1988). *Women and men in management.* Newbury Park, CA: Sage.

Quick, Thomas (1986, August). Process: Help or hindrance in guiding group training? *Trainer's Workshop* (American Management Association), pp. 55-58.

Rich, Adrienne (1979). *On lies, secrets, and silence: Selected prose 1966-1978.* New York: W. W. Norton.

Ridgeway, Cecilia L. (1983). *The dynamics of small groups.* New York: St. Martin's.

Rigby-Weinberg, Dorothe N. (1986). A future direction for radical feminist therapy. In Doris Howard (Ed.), *Guide to dynamics of feminist therapy* (2nd ed.). New York: Harrington.

Rowe, Mary P. (1977). The Saturn's rings phenomenon: Micro-inequities and unequal opportunity in the American economy. In P. Bourne & V. Parness (Eds.), *Proceedings of the National Science Foundation's Conference on Women's Leadership and Authority.* Santa Cruz: University of California.

Russell, Diana E. H., & Caputi, Jane (1990, March/April). Canadian massacre: It was political. *New Directions for Women, 19*, 17.

Sandler, Bernice, with Hall, Roberta (1986). *The campus climate revisited: Chilly for women faculty, administrators and graduate students.* Washington, DC: Association of American Colleges, Project on the Status and Education of Women.

Schafran, Lynn Hecht (1989a, January/February). How stereotypes about women influence judges. *AAUW Outlook, 83*, 10-17.

Schafran, Lynn Hecht (1989b, June 22). Sexual harassment isn't unusual; it's routine. *Star Tribune* (Minneapolis), p. 21A.

Schaper, Donna (1990, March 15). The new racism has a hard heart [Commentary]. *Star Tribune* (Minneapolis), op. pp.

Schmidt, Peggy J. (1982, October). Sexist schooling. *Working Woman*, pp. 101-102.

Schwenger, Peter (1987). Fatherhood and fiction. In Hilde L. Nelson & Marian Rengel (Eds.), *Gender and the curriculum: Theory and practice, selected papers* (pp. 13-25). St. Joseph/Collegeville, MN: College of Saint Benedict/Saint John's University.

Scott, Linda E. U. (1990). The cooperative active learning model: One answer to multicultural gender-fair education in math and science. In Sandra Keith & Phillip Keith (Eds.), *Proceedings of the National Conference on Women in Mathematics and the Sciences* (pp. 170-174). St. Cloud State University, St. Cloud, MN.

Sheldon, Amy (1990a). "Kings are royaler than queens": Language and socialization. *Young Children, 45*(2), 4-9.

Sheldon, Amy (1990b). Pickle fights: Gendered talk in preschool disputes. In Deborah Tannen (Ed.), Language and gender [Special issue]. *Discourse Processes, 13*(1), 5-31.

Shrewsbury, Carolyn (1984, June). *Feminist pedagogy: Teaching/learning for the entire academy.* Paper presented at the National Women's Studies Conference.

Smetanka, Mary Jane (1990, February 25). Cooperation, not competing, is key in class. *Star Tribune* (Minneapolis), p. 1B.

Smith, Manuel J. (1975). *When I say no, I feel guilty (How to cope—using the skills of systematic assertive therapy).* New York: Dial.

Spender, Dale (1980). *Man made language.* London: Routledge & Kegan Paul.

Steinem, Gloria (1983). *Outrageous acts and everyday rebellions.* New York: Holt, Rinehart & Winston.

Tannen, Deborah (1990). *You just don't understand: Women and men in conversation.* New York: William Morrow.

Tannen, Deborah (1991). *You just don't understand: women and men in conversation* [Audiocassette]. New York: Simon & Schuster.

Taylor, Peggy (1990, November/December). Can we talk? A *New Age Journal* interview with Deborah Tannen. *New Age Journal,* pp. 31-33, 60-64, 107-108.

Thompson, Doug Cooper (1985). *As boys become men: Learning new male roles (A curriculum for exploring male role stereotyping).* New York: Irvington.

Thompson, Jane L. (1983). *Learning liberation: Women's response to men's education.* London: Croom Helm.

Thornbury, Charles (1987). John Berryman's myth of his search for his father: From ritual to self portrait. In Hilde L. Nelson & Marian Rengel (Eds.), *Gender and the curriculum: Theory and practice, selected papers* (pp. 43-51). St. Joseph/Collegeville, MN: College of Saint Benedict/Saint John's University.

Turner, Judith Axler (1989, December 6). More women are earning doctorates in mathematics, but few are being hired by top universities. *Chronicle of Higher Education,* pp. A13-A14.

U of M sexual harassment study indicates bias. (1990, June 10). *St. Cloud* (Minnesota) *Times,* p. 8B.

University of Wisconsin—Madison. (1990-1991). *Social issues update.* Madison: Author.

Van Nostrand, Catharine H. (1986, June). *Changing men, catalytic women: How men are growing and what women have to do with it.* Paper presented on the panel, Men and Feminism (Jacqueline Flenner, Moderator), at the annual meeting of the National Women's Studies Association, University of Illinois, Champaign/Urbana.

Van Nostrand, Catharine H. (1987a, February). *Action or angst: Are men changing or merely paying lip service to gender justice?* Paper presented on the panel, Men and Feminism: Theoretical Aspects (Harry Brod, Moderator), at the conference, The New Gender Scholarship: Men's and Women's Studies, University of Southern California, Los Angeles.

Van Nostrand, Catharine H. (1987b, April). *Action or angst: Are men changing or merely paying lip service to gender justice?* Paper presented on the panel, Gender and the Male Experience (Peter Schwenger, Moderator), at the conference, Gender and the Curriculum: Theory and Practice, College of Saint Benedict/Saint John's University, St. Joseph/Collegeville, MN.

Van Nostrand, Catharine H. (1988, June). *No favorites? How group facilitators collude with gender-stereotyped participant behavior.* Paper presented on the panel, Gender-Linked Communication: Breaking the Barriers, at the annual meeting of the National Women's Studies Association, University of Minnesota, Minneapolis.

Van Nostrand, Catharine H. (1990a, June 30). *Gender-responsible leadership: Detecting bias, implementing interventions*. Featured address, including interactive workshop, presented at the national conference, Winning the Race in Science, Math and Technology: Passing the Torch to Women and Minorities, Sigma Delta Epsilon/Graduate Women in Science, College of St. Catherine, St. Paul.

Van Nostrand, Catharine H. (1990b). Gender-responsible leadership: Do your teaching methods empower women? In Sandra Keith & Phillip Keith (Eds.), *Proceedings of the National Conference on Women in Mathematics and the Sciences* (pp. 186-191). St. Cloud State University, St. Cloud, MN.

Van Nostrand, Catharine H. (1992a, March 7). *Expressing social displeasure: Interventions toward a peaceful society*. Interactive workshop presented at the conference, Creating a Violence-Free Community, Workplace, School, Church, Family, St. Cloud, MN.

Van Nostrand, Catharine H. (1992b, September). *Practicing gender-responsible medicine in the 90's*. Poster session including self-audit "Am I Biased?" for physicians and other healthcare professionals presented at the Sixth International Symposium on Obesity Surgery, Genoa, Italy.

Van Nostrand, Catharine H. (in press a). Practicing gender-responsible medicine in the 90's [abstract]. *Obesity Surgery (An International Surgical Journal for Research and Treatment of Massive Obesity)* (3)1.

Van Nostrand, Catharine H. (in press b). Gender-responsible leadership: Do your teaching methods empower women? *U. S.-Japan Women's Journal: A Journal for the International Exchange of Gender Studies* (13).

Van Nostrand, Catharine H., & Breitenbucher, Jean (1989, November). *Gender-responsible leadership: Females facilitating males in parenting groups*. Interactive workshop presented at the conference, The Daddy Track: Under Construction, Minnesota Council on Family Relations, University of Minnesota, St. Paul.

Van Nostrand, Catharine H., & Palm, Glen (1986, October). *Involving fathers in parenting programs*. Workshop presented for the Parent/Child Program, School District 742, St. Cloud, MN.

Wagner, David (1990). Some personal reflections on power equity. [Newsletter] *Understanding Equity* 4(1) p. 1. Laconia, NH: Equity Associates.

Warch, Richard (1990, Spring). Sex, gender and coeducation. *Lawrence Today* (Lawrence University, Appleton, WI), *70*, 14-19.

Witt, Linda (1990, August 16). Males communicate in authoritative tone. *St. Cloud* (Minnesota) *Times*, p. 8A.

Witt, Tom (1990, Summer). Sexism and militarism: Making the connections between war, masculinity, and the oppression of women. *Peace Notes* (Lutheran Fellowship quarterly newsletter), p. 4.

Woolf, Virginia (1957). *A room of one's own*. New York: Harcourt, Brace & World. (Original work published 1929)

Wright, F., & Gould, L. J. (1979). Recent research on sex-linked aspects of group behavior: Implications for group psychotherapy. In L. R. Wolberg & M. L. Aronson (Eds.), *Group therapy 1979: An overview* (pp. 208-218). New York: Stratton Intercontinental Medical.

Youngblood, Dick (1990a, September 2). For many women, executive ranks still out of reach. *Star Tribune* (Minneapolis), pp. 1D, 3D.

Youngblood, Dick (1990b, November 25). The key to women moving up is know [*sic*] laughing matter. *Star Tribune* (Minneapolis), p. 1D, 8D.

Zemke, R., & Zemke, S. (1981, June). 30 things we know for sure about adult learning. *Training: The Magazine of Human Resources Development,* pp. 115-117.

Zettersten, Rolf (1990, July). The new feminists. *Focus on the Family* [Magazine], p. 23.

Zimmerman, Donald H., & West, Candace (1975). Sex roles, interruptions, and silences in conversation. In B. Thorne & N. Henley (Eds.), *Language and sex: Difference and dominance.* Rowley, MA: Newbury House.

INDEX

Abrupt intervention, 205; purpose,
example and benefit of, 221-225;
tested in meeting, 129-132. For
other basic strategies, *see*
*GENDER-RESPONSIBLE
INTERVENTIONS (Table 7.1).
See also *INTERVENTION
TECHNIQUES

Advocacy (adversarial) mode of
leadership, 22-23—defined, 151;
contrasted with Response mode,
151-152. *See also* Justice/rights
mode; Peacock mode

American Association for the
Advancement of Science, 101

American Judicature Society, 158-159

American Medical Association (AMA),
101, 138n.2

American Society of Association
Executives, 64n.9

Assertiveness: process in assertion
training workshop (Case 3.1),
78-80; example; used to confront
assailant, 177-180; how to
encourage, 86; importance of
non-verbal communication in,
178; involves acknowledging
one's own power, 69-70. *See also*
Assertiveness techniques/skills;
Autonomy; Credibility of
women; Risk-taking; Self-esteem
in women

Assertiveness techniques/skills:
broken record, 195, 200n.8; "I
message"/"I statement", 56-57,
131, 195, 197; negative inquiry,
248, 251n.1; minimal assertion,
199. *See also* Assertiveness;
Compassionate precision;
*INTERVENTION TECHNIQUES

Association of American Colleges, 119,
138n.6

Autonomy, primary developmental
task for females, 68-70; helped by

AUTHOR"S NOTE: The majority of persons listed here are those quoted from
non-print sources; that is, I used words from their unpublished presentations, their
correspondence, or our personal conversations. Also listed are a few authorities
who, because they are mentioned in articles authored by others, cannot therefore
be located under their own names. In addition, I have included several nationally
prominent persons (Anita Hill, for example) who are featured in a case study or
interaction. All other authors and sources can be found in the references.

Several entries are "master" categories or "locator" topics. That is, they serve as
"directories" to help the reader find other major subject headings. These entries are
preceded by an asterisk (*) and printed in all capital letters; see, for example,
*MALES, or *DISCRIMINATORY LEADERSHIP PRACTICES.

ABOUT THE AUTHOR

Catharine Herr Van Nostrand, M.A., is founder of the consulting firm of Catharine Van Nostrand and Associates, which is located in St. Cloud, Minnesota. She is a trained educator with 20 years' experience in facilitating highly interactive employee empowerment seminars in such diverse populations as educators and health care providers, business executives and estate planners, and mental health professionals and county supervisors, among many other groups. She also designs and presents workshops on a wide variety of topics, including two-career families, women and men in the workplace, sexual harassment, and teaching methods that encourage women. She has facilitated assertiveness training workshops for groups of bank loan officers, battered women, men who batter, and the disabled.

Having researched issues in men's studies and the contemporary men's movement, she has been a presenter at regional men's conferences, meetings of the National Council on Family Relations, and a symposium on violence. She has also served as a panelist at National Women's Studies Association conferences, and at other academic symposia addressing gender issues and the curriculum. She is a guest lecturer at colleges and universities for classes in women's studies, small group communication theory, and other subjects.

Her special interest is the subtle and blatant bias women face in such male-dominated fields as medicine, law, and technology. She has been a presenter at an international surgery symposium, and Keynote speaker or workshop facilitator at regional meetings of legal administrators and national conferences for women in science, math, and technology. Her presentations are geared to helping leaders—educators, community activists, parents, human services practitioners, and others—to become more credible by recognizing and admitting their own personal biases even as they try to confront sexism in the groups they lead. Her paper "Practicing Gender-Responsible Medicine in the 90's" was presented as a poster session at the Sixth International Symposium on Obesity Surgery (Genoa, Italy, 1992), and an abstract of this paper will be published in the journal *Obesity Surgery: An International Surgical Journal for Research and Treatment of Massive Obesity* (in press a).

Her article "Gender-Responsible Leadership: Do Your Teaching Methods Empower Women?" was first published in the *Proceedings of the National Conference on Women in Mathematics and the Sciences* (St. Cloud State University, 1989), and subsequently published in *U.S.-Japan Women's Journal: A Journal for the International Exchange of Gender Studies* (in press b). In addition, her work has appeared in the "Feminist Forum" of the *Women's Studies International Forum* (1986). Her articles on women in business, women in the arts, physical fitness for women, and innovative methods in assertiveness training have appeared in the popular press.